Business Administration

A textbook for the
computer age

Also from Heinemann, By the same author

Quantitative Methods for Business Students

Model Answers to Business Administration Assignments

Model Answers
To Business Administration
Assignments

The Model Answers are intended as a guide for lecturers and students using the *Business Administration* textbook. The material in the Model Answers follows the same sequence of topics as the main text and include examples of business documents, the applications of a computer to a small business, O & M and job enrichment principles. Both students and lecturers will find the Model Answers a useful source of additional material to supplement the main *Business Administration* text and a guide to methods of handling the assignments.

Business Administration

A textbook for the
computer age

ROGER CARTER
BSc (Hons)

HEINEMANN : LONDON

Acknowledgements

The author wishes to thank the organizations that assisted in the preparation of case study material for this text. They include:

Alphamed Ltd
British Airways
Lloyds & Scottish Finance Ltd
Reldan Ltd
The Pine Workshop (Great Missenden)

William Heinemann Ltd
10 Upper Grosvenor Street, London W1X 9PA
LONDON MELBOURNE TORONTO
JOHANNESBURG AUCKLAND

First published 1982
Reprinted 1984
© Roger Carter 1982

434 90219 5

Printed in Great Britain by Redwood Burn Ltd,
Trowbridge, Wiltshire

Preface

Over the next decade there will be a revolution in all types of business activity, and nowhere will the revolution be more keenly felt than in the office. In five years from now even the smallest business will have access to vast databases and computing power over the telephone network, simply by connecting to it a word processor costing around £2,000 at today's prices. Its need for paper will be dramatically reduced, for its accounts, files, and other documentation will be processed and stored electronically, either in the low-cost micro-electronic office equipment that is now becoming available or in the telephone network itself.

60% of all workers are employed in offices and their jobs will be radically changed. Routine tasks, which at present comprise a large part of their workload, will disappear, and much more time than at present will be spent on decision-making − asking questions of the databases, analysing the information received, and choosing appropriate courses of action.

The Business Education Council, realizing the importance of this revolution, has recently stressed the need to give business students a proper appreciation of its implications and an awareness of the applications of the new technology in the office. This text is firmly orientated towards preparing students to meet the challenge of the new age. It is designed both for students taking the Business Education Council's 'Administration in Business' course and for students on professional courses who require an introduction to administration in the age of the computer and the intelligent office machine. It also meets the needs of students taking the BEC/TEC National Award in Computer Studies module 'Information in Organizations' and students on BEC Higher National courses.

Student activity based upon case studies should form an important element of a business administration course. Following the main body of the text is an activity and assignment programme (consisting of seven business administration assignments and two cross-modular assignments) based upon a study of Pinecrafts, a small furniture business. This programme has been thoroughly tested in the classroom on both full-time and day-release courses. It is intended for students taking the BEC 'Administration in Business' module, though it can be adapted for other courses, in particular the BEC 'Information in Organizations' module.

Case studies are also included in the body of the text to illustrate important principles and to reinforce student learning. All these studies describe factual situations (although fictitious names are used) and were specially written for this book.

The Pinecrafts case study and assignment programme, together with a selection of other case studies from the book, were a winning entry for the 'Case Study of the Year − 1980' competition organized by the Case Clearing House of Great Britain and Ireland and sponsored by Unilever Limited.

Roger Carter

v

Structure of the Text

Administration is the total system of office activities and procedures within a business. The purpose of this system is to enable management to organize and control the physical resources of the business:

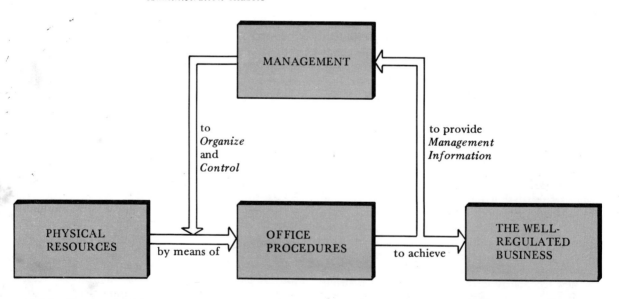

This diagram (which is explained in Chapter 2) forms the organizing framework for this book, which deals with administration in business under the following main headings:

Part I: The Organization and Control of Physical Resources

Part II: Office Procedures and Management Information

Part III: The Well-Regulated Business.

Contents

processing example: invoicing. Business applications of computing. The electronic architecture of the integrated office. Telecommunications: public packet switched networks; value-added networks. Viewdata. The integrated office. Information privacy. Information security.

PART III THE WELL-REGULATED BUSINESS

Part One

The
Organization and Control
of
Physical Resources

1 The Organization of Production

The high standard of living enjoyed by so many today is the fruit of man's efficiency in the production and exchange of goods and services. This efficiency is based upon division of labour, and in this chapter we show how division of labour has developed over the centuries, and how it is applied in business today.

Technology and the Organization of Production

Efficient production – and hence a high standard of living – comes about when people organize themselves to make the best use of the available technology. The standard of living attained at any point in history is dependent, therefore, upon the stage reached in the development of

1 the organization of production, and
2 technology.

The latter is the key factor, for the level of technology largely dictates the way in which production is organized, and so we begin our study with a brief review of the historical development of technology and its impact upon production and wealth.

Technology has advanced by a process of revolution rather than evolution. The first technological revolution led to the stone age, which was characterized by the widespread use of stone tools and weapons. The typical productive organization that developed to meet the needs of that age was the hunting party: man had learned that *co-operation* in production (of meat and skins) resulted in greater productivity, and therefore more wealth, than trying to go it alone.

The next revolution led to the new stone age, which was characterized by the spread of agriculture. The type of productive organization that appeared in that age was the agricultural settlement. By this time man had learned that in order to achieve high productivity, and therefore substantial wealth, co-operation in production must be based upon:

1 Division of labour, each man specializing in one type of activity only (farming, tool-making, healing, etc.), the advantage of this being that he becomes very skilled at that activity, it is worth his while to buy or make special tools and equipment to increase production, and he does not waste time switching from one activity to another.

2 Trade, each man exchanging his output for that of other specialists in order to acquire the things he does not produce.

Next came metal tools (the bronze age and the iron age), and with them came larger and more complex forms of productive organizations employing, in some instances, many hundreds or thousands of people. The first step towards the development of the modern busi-

3

ness organization came when the domestic system of production appeared in the fifteenth century A.D. Under this system an entrepreneur ('promoter') took care of all the trade (buying the raw materials, transporting them to the workers' homes for processing, and collecting and selling the finished goods), leaving the workers free to devote all their working hours to their specialisms, for which he paid them a wage. All profits from the business went to the entrepreneur, and from them he obtained his living and financed any expansion of the business.

This separation of the commercial functions of finance and trade from the physical production of goods enabled commerce to expand, during the next century, and thus take advantage of the new markets that were opening up overseas. Physical production also increased as a result of the greater specialisation that the domestic system allowed; but it failed to match the growth of commerce and the demands of the new markets. This state of affairs provided the impetus for the invention and application of large power-driven machines at the end of the eighteenth century, and the industrial revolution was born.

The type of productive organization that developed to take advantage of this revolution was the business enterprise as we know it today. Its main features are:

1 *Very high productivity*, resulting in wealth that is, by all previous standards, unbelievable.

2 *Machine-based production*, workers being required to carry out their occupations in 'manufactories'. This has resulted in a clear separation of an individual's work from his other activities.

3 *Division of labour taken to its limits*, workers being organized into specialist departments, each individual being responsible for a tiny part only of the total task. Because of this, workers often have difficulty in identifying with the end-product and therefore cannot take a pride in their work, and the work itself often lacks interest and fails to fulfil their inner needs. The frequent result is that the worker is alienated from his work, which becomes merely a necessary evil to be endured for the sake of the wages he needs to finance his out-of-work activities.

4 *Problems of co-ordination*, i.e. failure by the various parts of the organization to integrate their efforts in pursuit of the common goal, caused by the fragmented nature of the organization. Each department is, to some extent, an autonomous unit, and communications between departments are often inadequate. The result is lack of co-ordination in decision-making, so that departments tend to pursue conflicting goals, to the detriment of the overall performance of the business.

The Next Revolution: Micro-Electronics

We are now on the verge of the next technological revolution − the micro-electronics revolution − which will be based upon the spread of 'intelligent' machines. 'Intelligent' in this context does not mean that these machines can think in a creative or original way. It means that they can be programmed to respond in appropriate ways to various stimuli, rather as living organisms are genetically programmed to respond to their environment.

The 'brain' of an intelligent machine is a tiny device called a **microprocessor**. This is, in effect, a computer etched onto the surface of a fingernail-sized slice of silicon − the so-called silicon chip. The tiny size, low cost (measured in pence rather than pounds), extreme reliability (it has no moving parts and so will never wear out), and enormous computing power (equivalent to that of a room-sized computer costing hundreds of thousand of pounds only a decade or two ago) mean that this device will revolutionize our tools and technology and therefore our productive organizations.

Stimuli (information) are picked up and fed into the microprocessor by electronic sensors connected to the machine − such a sensor might be a video camera in the case of an industrial robot, or a keyboard in the case of an office machine. The microprocessor makes a decision on the basis of this information and sends appropriate commands via electronic circuitry to switches, visual display units, or other parts of the machine.

Intelligent machines will affect everybody's job. In the past, automation was only possible for mass-production processes, because non-intelligent machines are purpose-built for one task only, and enormous production runs are essential if the capital invested in such machines is to be recouped. Intelligent machines, on the other hand, can be repro-

THE FIRST REVOLUTION AND THE LAST REVOLUTION COMPARED

The Stone Age Revolution
Based upon *flint chips*, which were produced very cheaply and on a large scale at a few centres, such as the flint workings of southern England. From these centres the chips were distributed everywhere and transformed every aspect of man's life.

Flint chips were, in effect, *stone extensions of man's hands,* and they greatly increased his physical capabilities and hence his control over his environment. They formed the basis of man's *first tools* and resulted in greatly increased productivity.

The result was increased wealth and leisure and significant developments in all aspects of society. Weapons were also developed which assisted the rise of powerful communities whose leaders were able to exercise a tight central control. These communities were the forerunners of the vast empires that straddled the Middle and Near East in bronze age and later times.

The Micro-electronics Revolution
Based upon *silicon chips*, produced very cheaply and on a large scale at a few centres, such as Silicon Valley in Texas. They are likely to become, over the next few decades, as pervasive as the flint chips of the first revolution. Typical applications are digital watches, TV games, and washing machine controls.

Silicon chips are, in effect, *electronic extensions of man's brain*, and they increase his mental capabilities and hence his control over his environment. They form the basis of man's *first intelligent tools* and will greatly increase his productivity. Typical of these tools are electronic calculators, word processors, and industrial robots.

The result is likely to be increased wealth and leisure, and also sophisticated new weapons and advanced techniques for monitoring and controlling all members of society. The enormous power of today's telecommunications and data processing facilities makes the possibility of a centrally-controlled empire straddling the four corners of the earth very real.

grammed very easily, and so production lines can be changed cheaply and quickly to incorporate new designs and to introduce variety into mass-produced goods. This means that automation of small batch-production processes is now possible. Much office work can also be automated.

The intelligent machine tool and the industrial robot will, over the next twenty years, take over many factory jobs. So big is the potential demand for such devices that it is reckoned that robotics will soon be one of the world's biggest growth industries. At present, an

industrial robot costs about £30,000, but, as with other microprocessor-based devices, this cost can be expected to fall dramatically when the industry takes off.

Most workers today are employed in offices, and it is this sector that will be most affected by micro-electronics. It is predicted that paper will be a thing of the past in most offices by 1995. Communication, storage, and other processing of information will take place entirely electronically.

The effect of this revolution on the worker will be

similar to that of previous technological revolutions:

1 It will increase his productivity, and therefore the wealth-creating capabilities of productive organizations.

2 It will produce a substantial shift in employment from one type of occupation to another. In particular, the worst feature of the industrial revolution − monotonous work in poor conditions − will largely disappear.

3 Although previous technological revolutions created no long-term unemployment, it would be perhaps too optimistic to hope that history will repeat itself in this case. However, the massive unemployment predicted by some is unlikely to materialize, provided the economy grows and is able to absorb the increased wealth that industry can produce. Even in the office, where the micro-electronics revolution will have its greatest impact, there is likely to be little reduction in the total number of workers, at least during the 1980s. Instead, a substantial improvement in the quality and quantity of work produced is expected. It is estimated that if this revolution had not occurred, then office staff would have had to increase by some 30% over the next decade to keep pace with the demands made of it; as it is, numbers employed are expected to remain at roughly their present levels. In the longer term, any unemployment generated by the revolution may well take the form of a reduction in the working week rather than a substantial drop in the numbers employed.

The Structure of Productive Organizations

The computer, with its enormous data-processing capabilities, provides a solution to the communication and co-ordination problems encountered by present-day productive organizations. Businesses are beginning to reorganize themselves to take advantage of the new technology. In the best organizational structures that are now emerging, departments are grouped in ways which enable decision-making to be carried out in an integrated manner (so that departmental goals do not conflict, activities are co-ordinated, and overall performance is optimized), and the computer is being used to provide the information needed for this decision-making.

The degree to which decision-making can be co-ordinated is limited at the moment by human span-of-control limitations (the number of people that a single individual can control); the great potential of the computer lies in the fact that it can overcome these limitations. We can expect to see emerging, in the 1990s, fully integrated businesses in which the various intelligent machines in the office and factory will be linked to a central computer which will enable management to co-ordinate activities throughout the organization (see Figure 4.1 and the accompanying text).

Thus the traditional ways of organizing and administering business enterprises are fast disappearing, and we are entering a new age in which administrative processes will centre upon the computer and the intelligent office machine. The main aim of Parts I and II of this text is to enable the student to understand the principles underlying the control and organization of the new business structures that are emerging, and the way in which the new generation of machines will be used in those structures.

The steps involved in the design of organization structures are dealt with in Chapter 3. The first step is to identify the operations the business must carry out in order to achieve its main goals. These operations will differ from business to business, and will give rise to the **division of labour** within the organization. The second step is to design the decision-making apparatus needed to control these operations, and this gives rise to the **distribution of authority** in the organization.

These two main characteristics of an organization can be portrayed by means of an **organization chart**, examples of which are shown in Figures 1.1 to 1.3. The division of labour can be seen by reading the chart across horizontally (except in Figure 1.3, where it is shown listed vertically). Read downwards vertically, the chart shows the distribution of authority (except in Figure 1.3, which should be read across horizontally). The network of lines joining the posts in the chart indicate the relationships between posts: decisions made by superiors are communicated downwards to subordinates via these lines; feedback on the effects of these decisions upwards via the same lines; horizontal liaison between posts reporting to a common superior also take place along these lines. Other communication channels exist in the organization, of course, and are discussed in Chapter 3.

In an organization chart there is no indication of the

specific duties of individual posts. For this **job descriptions** are needed, and an example of one is given overleaf (it applies to the post of European Sales Manager referred to in the case study given in the next section). Besides a list of duties, a job description might specify the materials and equipment required for the job, the working conditions and the rates of pay, the personal qualities, qualifications, and experience necessary, and the job's relationships with other posts.

The Growth of a Business: Stage I

The growth of the individual business reflects the historical development of productive organizations. Pinecrafts, the business described in the case study and assignment programme in Appendix II, typifies the infancy of many businesses: two or three partners co-operating on an informal basis − co-operation similar in type to that of the earliest forms of productive enter-prise − to carry out all the tasks of buying, producing goods or services, selling, bookkeeping, sweeping the floors, and so on. Many businesses, of course, start off on an even smaller scale, one man (the sole proprietor) carrying out all of these tasks himself.

Unfortunately, the infant mortality rate amongst businesses is high − one-third fail within the first year of starting up. If, however, the line of business is well-chosen, and the owner or owners have adequate savings behind them, and they work hard and run their business efficiently, then, other things being equal, sales (and work) will gradually increase, and the time will come when some staff will have to be employed.

The decision to expand the business cannot be taken lightly. Staff require not only pay but also accommodation and equipment, and they introduce the possibility of conflict into the business. Many one-man outfits remain that way because the owner is unwilling to risk expansion, or because he has no stomach for the complications and increased responsibility that expansion brings. Others grow quite fast and diversify their operations because the owner has a driving ambition and is prepared to take risks.

The course that a business follows depends, therefore, upon the *aims* of its owner. He may seek a busy and prosperous life, or status, or a good reputation, or he may desire a quiet life with a steady income. These aims will determine his *objectives*, or goals (which might be, for example, to make a large profit by expanding into a certain market), and his *policies*, or 'code of behaviour', which govern the way in which he will achieve his objectives (for example, a business with a 'no redundancy' policy will achieve reduced labour costs by natural wastage).

CASE STUDY: MEDTECH LTD.

In 1973 David joined Betapacers Inc., an American pacemaker manufacturer, as the European Sales Manager. (A pacemaker is a small battery-powered device implanted into a patient to ensure correct heart functioning.) In spite of his title (and in spite of his job description − see over), David did not 'manage' anyone. He was the sole sales representative of Betapacers in the U.K., and on the Continent his duties were limited to giving technical assistance to the various small companies that acted as distributers for Betapacers' products. He was, therefore, a lone operator, but he lacked the job satisfaction and the freedom to plan his own objectives that is often enjoyed by the sole proprietor who runs his own business. He remained with the company for five years, and, as we shall see in the case study at the end of Chapter 3, he was very frustrated during that time.

During his final year or two with Betapacers David experienced considerable difficulties in selling his product. There were by then some twenty competing brands on the U.K. market, and doctors no longer wanted to see pacemaker sales-men. In order to get their foot in the door salesmen had to demonstrate other medical products to doctors and then, having gained their confidence, bring up

Job Description of European Sales Manager, Betapacers Inc.

Title: EUROPEAN SALES MANAGER

Responsible to: DIRECTOR OF INTERNATIONAL SALES

Objective: To make Betapacers' product line accepted as a major choice for treatment of pacemaker indications.

General Responsibilities: Complete responsibility for sales and business management for Betapacers in Europe.

Specific Responsibilities:

1   Hiring, training, directing, controlling, and motivating sales and office staff.

2   Liaison with and training of agents of the Company.

3   Developing and executing marketing plans and strategies.

4   Preparing forecasts and budgets.

5   Controlling expense expenditure.

6   Maintaining a Management by Objectives system.

7   Planning and attending medical seminars with emphasis on highlighting Betapacers' products.

8   Ensuring that goods are distributed to customers, and that adequate invoicing and accounting procedures are followed.

9   Developing adequate inventory and stocking procedures.

10 Developing knowledge of and rapport with key government agencies that control prosthetic devices, and familiarity with the laws and procedures relating thereto.

Immediate Subordinates: All sales and office staff in Western Europe.

the matter of *their* brand of pacemaker. Betapacers, however, manufactured only pacemakers, and so with no other products to sell David found himself at a disadvantage.

By the end of 1977 David's frustrations with his job caused him to suggest, during a visit to Betapacers' head office in America, that he leave the company and become an independent agent for their pacemakers in the U.K. (this would enable him to sell other companies' medical products and thus gain easier access to doctors). Rather to his surprise, Betapacers reacted sympathetically. It transpired that its selling policy for the American market was shifting to this approach – the company was cutting back on its representatives and appointing independent agents instead.

Eventually, after numerous delays by the company, contracts were signed, and in November 1978 David set up Medtech Ltd. (a private limited company with his wife and himself as owner-directors), the sole U.K. agent for Betapacers' products. The new company was run from David's home, the registered address being that of his chartered accountants in Marlow.

As is frequently the case when a small business is set up with virtually no capital, David faced an immediate cash flow problem. He had to hold a stock of pacemakers to supply to customers, and stock costs money. Furthermore, the terms of his contract with Betapacers specified that he should pay for any pacemakers within thirty days of despatch from the factory in America, whereas he was in no position to insist that his customers settle their accounts so promptly. He calculated that he needed to borrow £15,000 to cover this cash flow problem, but his application to a bank for a loan for this amount was unsuccessful. In desperation he asked Betapacers for less rigorous terms, and the company finally agreed to accept fifty per cent within the thirty days, and the remainder within sixty days. In addition, he managed to raise a short-term loan of £6,000 from a private source (at a high interest rate), and his immediate cash problem was solved.

David quickly took advantage of his independent status to diversify, taking on several products in the cardiology and radiology fields. This gave him ready access to doctors and, of course, increased his total sales, but the purchase of this additional stock added to his cash flow problems. However, he was able to replace his £6,000 loan by a long-term loan of £10,000 at a favourable interest rate, and in this way managed to finance this diversification – although he now faced the problem of servicing this loan.

Shortly after this he received the offer of a further substantial loan from a friend, and he had to decide whether to take up this loan to finance further diversification and to take on a salesman to handle the increased sales, or take the alternative course of consolidating his position and financing further expansion as and when he could out of profits. A decision in favour of taking up the loan could result in his inability to service it, and eventual failure, or it could lead to his company taking off, with the prospect of employing further salesmen in the future to handle greatly increased sales. The decision he came to was based upon:

(a) His main business objectives
(b) His experience as a salesman in the medical field telling him how well the products he was thinking of moving into would sell
(c) A forecast of the future cash flows that this level of sales would generate.

At the time when this decision had to be made David was asked to state his main objectives in order of importance. He produced the following list:

1 *Sales* He wanted to achieve as large a market share as possible. Profit was of lesser importance to him, and he was prepared to increase sales (by trimming his prices as much as possible and by employing salesmen) even if this did not increase his total net profit. He admitted that this desire for a large market share was really a desire for prestige.

2 *Growth* Related to his desire for a large market share was the desire to increase the size of his company by employing salesmen and moving into proper offices.

3 *Profit* David had no great desire to become very rich, but would be content with a level of profit that would give him what he regarded as a reasonable standard of living.

4 *Welfare* David has a strong medical background (he worked for a number of years in the hospital service), and underlying much of what he was doing lay a desire to help the sick.

The way in which David had developed his business up to this point was a direct result of these objectives. The marketing policies he had adopted were as follows:

1 *Low profit margins*

In order to increase sales his average mark-up was 15%.

2 *Product-diversification*

    (a) He was seeking the U.K. selling rights on a number of technically sophisticated medical products being developed on the Continent and in America.

    (b) He had initiated the development of, and was about to market, a closed-circuit TV system for the partially-sighted.

    (c) He was considering taking up the selling rights on a certain brand of disposables (these include disposable syringes, theatre gowns, and catheters). Disposables are in constant demand, and they provide the salesman with a steady income. However, they are low-priced items, and selling them is labour-intensive (hospitals require supplies on a regular and frequent basis). In addition, large quantities have to be stocked, and this creates major storage problems for someone operating from his own home.

EXERCISES
(Suitable for a cross-modular assignment)

1 If you owned David's business, what would be your main objectives (in order of importance)? What marketing policies would you adopt?

2 'The principal objective of any business is to make a profit.' To what extent is this true of (a) a public company, (b) a nationalized industry?

3 You have the following information on the market for medical products:

    A number of new disposable products have recently come on to the market, and a period of good, steady sales in this segment seems assured, at least in the short term. At the high-technology end of the market a number of innovations are around the corner, and although profitability is, initially, uncertain, it seems likely that a company getting in on the ground floor and operating successfully now will make excellent profits in the long term.

You are at the point in the case study where you have to decide whether to take up the offer of a further loan and expand the business, and if so, how you would expand it. In the light of this market information, and your list of objectives in Question 1, what decision would you make? The following financial information is relevant:

Proprietor's overheads (living expenses, car, etc.)	£10,000 p.a.
Cost of employing a salesman (including car)	10,000 p.a.
Present level of sales	100,000 p.a.
Present value of stock	20,000
Cash in bank at present	4,000
Debtors	6,000
Creditors	5,000

The Growth of a Business: Stage II

If the owner of a one-man business wishes to expand, then, if he is in the business of making things, he might begin by employing one or two workers (operatives) on the production side, then later perhaps a salesman, and a clerk/typist to deal with the bookkeeping, filing, typing, and other office duties. He will directly supervise all of these employees, will continue to do all of the buying and some of the selling, and will personally sort out any production problems and initiate any product-innovations. But he will delegate to his subordinates responsibility for the routine production, selling, and office work.

The type of co-operation that the business exhibits at this stage of its growth reflects that developed in the history of productive organizations when the production function was separated from the commercial function.

After further years of continued expansion the organization chart of this business might be as shown in Figure 1.1. At this stage of growth the owner will find himself becoming increasingly divorced from the day-to-day work of the business. Production is handled by a dozen or so operatives under the control of a foreman, the owner becoming involved only when production changes are necessary or problems arise. The market for his products has been split into two sectors (probably on a geographical basis), each handled by a salesman.

The Manager's personal secretary will probably be a lady of some maturity, who deals with his correspondence, keeps his diary, and perhaps deals with customers and other enquirers in his absence. She also supervises the other two office workers who keep the sales ledger and the purchases ledger, look after the accounts, send out invoices and keep records of payments made, order materials required and deal with the purchase invoices, calculate and record the wages, and so on.

As for the Manager, his duties will be as follows:

1 Obtaining and reading the information on which his plans for the business must be based (information such as the salesmen's reports of their visits to customers, the latest sales figures, relevant trade journals and technical journals, and so on) and trying to anticipate the future conditions of the various markets that affect his business.

2 Planning the future development of the business – seeking ways to improve its competitive edge (product-innovation, altering price and quality, etc.), exploiting opportunities for growth (e.g. entering new markets), seeking ways to increase efficiency (e.g.

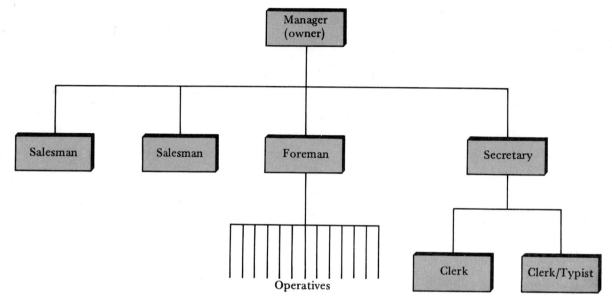

Figure 1.1   Organization chart of a small manufacturing business

installing new equipment).

3 Drawing up budgets based upon these plans, and modifying the plans if they are not financially viable.

4 Planning the day-to-day operations of the business – scheduling customers' orders through the workshops, deciding what quantities of materials and bought-in parts should be ordered, making decisions on technical problems, and so on.

5 Organizing the resources of the business so that the plans can be put into effect – arranging finance, recruiting staff and purchasing equipment, installing new working procedures, allocating duties and responsibilities to staff, and so on.

6 Controlling the business – communicating the plans to the staff, and ensuring that they are carried out. For example, he must ensure that delivery dates are adhered to, that customers' accounts are being settled, that appropriate stock levels are being maintained, that all the routine work of the business is being efficiently carried out and that the activities of all parts of the business are properly co-ordinated.

7 Attending to staff matters – motivating employees to give of their best, looking after their welfare, and dealing with problems of discipline.

ASSIGNMENT GROUP WORK

Discuss and determine the solution to Assignment 1(a), page 190 (organization chart for Pinecrafts).

The Growth of a Business: Stage III

If the business continues to grow, then the Manager will find himself increasingly overloaded with work and unable to deal adequately with all the planning and control matters that require his attention. He will therefore find it necessary to employ other managers to share his burden of work. The usual and simplest way of sharing managerial work is by specialist function: a Marketing Manager will plan and control all the marketing and sales of the business, a Production Manager will control the factory, and an Office Manager or Accountant will control the accounting and other office work.

Clearly-defined departments are now beginning to emerge, and the business is exhibiting the type of co-operation that developed in the history of productive organizations when the industrial revolution occurred. Tasks are becoming more specialized, production is

WHAT IS MANAGEMENT?

Management can be regarded as the process of planning business objectives, policies, and activities, organizing business resources to enable the plans to be executed, and controlling the business to ensure that the planned objectives are achieved. The elements (or stages) of this process are listed below (the numbers refer to the duties in the text).

Planning the objectives and the operations of the business

FORECASTING future values of relevant variables (1)

LONG-RANGE STRATEGIC PLANNING based upon these forecasts (2)

SHORT-TERM BUDGETING to implement the long-range plans (3)

OPERATIONAL PLANNING of day-to-day activities (4)

Organizing the staff and other resources of the business and directing efforts to execute the plans

ORGANIZING resources and allocating duties and responsibilities (5)

DIRECTING the efforts of staff towards achieving the plans (6)

CO-ORDINATING these efforts so that all are working in unison (6)

MOTIVATING staff so that resources are utilized most effectively (7)

Controlling the business so that the plans are achieved

MONITORING performance against the plans (6)

ADJUSTING resources and **REDIRECTING** efforts in the event of under-achievement of plans (6)

Note that **DECISION-MAKING** is the subsidiary process of choosing between alternative courses of action. It encompasses the drawing up of plans, the organizing of resources, and the adjusting of resources. It lies at the heart of the total management process.

becoming more mechanized, and communications and co-ordination problems between the various parts of the organization are beginning to manifest themselves.

A chart of the organization at this stage of growth is shown in Figure 1.2. A Board of Directors is included in this chart – by this time the business will have become a limited company, the previous owner/manager being now just one among a number of shareholders. Overall control is in the hands of the Board, which represents the shareholders, the previous owner/manager now being the **Managing Director** (or Chief Executive): as well as being a director, he holds the highest management (executive) position in the company.

The Marketing Manager (or Marketing Director, if he is a member of the Board) will control the office work associated with the receipt of customers' orders and the production of related documentation, and a clerk will be employed in his office to look after this work. Credit control will have become an important task, and if this, and sales invoicing, are brought under his control, a further clerk will be needed (although to minimize the possibility of fraud these tasks are often controlled by the Office Manager/Accountant). By this time the business may have its own lorries, in which case the drivers will probably be under the control of the Marketing Manager.

Production will now be housed in quite a large factory, with a hundred or so operatives under the control of a number of foremen or chargehands. The functions of technical development and maintenance will be under the control of an engineer, assisted by a number of technicians and operatives. Much of the paperwork required to keep things moving in the factory will be under the control of the Chief Works Clerk, who will probably supervise the stores, wages, cost control, and production control clerks.

The Office Manager will be in charge of the 'General Office', which will probably handle the accounts as well as services such as mail, filing, typing, reception, and possibly buying. The Managing Director will probably generate enough work to keep his personal secretary fully occupied on his personal correspondence, filing, diary, etc.

As the business continues to grow the functions of production engineering, accounts, and personnel become separated out into specialist departments, each under a departmental manager, and Work Study, O & M, and Legal departments may be set up. By this time

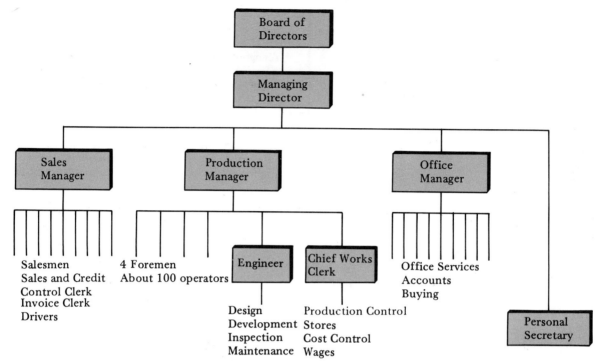

Figure 1.2   Organization chart of a medium-sized manufacturing business

the company will have a computer, and so there will be a data processing department. A possible organization chart showing the top management structure and the departments is shown in Figure 1.3. (Note that in this chart the distribution of control is shown as a horizontal breakdown instead of a vertical breakdown.)

Note the personal assistants to the Managing Director shown on the chart. These are advisory posts, exercising no control over the various departments. Their duties include undertaking research into economic and statistical matters in order to assist the Managing Director in his long-term planning, and they will assist in some of his administrative duties.

The work of the departments shown in Figure 1.3 is outlined below. Detail on many aspects of this work is given at appropriate points in subsequent chapters. For example: control and organization are dealt with in Chapters 2 and 3; statistical techniques employed in marketing, quality control, and forecasting in the section on statistics in Chapter 4; office procedures and forms in Chapter 5; computerized systems in Chapter 6 and 7; production control, costing and budgetary control, work measurement, linear programming, and other planning techniques in Chapter 8; method study, O & M techniques, and motivation in Chapter 9; the working environment in Chapter 10; and personnel matters in Chapter 11.

Marketing

Marketing is the function concerned with determining consumer wants so that the research, development, and production activities of the organization are directed towards producing goods for which there is a viable market, and selling at a profit the goods so produced. It includes the following departments:

1 Market Research – investigating marketing possibilities and consumer preferences. This will involve collecting either secondary data, i.e. 'secondhand' data published by the government or the trade, or extracted from the company's internal records; or, if this is not available or not suitable,

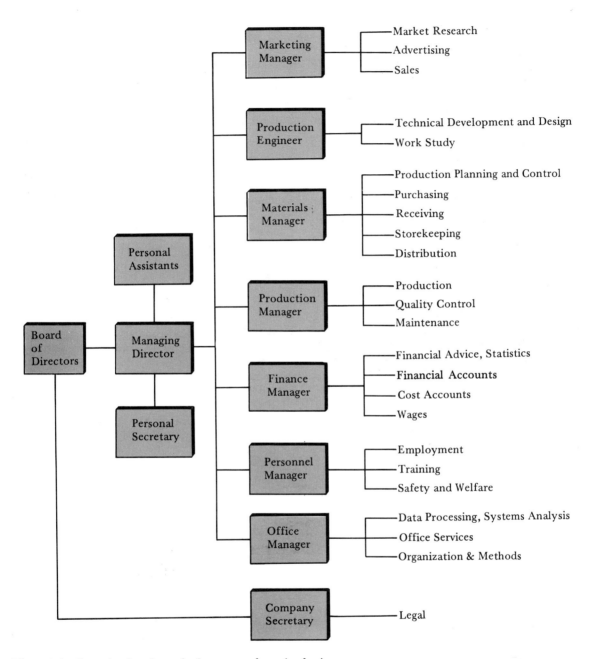

Figure 1.3 Organization chart of a large manufacturing business

primary data, i.e. data collected first-hand by means of sample surveys of consumers. Sample surveys, which would normally be carried out by specialist market research agencies, are expensive but are often the only way of obtaining the information required.

Market research seeks to find answers to questions such as: the amount and type of advertising needed to promote the company's products; the type and degree of competition faced by the company, and the market share enjoyed by the company and by its competitors; the appropriate price/quantity combination for each product made; the long-term trend in demand and the effects of seasonal influences.

2 Advertising – bringing the company's products to the attention of the market in order to promote their sale. Market research indicates the most appropriate type and methods of advertising, the amount spent on advertising being determined by the company's budgets. Many companies adopt a fixed sales/advertising ratio, so that the budgeted level of advertising is geared to the expected sales revenue during the budget period. The use of such a blanket formula, although easy to administer, is unlikely to result in optimal levels of advertising, and a more rational approach is indicated on page 65.

Companies often hire the services of specialist advertising agencies to run their advertising campaigns. The methods used include press and television advertising, circulars, brochures and catalogues, exhibitions, and branding of goods.

3 Sales – obtaining orders for the company's products. Orders may be obtained over the telephone, at an exhibition, or as the result of a visit by a sales representative. Large companies often employ a substantial number of representatives, each of whom will be assigned a certain geographical territory, and possibly a certain product range or a certain type of customer. Each salesman's itinerary will be planned in advance in consultation with the area sales manager, and reports will be submitted on the results of each call. The insight a salesman gains into customers' opinions and problems can be invaluable to the company in formulating its sales policy and its servicing policy, and improving its products.

The responsibilities of the Sales Department include producing brochures and catalogues, staging exhibitions, managing the showroom, and dealing with customers' complaints.

Production Engineering

Production Engineering is the function concerned with developing the company's products and production equipment so that consumer wants are met, and ensuring that the products are produced by the most efficient methods. It includes the following:

1 Technical Development and Design – designing and developing the product so that consumer wants (as indicated by market research) are met, and designing and developing special tools and equipment so that the Production Department can manufacture the goods efficiently. Possibly included in the work of this department will be research into new processes and products, though in the case of high-technology companies this will normally be undertaken by a specialist research department staffed by scientists and engineers.

The micro-electronics revolution is making a major impact on design work – computer-assisted design is resulting, in many instances, in a fourfold increase in productivity, and the interval between the inception of an idea and its translation into detailed technical drawings is being substantially reduced.

2 Work Study – laying down the methods to be used by production workers to make the products, and establishing output targets. The work of this department is normally split into two sections: method study, which has the task of critically examining existing methods in order to eliminate inefficiency and waste and to lay down good working procedures; and time study, which has the task of establishing optimum staffing levels, fixing work norms (output targets), and running bonus incentive schemes.

Materials Management

Materials management is the function concerned with controlling the movement and processing of materials through the organization from their initial supply to the final distribution of finished goods to the customer. It includes the following departments:

1 Production Planning and Control – controlling the flow of work through the Production Department so that the orders achieved by the Sales Department are met in the most economical way. Its main activities are:

(a) Scheduling (programming) the work through the Production Department so that delivery dates are met
(b) Loading each section or machine so that each has a

balanced workload and bottlenecks do not occur

(c) Determining what raw materials and bought-in parts are required, and at what times, by the production programme; also making arrangements as necessary to contract out work, in order to achieve the programme.

The 'control' part of the department's work involves ensuring that the planned programme is being achieved. It entails progressing (or 'chasing') late deliveries of essential supplies, ensuring that absences are covered in critical areas, making arrangements for the speedy accomplishment of late work, and so on.

2 Purchasing – buying the materials and bought-in parts specified by Production Planning and Control, and also machinery and other items required by other departments. The timing of orders and the quantities ordered have to be carefully calculated: materials and parts ordered too far ahead of requirements will tie up cash and storage space, whereas orders delayed to the last moment may result in production hold-ups if deliveries are delayed. If the quantities ordered are large, this will again tie up cash and storage space; small orders, on the other hand, will result in frequent re-ordering (which is administratively expensive) and failure to take advantage of any quantity discounts available. For each item there is an optimum re-order quantity, and the method for arriving at this is given on page 136.

For high-value items which are not purchased on a regular basis it is normal to request quotations from a number of suppliers and to place an order with the one offering the most favourable terms. For low-value items, and items which are re-ordered from a regular supplier, a quotation will not normally be required – a routine order will be send through the post, placed over the telephone, or given to the supplier's sales representative when he calls.

Although buying is sometimes organized so that each department is responsible for ordering its own supplies, it is normal practice to set up a centralized purchasing department. In addition to the usual benefits that result from centralization (see page 41), centralized buying has the following advantages:

(a) A central buying department has expert knowledge of the various sources of supply, and is better able to select the most suitable products.

(b) Centralized buying results in smaller numbers of orders (since the various small orders from individual departments will be combined into a few large orders), and this leads to lower administrative costs. In addition, since orders tend to be larger, better terms can often be obtained from suppliers.

(c) Better control over expenditure can be achieved.

3 Receiving – the task of the Receiving (or Goods Inwards) Department is to ensure that the materials, bought-in parts, and other items of goods and equipment received are as ordered, i.e. that they are of the right quantity and quality, and undamaged. Typically, each consignment is checked against the supplier's delivery note and the internal copy of the original order, and a document called the Goods Received Note (G.R.N.) is made out detailing the contents (see Chapter 5 for detail on the procedure). The items received are then routed to the requisitioning departments, or stored until needed.

4 Storekeeping – storing materials and parts prior to issue to the production or other user departments in suitable conditions and in optimum quantities. We can also include under this heading **stockkeeping**, which is concerned with receiving and storing finished goods from production (or from outside suppliers) and making issues for delivery to customers. All receipts and issues, as well as the balance left in stock, must be recorded on stock record cards or keyed into a computer terminal. The re-order level must be recorded on the cards, and an order placed as soon as the balance reaches this level. The re-order level will vary from item to item, for it will depend on the rate of usage and the average interval between ordering and receiving the items. A re-order level which is too high will result in unnecessarily large quantities of the item being held, which increases costs; a re-order level which is too low will result in frequent stock-outs (i.e. the item being out of stock), which will cause hold-ups in production or delivery.

5 Distribution – packaging and despatching goods, and delivering them to customers. In large organizations two departments are normally set up to handle this work: the Despatch Department, which deals with the despatch documentation and packages the goods, and the Transport Department, which includes not only the drivers who deliver the goods but also office staff responsible for planning the transport programme.

Transport programming involves determining the optimum routing of vehicles (so that delivery requirements are met in the most economical manner), and allocating the programme to vehicles and drivers. The optimum routing will often be determined by computer, using the technique of linear programming. The programme of deliveries for each day is drawn up on destination sheets, which include the route for each vehicle, the name of the driver, and the collection and delivery addresses.

Production

Production is the function concerned with manufacturing the goods required by customers in accordance with the specifications and methods laid down by Production Engineering and the programme drawn up by Production Planning and Control. It includes the following departments:

1 *Production* – this normally includes the work of machining the parts required, assembling the goods, and finishing (e.g. painting) them, and three departments may be set up for this purpose. Detailed instructions for each job that has to be done are recorded on job cards issued by Production Planning and Control; these are passed to the foremen or chargehands, who are normally responsible for allocating specific tasks to operatives.

There are three main types of production process:

(a) **Job production** (jobbing). This refers to the manufacture of goods which are tailor-made to fit the requirements of individual customers. Since few jobs will be the same, the main requirement for this type of production is flexibility in the use of equipment and labour; the highly variable nature of the work limits the use of work study to improve efficiency and fix output targets.

(b) **Batch production**. This refers to the production of a fixed quantity, or batch, of identical items to fulfil a special order or to build up the company's stocks. Continuous production (see below) may be organized on a batch basis, batches of identical products following each other continuously off the production lines; the advantage of this is that handling, checking,

etc. is often made easier if work is broken down into manageable lots (paperwork in an office may be batched for similar reasons; see page 87).

Owing to the larger quantities involved, batch production requires less flexibility in the use of operators and machines than job production, but greater attention needs to be given to the adoption of efficient methods and the setting of output targets. When a batch is being produced to build up the company's own stocks, the size of batch will be determined by balancing the need to produce in large quantities to achieve economies of production, on the one hand, against the cost of storing large quantities and the possibility of deterioration and obsolescence, on the other.

(c) **Continuous (or flow) production**. This refers to the large-scale production of items, which 'flow' from one operation in the process to the next (often on a conveyor belt). Little flexibility in the use of equipment and operatives is required, each operation being carried out by specialized machines and operators. Work study is most important in this type of production, as method improvements can achieve substantial economies, and properly-set output targets are essential.

The micro-electronics revolution will have a major impact on all three types of production, for a single industrial robot can perform a highly complex sequence of operations that up till now has required a number of specialized machines under the control of human operators. Moreover, product changes no longer necessitate extensive – and expensive – retooling: it is necessary merely to reprogram the machine.

2 *Quality Control (Inspection)* – ensuring that the items produced by the Production Department (or purchased from outside suppliers) are within the design tolerances laid down by the Technical Development and Design Department. For job production, this task will involve inspecting and testing every item produced; for continuous production a sample of the output will be tested and conclusions drawn about the total output on the basis of the sample results. The usual practice is to take small samples at frequent intervals and plot the results on a quality control chart. Early warning of any serious breakdown in quality standards will be given by indications on the chart of a consistent trend in the

plotted points towards either the upper or the lower tolerance limits.

Quality control can be carried out either by sending work to a central inspection bay before it is passed to the next stage in the production process, or by carrying out inspections at the point of work.

3 Maintenance – the servicing of machines according to a pre-determined maintenance programme (preventive maintenance), and the repairing of machines when they develop faults (breakdown maintenance); also included in the work of this department is the maintenance of buildings. In factories today the cost of hold-ups due to machine breakdown is such that some parts may be replaced after a fixed number of hours' wear even if they appear to be perfect. The calculation of the optimum interval between services is based upon probability theory, the probabilities used in the calculations being derived from past records.

Maintenance record cards must be kept for each machine, and on these is entered the preventive maintenance programme, as well as the actual maintenance that is carried out. Any breakdown maintenance that has to be undertaken is also entered – too high a breakdown rate will indicate a need to revise the preventive maintenance programme.

Maintenance work involves many skills, and the maintenance staff may include electricians, carpenters, bricklayers, etc. As in most other areas of business, the micro-electronics revolution is already making its presence felt: electronic monitoring devices are now being built into machines to give instant warning and automatic diagnosis of faults, thus reducing the numbers and quality of the maintenance staff required.

Finance

Finance (or Accounting) is the function concerned with producing the financial and cost information needed to plan and control the operations of the business, and with recording and summarizing all financial transactions in a form suitable for use by the tax authorities, the shareholders, and the managers. It may include the following departments:

1 Financial Advice and Statistics – the production of the financial information needed by management for planning and controlling business operations.

From past and present figures on sales, purchases, costs, etc., trends can be discerned and forecasts can be made. These forecasts enable management to draw up realistic plans and budgets, and control is then exercised by comparing the actual performance of the business against the plans and budgets.

Other types of advice which the department can give include: the financial effects of terminating particular activities; the evaluation of proposed investment projects; the raising of capital.

2 Financial Accounts – the recording of all financial transactions, the determination from these records of the amounts owed by customers and other debtors and owing to suppliers and other creditors, the value of assets, and the income and expenditure of the business. The department also produces the financial statements required by the Companies Act (the Profit and Loss Account and the Balance Sheet), but as these annual statements are of only marginal value to management it is normally required to produce in addition more directly useful summaries, such as monthly profit statements. Other analyses which management may require include the various measures of operating efficiency, capital structure, and liquidity (profit to capital employed ratio, working capital ratio, etc.).

In addition to this accounting work the department will normally handle sales invoicing and the issuing of monthly statements, the receipt of payments from customers, and the making of payments to suppliers. A further important task is **credit control**. Many businesses experience cash flow problems because effective follow-up of customers who delay settling their accounts is not exercised. The work of the credit control section involves ensuring that

(a) goods are not sold to customers who are unlikely to pay, and
(b) payment for goods that are sold is received within a reasonable period.

With regard to (a), a new customer may be required to pay in advance for goods, or he may be required to supply references from other traders or from his bank. Also, supplies to customers whose accounts are long overdue may be withheld. Close liaison with the Sales Department is obviously required for this aspect of the work, and in many companies the credit control section is part of that department.

With regard to (b), the credit control section will follow up customers who fail to settle their accounts within the stipulated credit period (payment is normally required within one month of receipt of the statement of the amount due). This is done by drawing up 'aged' lists of customers whose payments are one month, two months, and three or more months overdue, and taking appropriate action, beginning with letters requesting prompt settlement, and ending, if necessary, with legal action.

Traditional 'bookkeeping' is rapidly disappearing (even in quite small businesses), being replaced by computerized accounting systems, the ledgers being held on magnetic disks. All the work of double entry, adjusting balances, etc., is done automatically. The operator keys in, for example, a sales transaction, and the computer automatically posts the transaction to the sales ledger, adjusts the stock balance on the stock record file, and produces as required the invoice, the end-of-month statement of account, as well as aged debtors lists, sales analyses, stock reports, and other information required by management for its work of controlling the business.

3 Cost Accounts – the collection of costs for every job or process to assist management in planning and controlling the work of the business. Cost accounting involves determining the costs of materials, labour, and overheads for the various 'cost centres' of the business (which may be work sections, machines, processes, or individual jobs). Costs, such as factory rent, which apply to more than one cost centre, must be apportioned in some way.

This information is used in the following ways:

(a) To determine the true cost of each product sold by the company. Many companies use this to fix the selling price by means of the formula

selling price = cost price + a fixed percentage mark-up.

In many cases the selling price is governed by market forces, and knowledge of the cost price then gives management the level of profit on each product line. This indicates what action, if any, should be taken for that line (expansion, contraction, efficiency improvements, etc.).

(b) To draw up budgets and control the performance of the business. Costing information is used to draw up budgets for each department and for the business as a whole for the forthcoming (annual) budget period. Budgetary control is then exercised by comparing, each month, the actual costs with the budgeted costs and taking action, where appropriate, if significant adverse variations occur.

4 Wages – determining from the clockcards, output records, and other relevant documents the wages due to each employee, and making arrangements for these to be paid. The hours worked and gross wages due to each employee are calculated and entered on the master record (the payroll), together with the various deductions (such as income tax) and the net pay. This information is also entered on the employee record cards and on the payslips (using carbonized paper in manual/mechanical wages systems, automatically in computerized systems).

If payment is by cash, a note and coin analysis is made, the required cash is drawn from the bank, and the payslips plus the pay are inserted in pay envelopes and passed to the employees. Where wages are paid by credit transfer instead of cash, the procedure is much simpler: the company's bank receives a copy of the payroll, and it transfers from the company's account to each employee's account the wages due.

Today, payroll work is often computerized. Fixed details relating to each employee (rate of pay, tax code, standard deductions, etc.) are held in the computer on the employee file, and on the wages run this is merged with the variable data relating to each employee (the standard hours and overtime hours worked), and the payroll and other documentation produced automatically.

Personnel

People are the most important resource of a company (they are also the most expensive – wages and salaries often account for about half a company's costs). Personnel is the function concerned with ensuring that the right people are employed in the right posts at the right pay and conditions, and that they are properly trained and are able to give of their best.

Every manager, in every department, is responsible for those placed under his charge, and he therefore has a direct interest in personnel matters. A Personnel Department, where it exists, impinges on these areas of a manager's authority, and its purpose is (a) to ensure that company personnel policy (on employment, training, and so on) is properly implemented throughout the organization, and (b) to provide specialist advice and assistance to managers on personnel matters. The type of authority exercised by the personnel manager over this aspect of the work of other departments is known as *functional* authority (see page 42).

The Personnel function is concerned with the following matters:

1 Employment. This includes recruitment, promotions, dismissals, grading, and remuneration.

Recruitment − obtaining the right person for the job − begins with an examination of the job description of the post to be filled. From this a personnel specification is drawn up, giving the attributes required of the individual who is to fill the post: his physical and intellectual qualities, his general disposition, his educational attainments and experience, and any desirable special skills or aptitudes. The most suitable recruitment method can then be decided upon (advertising in the local press, for example, or using the services of an employment agency), and an advertisement and information sheet for the post drawn up. In most cases applicants for the post are required to complete standard application forms, from which applicants who most closely match the personnel specification are selected and invited to attend an interview. The purpose of this is to describe the duties of the post in more detail than is possible on an information sheet, answer any queries that applicants may have, and select the one considered to be most suitable for the job.

Promotion − movement to a higher post in the company hierarchy − is sometimes made solely on the basis of seniority (number of years' service with the company). It is generally recognized, however, that the most satisfactory policy is to promote according to ability, i.e. to choose the individual who most closely matches the personnel specification for the post, seniority prevailing only when there are two or more equally suitable applicants. It is important for morale that the company offers all employees the opportunity to reach the highest grades, that all are aware of the promotion avenues open to them, and that promotions are seen to be made on an equitable basis, i.e. merit and seniority.

Discipline − ensuring that employees conform to company norms of behaviour and work − is best achieved by motivating employees to give willingly of their best. However, in certain types of job it can only be achieved by coercing them to 'toe the line'. In the case of disobedience the possible courses of action are:

(a) Reprimand with no further action (for the occasional minor lapse)
(b) Reprimand with a 'black mark' on the employee's record card (written evidence of misdemeanors and reprimands is necessary if it is desired subsequently to sack the employee)
(c) Suspension, i.e. removal from the post for a period
(d) Dismissal, in the event of very serious offences.

Grading − placing posts in rank order − is, in many companies, done on the basis of a points system (points being awarded for the degree of responsibility entailed in the job, the educational qualifications and the skills required, and other factors as indicated in the job description and the personnel specification). In general, a uniform grading scheme should operate throughout the company.

Remuneration − the pay received for the job − may be by means of a fixed annual salary based on the grade and paid monthly; or, in the case of shop-floor and similar workers, at a fixed hourly rate (based upon grade) paid weekly for the number of hours actually worked. In many companies, however, an individual's pay is linked not only to the grade of his post but to his ability and the effort he puts into the job. Possible schemes are:

(a) Piecework, in which pay is geared entirely to output
(b) Bonus schemes, in which workers are paid at a fixed hourly rate plus a bonus which is determined by the speed of work (see page 129)
(c) Merit-rating schemes, in which effort and ability assessed over a long period are rewarded by adjustments to the employee's rate of pay.

2 Training. This ensures that each worker acquires the knowledge and skills to perform his job to the best of his ability. The design of a training programme must begin with an examination of the company's plans, for these will indicate the way in which jobs are likely to change in the future, both in terms of type of work done and numbers of personnel required. Next, it is necessary to examine the job descriptions, which will indicate what training objectives trainees must achieve in order to carry out their duties efficiently.

The programme is then designed so that these objectives are met. The final stage is to evaluate (and if necessary modify) the programme by assessing, against these objectives, the performance of individuals who have completed it.

Types of training include:

(a) Induction training – introducing new employees to the company by means of lectures, films, tours, etc.
(b) Job training – imparting skills necessary to the job by means of company-run training courses, college courses, or on-the-job training by supervisors.
(c) Supervisory training – e.g. by N.E.B.S.S. courses run by colleges.
(d) Management training – e.g. by part-time D.M.S. courses at colleges.

3 Safety and Welfare – ensuring that the working environment is as safe and pleasant as is reasonably possible, and providing canteen and social facilities. These matters are important to a company, because:

(a) it may be liable to damages in the event of an injury to an employee,
(b) it may be fined if it infringes the provisions of the Health and Safety at Work Act and other legislation, and
(c) the working environment and welfare facilities affect the morale and the productivity of the workforce.

Most large companies will employ a full-time safety officer. The duties of this post include training staff in accident-prevention, advising on safety aspects of plant and machinery, inspecting plant, buildings, and safety devices, and recording and investigating accidents. In addition, a nurse will normally be employed to deal with any injuries or sickness at work.

Office Management

Office costs (which include all administrative, secretarial, and clerical costs) account, overall, for some 60% of business costs, and it is therefore essential that this side of the company's work is run efficiently. Office management is the function concerned with the provision of centralized office services such as data processing, word processing and typing, filing, reprography, mail and messenger services, the telephone switchboard, and reception. It is also concerned with ensuring that office procedures throughout the company operate efficiently.

Every department is involved with office work of some description, and the Office Manager's authority in this area impinges upon that of the departmental manager: like the Personnel Manager, he exercises *functional* authority over a particular aspect of the work of other departments, in this case the documentation procedures and equipment used. Clearly the extent of this authority will vary from company to company.

Office Management may include the following departments:

1 Data Processing and Systems Analysis – designing computer-based systems for processing the data flowing through the business and for providing management with the planning and control information that it needs, writing the computer programs, and running the day-to-day operations of the computer. The Data Processing Department normally has three sections:

(a) **Systems analysis**, which is concerned with analysing existing information systems in the company, determining how these systems should be organized and what their information outputs should be, and redesigning the systems and the documentation used so that this output is achieved in the most efficient way. Traditional departmental boundaries tend to be ignored, the organization being viewed instead as a network of 'decision-centres' – points at which control is exercised – linked by information channels. The approach is to reorganize the company's administration around a computer-based method of supplying each decision-centre with its information requirements, designing the necessary information systems, and ensuring that the network of decision-centres is arranged so that control is exercised in the most effective way throughout the organization.
(b) **Computer programming**, i.e. writing the sequence of instructions needed by the computer to carry out the data processing tasks required. The systems analyst, having designed a system and specified what its data inputs and outputs should be, hands over the task of program-writing to specialist programmers.
(c) **Computer operations**, which is concerned with the day-to-day operations of collecting and verifying the input data, transferring the data from the source

documents onto punched cards or tape (or keying it directly into the computer), setting up the computer runs, and preparing the output for despatch to the user departments.

As a result of the micro-electronics revolution, computer data processing is steadily becoming decentralized. The pattern emerging is of each department having direct and constant access to the central computer via its own 'intelligent' computer terminals. It will key in its own input data, run programs as required, and receive on its own V.D.Us (visual display units) or printers the output it requires. Centralized computer operations sections can be largely expected to disappear.

2 Office Services – providing, on a centralized basis, typing, filing, reprographic, mailing, reception and similar services. The micro-electronics revolution, which is bringing in its wake the electronic office and the virtual disappearance of paper, will, over the next decade, make many of these services largely redundant.

3 Organization and Methods (O & M) – examining and improving office procedures and organization so that unnecessary activities are eliminated and productivity is increased, establishing staffing levels and output targets, and, where appropriate, installing bonus incentive schemes. There is obviously a close relationship between O & M and work study, and in some organizations both tasks are carried out by the same department.

Systems analysis is also related to O & M, and in some companies it is carried out by the O & M Department. O & M, however, is concerned mainly with making improvements to specific procedures or situations – e.g. improving the work-flow and the clerical methods in an office, or setting up a centralized typing service – whereas systems analysis is concerned mainly with designing information systems and improving business control.

The Company Secretary

All companies must, by law, have a Company Secretary, though in smaller companies the Finance Manager or Office Manager will combine this job with his other duties. He is the secretary of the Board of Directors, and he is responsible for convening and minuting the meetings of the Board as well as the Annual General Meetings of the shareholders. He is also responsible for conducting the correspondence of the Board, completing the various statutory books and returns (such as the register of shareholders), and attending to the legal aspects of the company's work (drawing up contracts, administering property investments and patents, conducting legal negotiations, and so on). In a large company the volume of such work may justify the establishment of a Legal Department, as shown in the organization chart in Figure 1.3.

ASSIGNMENT GROUP WORK

Discuss and determine the solution to Assignment 1 (b) & (c) (page 190).

2
The
Systems Approach
to
Organization
and Control

The purpose of the administrative procedures of a business is to enable managers to organize the business and exercise control over it. These procedures are the means by which diverse physical resources such as labour, capital, equipment, and materials are welded together into a well-regulated and smoothly functioning business machine.

This may sound mechanistic. But the theory on which the control of engineering systems is based can be applied with equal validity to running a business. Moreover, it is a theory which has particular relevance to business administration in the computer age. It is called **systems theory**, and it has its origin in a branch of applied mathematics known as cybernetics.

Like all good theories, the underlying idea is simple and elegant: a business, or a work-centre within a business, is viewed as a 'black box' which converts inputs received from its environment to outputs transmitted to its environment:

Control is exercised, not by monitoring what goes on inside the black box, but by monitoring the output that emerges from it, and adjusting the input in the event of undesirable output variations.

Systems Theory Applied to a Simple Productive Organization

Many college students have perhaps only a vague understanding of what goes on in business, and to illustrate the implications of the systems approach by applying it to something as complex as a modern business enterprise would serve only to confuse. We have chosen therefore as a teaching model the earliest and simplest productive organization devised by man, namely the stone-age hunting party. (A recent and familiar example of this type of productive organization is provided by the North American Indians.)

A hunting party is a system for converting wild animals (game) received from its hunting-ground environment into meat and skins transmitted to its tribal environment. The characteristics of this system, which it shares with modern business systems, are as follows (see Figure 2.1):

1 It exists within the framework of a number of larger systems, which collectively comprise its environment. In this example these include the tribal system and the ecological system of its hunting grounds.

2 It is made up of a number of smaller systems, called 'subsystems'. Two of these subsystems are the weapons system used to kill the prey, and an infor-

24

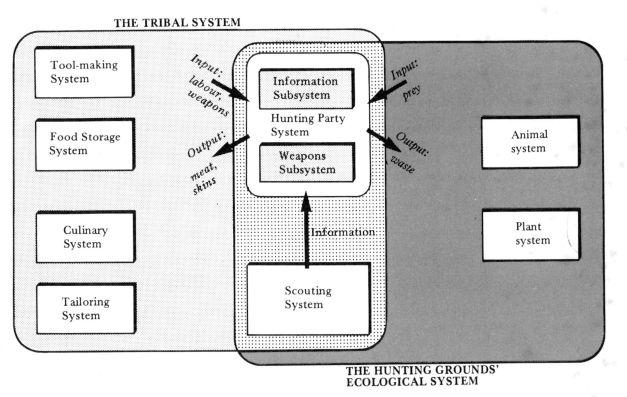

THE TRIBAL SYSTEM

Tool-making System

Food Storage System

Culinary System

Tailoring System

Input: labour, weapons

Output: meat, skins

Information Subsystem

Hunting Party System

Weapons Subsystem

Input: prey

Output: waste

Information

Scouting System

Animal system

Plant system

**THE HUNTING GROUNDS'
ECOLOGICAL SYSTEM**

Figure 2.1   A productive system: the hunting party

mation system of hand signals, whistles, etc. used to coordinate and control the attack. (Note that the hunting party is itself a subsystem of the larger tribal system.)

3 It uses inputs that are received from other systems in its environment. For example, its weapons are provided by the tribal tool-making system, and its prey is provided by the animal system that is part of the local ecology.

4 It utilizes these inputs to produce outputs which in turn form inputs to other systems in its environment. The meat from the prey forms an input to the tribal culinary system, and the skins form an input to the tribal tailoring system.

5 Its inputs, outputs, and operations have to be planned and organized. This involves:

(a) **Planning the specific objectives of the**

hunt. These objectives are the target output – the quantity and type of prey it should obtain within a given time if the tribe is to be adequately fed and clothed. In order to plan these objectives, the hunting party needs information from other tribal subsystems: from the food storage system it needs to know the current food-stock levels and the rate of depletion; from the culinary system it requires information on consumer preferences; and it needs forecasts of game availability from the scouting system and by extrapolation from the records of previous hunts.

(b) **Planning and organizing the inputs to and the operations of the hunt to enable the target output to be achieved.** This involves deciding upon and making available the resources of men, weapons, food supplies, etc. needed for the hunt, and deciding upon the area of the hunting grounds to travel to and the most suitable hunting or trapping methods to be employed. Again, information from other tribal subsystems will be needed to make these decisions: records of previous hunts, information on the availability of men, weapons, and food supplies, and information from the scouting system.

Note that the process of planning the outputs − (a) above − must be integrated with the process of planning the inputs and the operations of the hunt − (b) above. For example, if the labour input (the number of available hunters) is limited, then this will place constraints upon the target output and upon the methods employed. Also, the tribe will not attempt to maximize the output of the hunting party by sending on the hunt all the adult males, for this would seriously impair the operations of other tribal subsystems such as defence and tool-making. What it will attempt to do is to plan the outputs of *all* its subsystems so that total tribal welfare is maximized. The total physical resources of manpower, tools, etc. will then have to be shared among the various subsystems in such a way that this overall objective is achieved. This, in its modern business context, is the process of budgeting, and it is

enlarged upon in a subsequent section of this chapter and in Chapter 8.

6 It is made up of a number of components, shown in Figure 2.2.   This figure isolates the hunting party system from its environment and shows it as a configuration of **input**, **processing**, **output**, and **control** elements. The flow through the system is indicated by the arrows. The inputs (labour, weapons, prey, information) are utilized in the hunting process to produce the outputs (meat, skins). These outputs are monitored by the controller (the hunting-party leader) and compared with the target output. If it appears that the target output is not being achieved, then he will make suitable adjustments to the inputs, e.g. by issuing directions that the number of hours spent each day on hunting are increased, or that different hunting techniques are employed, or that the party moves on to another area of the hunting grounds.

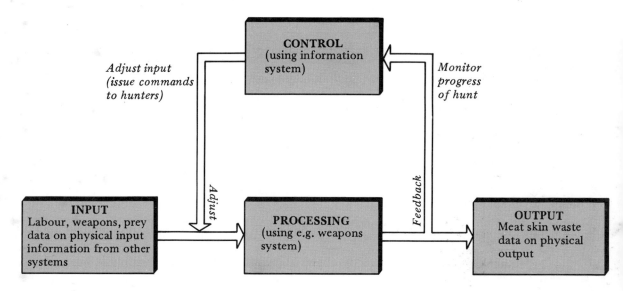

Figure 2.2   The elements of a system: the hunting party

CASE STUDY: A BUSINESS SUBSYSTEM

This case study, and a number of other case studies in this text, describe aspects of the work of the Materials Management function of the world's leading manufacturer of cigarette-making machines. Cigarette-making machines are extremely complex — each one comprises between 2,000 and 4,000 individual items, many of which are 'variable' (that is, customers can choose between a number of alternatives to suit their individual requirements). Production is on a small-batch basis.

Production is planned in monthly 'bites'. The parts for machines to be 'built' (i.e. assembled) in any particular build month have to be made (or bought in) and at hand by the first day of the month prior to the build month, and an important subsystem within the materials management function is that concerned with producing, from the sales programme, lists of parts and machines that are to be built in the build month lying seven months ahead (this list is called the layout — *see* below) and in the build month lying three months ahead (this list is called the lookout).

This task is part of the work of the Engineering Issues Department, which consists of a manager, five supervisors, and thirty-four clerks. The main inputs and outputs are shown in the diagram of the system in Figure 2.3. (Note that the work of planning the manufacture of the parts required for the build programme is carried out by the Production Control Department.)

The various parts of this system are as follows:

1 INPUT

This includes physical inputs (labour, office accommodation, etc.) and the following data inputs:

    (a) The sales plan for the next twelve months produced (and if necessary modified) at the monthly meetings of the Sales Review Committee (made up of senior management members, including the Engineering Issues Manager).

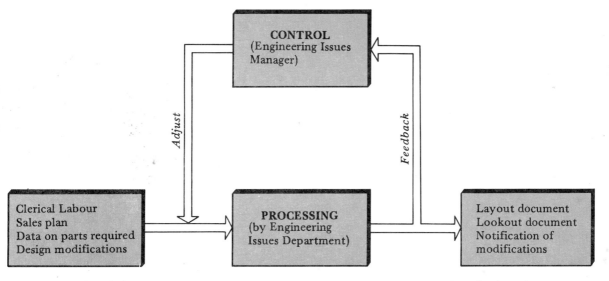

Figure 2.3   System for producing the forward build programme and parts list in a batch production company

This specifies the machines to be built and, for each machine, individual customer requirements (obtained from the Sales Department).

(b) Data on parts required for machines, held on a computer file (this data takes the form of lists of part numbers).

(c) Design modifications (part numbers and specifications) issued by the Design Department.

2 OUTPUT

Each month, the following documentation has to be produced:

(a) The LAYOUT document, covering a single build month, produced at least seven months prior to the first day of the build month. This document lists and totals all parts required, and machines to be assembled, in the build month. All modifications received over the next three months have to be incorporated in the layout. This document forms the advance forward plan to which Production Control (for example) works.

(b) The LOOKOUT document, similar to the layout but produced three months prior to the first day of build and incorporating all modifications and planning changes. This forms the final plan for the build month, and is used in particular by Stores to 'look out' (i.e. make available) the parts required during the build month. As a general rule, no modifications are accepted within four months of the first day of build, and so no alterations to the lookout will be made.

3 PROCESSING (I.E. DOCUMENT GENERATION)

This is carried out by two sections within the Engineering Issues Department, each under a supervisor: the Engineering Issues section, which produces the layout and the lookout, and the Modifications Control section, which incorporates all modifications into the system and notifies all interested parties (such as Production Control). The lists of parts required for each machine and the totals of each part (which form the basis of the layout and the lookout) are produced by computer.

4 CONTROL

This is carried out by the Engineering Issues Manager, who monitors the progress of the work of preparing the layout and the lookout, and of incorporating modifications, against the target issuing dates (seven months and three months prior to the build month). This monitoring is by means of:

(a) Regular feedback from the two sections on the status of the work and on any relevant problems

(b) A weekly Modification Report giving the number of modifications in the system and the number cleared in the past week.

In the event of the work falling behind, he makes adjustments by re-allocating work and re-assessing priorities.

EXERCISE

The aim of a BEC course is that students should achieve the specified learning objectives. Feedback (monitoring) is by means of assignments submitted to the lecturer. What is the input, how is the input processed, and how is the system controlled?

Motivation and Authority

If productive organizations were operated and run entirely by machines, then they could be controlled purely on the basis of engineering principles. However, organizations are made up of people: it is through people that business objectives (system outputs) are achieved, and it is by people that control is exercised. Therefore, for a proper application of systems theory to business administration, account must be taken of the fact that people must be *motivated* to achieve business objectives, and that control can only be exercised if people are prepared both to wield *authority* over others, and to accept the authority of others over them. An understanding of human needs and abilities in these two areas is therefore vitally important, and a full discussion is given in Chapters 9 and 11. We can summarize the main points made in those chapters as follows:

1 Motivation. If the individuals who make up an organization are highly motivated, then they will probably overcome organizational deficiencies or weak control in their efforts to achieve organizational objectives. On the other hand, good control and a well-structured organization will not overcome problems caused by poor motivation. Although individuals vary greatly in the extent to which they can be motivated towards achieving organizational objectives, for most people the following factors are important:

(a) **The reward for the work**. For the hungry hunter the prospect of a full stomach is a very powerful motivator – as is the prospect of an appreciative wife at the end of a successful hunt. For the modern worker, rewards include pay, promotion, status, and the praise and esteem of others.

(b) **The work group**. Most people desire to carry out their tasks as part of a small work group which accepts and values them and fulfils their need for companionship. This is also a powerful motivator, for in order to gain acceptance by the group the individual will strive to achieve the group's objectives.

(c) **The nature of the work**. Most people desire to perform satisfying work, that is work which enables them to exercise their natural abilities and fulfil their potential, which enables them to perform a 'whole' task (rather than a tiny – and meaningless – part of a task), and which produces an end-product that gives a sense of achievement. It is this that motivates artists to

paint and writers to write, despite the poor material rewards that such activities often produce.

2 Authority. The control of a business system involves planning its outputs (objectives) and adjusting its inputs so that the planned outputs are achieved. In the case of the labour input, this adjustment is achieved by issuing instructions and commands – in other words, by the exercise of *authority* by a manager or supervisor over his subordinates. The main factors to be noted in this connection are:

(a) **Span of control**. A single individual can accomplish only a limited amount of work and control only a limited number of people. The number of subordinates that a manager can control is called his 'span of control', and varies according to both the ability of the manager and the difficulty of the work. A foreman may be able to control twenty or thirty operatives if the work being done is of a very routine nature; whereas the leader of an O & M team may be able to control only three or four O & M analysts. These span of control limitations inevitably result in a hierarchical (pyramid) authority structure in large organizations – the Managing Director exercises authority over the functional managers, who in turn exercise authority over departmental managers, and so on down to the shop-floor or office-floor level. This type of control structure has been a feature of human organizations from earliest times.

(b) **Leadership Style**. This refers to the way in

HIERARCHICAL CONTROL IN ANCIENT TIMES

'Moses, this job is too heavy a burden for you to try to handle all by yourself. Find some capable, godly, honest men who hate bribes, and appoint them as judges, one judge for each 1000 people; he in turn will have ten judges under him, each in charge of a hundred; and under each of them will be two judges, each responsible for the affairs of fifty people; and each of these will have five judges beneath him, each counselling ten persons.'

(Extract from Exodus, Ch. 18, *Living Bible*)

which the objectives are planned and the adjustment of the labour input is achieved. At the lowest level in the organization the planning and adjustment process is often carried out by issuing commands without any consultation with subordinates, the style of leadership adopted being known as 'authoritarian'. It is a style that tends to quench individual initiative and to reduce motivation. Further up the organization a more 'democratic' leadership style will be adopted, superiors consulting with subordinates before making plans and adjustments. Improved decision-making can result, as more brains are brought to bear on the problem, and subordinates feel involved in the planning and control process and will endeavour to achieve objectives more enthusiastically. If a manager leaves subordinates completely free to plan their own objectives and to control themselves, the leadership style adopted is known as 'laissez-faire'. The absence of central planning and control in such situations may result in subordinates pursuing conflicting objectives, and reduced morale and lack of coordination are frequent consequences.

The Systems View of a Modern Productive Organization

To describe completely all the inputs, outputs, and subsystems of such a complex system as a modern busi-

ness would be a Herculean task. In Figure 2.4 we show just the main inputs and outputs and the main organ of control (top management).

As far as the Board of Directors and the top management are concerned the main output is, of course, profit. Control is exercised by comparing the actual profitability of the business against the level of profitability anticipated by the long-term plans, and issuing from time to time short-term plans and budgets to keep the business on course.

Figure 2.5 shows a simplified view of just a few of the main subsystems of the business, together with some of their main inputs and outputs. As has been emphasized previously, each subsystem is a system in its own right, complete with control and processing elements, the outputs of one subsystem forming the inputs of others.

If we extended this diagram to show all of the main subsystems of the business it would be apparent that, although some of the inputs and outputs would be of a physical nature (labour, equipment, raw materials, parts, finished goods), the overwhelming majority would consist of data and information. Most business activities are concerned with handling data and information. This is why office costs account for over half of all business costs, why computer data processing has had such a substantial impact on business, and why properly-designed information systems are so impor-

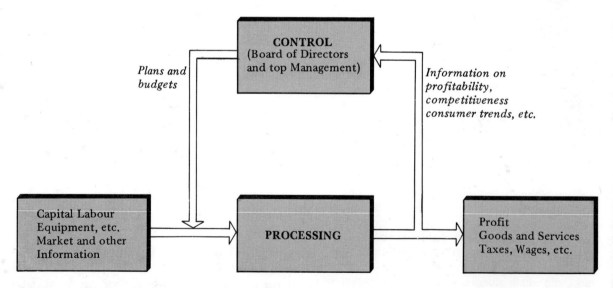

Figure 2.4   The systems view of a modern business

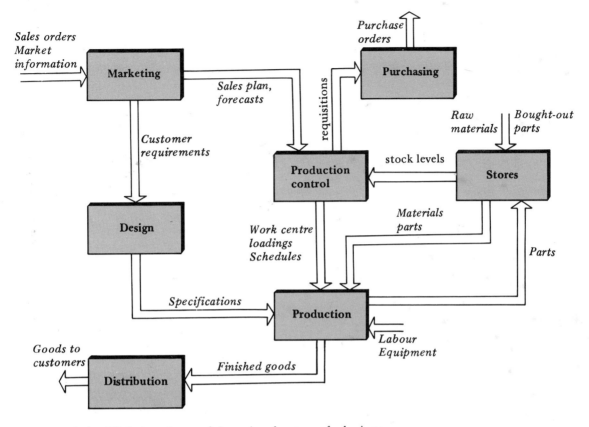

Figure 2.5   A simplified view of some of the main subsystems of a business

tant. It is also the reason for the current emphasis upon the teaching of business administration.

In the remainder of this chapter we consider in detail the input, output, processing, and control elements of business subsystems, together with the factors that determine subsystem boundaries (the dividing lines between one subsystem and another). In Chapters 3 and 4 we move on to the applications of this approach to the design of organization structures and information systems.

System Inputs

There are three types of input to a business system:

1 The prime inputs of labour, equipment, materials, etc. from which are produced the prime outputs of goods and services. Some of these prime inputs may take the form of data, for example, account trans-

actions in the case of a bank.
2 Data on these prime inputs.
3 Information on the system's environment.

We need at this point to distinguish between data and information. **Data** means raw facts received in an unprocessed form – for example, a customer's order consists of data: the customer's name, address, and the quantity and type of goods ordered. **Information** means data that has been processed (analysed and summarized) to a meaningful form to enable managers to make decisions – for example, sales analyses might give total sales by area, product, type of customer, etc., and comparisons with previous sales periods.

It is helpful to consider these three types of input by reference to our simple hunting-party model. 1. The prime inputs to this system are the hunters, the weapons, and the prey. 2. The data on these inputs include the number of hunters and their deployment, the number and type of weapons available, and spoor

---

WHAT IS ADMINISTRATION?

Administration can be regarded as a system, controlled by managers, for organizing and controlling labour and other physical inputs so that they form a well-regulated business enterprise, every part of which works harmoniously towards the achievement of the common objectives (which have been planned by management). The elements of this system are shown in the Figure in the Preface to this text.

The processing element is the network of 'office' (or administrative) procedures, which extend to every business activity. These procedures entail the collection and processing of data and the communication and presentation of information, and they include procedures for acquiring and utilizing the physical inputs to the business, procedures for providing managers with information for decision-making, and procedures for disposing of the goods, services, and other outputs of the business.

As stated in the Preface, the elements of this system form the organizing framework for this text. Part I of the text deals with the organization and control of physical inputs: the most important of these is labour, and so we are largely concerned here with the division of labour and the structure of authority. Part II deals with office procedures and management information, and Part III with the well-regulated business (that is, with the requirements that have to be satisfied for the main physical input — labour — to work efficiently and harmoniously towards achieving the objectives of the business).

---

environment (the tribe and the hunting grounds). The main information he requires on the tribe is the quantity of meat that must be produced within a given time in order to raise the tribal food stocks to an adequate level; the main information he needs on the hunting grounds is the location of the game herds. Both types of information are provided by other tribal subsystems: information on food stocks is received from the stock-keeping system; information on the location of game herds is received from the scouting system. In the case of North American Indians the scouts were sent out in various directions to collect data on the location of game and to summarize the data and transmit it to the hunting party by means of smoke signals.

The purpose of many of the systems that make up a modern business is to capture data from within the business itself or from its environment and convert it to meaningful information to assist the controllers of other systems to make their planning and control decisions. These information systems are discussed in Chapter 4; they include, for example, market research and management accounting.

System Processing

The processing element of a business system is concerned with converting the prime inputs to the prime outputs. It is known as the **operating system**, and in the case of the hunting-party system it includes the operations of locating, tracking, cornering, and killing the prey. Each of these operations is carried out by a subsystem of the hunting-party system — the prey-tracking and cornering subsystem is shown in Figure 2.6. Every system can be broken down indefinitely in this way into a hierarchy of smaller and smaller subsystems — although there is normally little to be gained in practice by considering more than two or three levels of subsystems.

The process of designing organizations as described in the next chapter works from the bottom up: it begins by analysing the operations that a business has to perform and the subsystems needed for undertaking and controlling these operations, and builds up these subsystems into larger systems in ways which best facilitate coordination and control, repeating this process until the highest system level — the total business — is reached.

and sightings of the prey — the hunt controller needs all this data in order to adjust the physical inputs to achieve the system's objectives. 3. To plan the hunt the controller needs, in addition, information on his

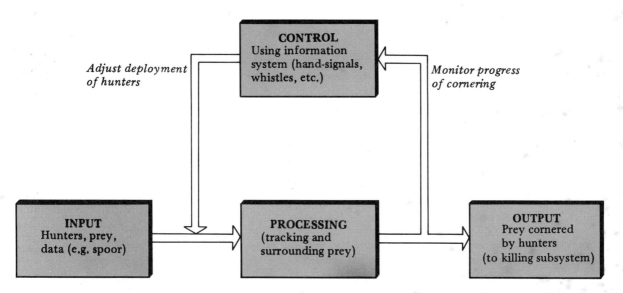

Figure 2.6   The hunting party; prey tracking and cornering subsystem

System Outputs

The output that the hunting party transmits to its environment includes its prime outputs of meat and skins, data relating to these prime outputs (quantity and type of meat and skins), and information on variations in the supply of game, the effectiveness of the hunting methods used, and so on.

In a well-regulated business each system will be set objectives, or target outputs, which form standards against which the prime outputs are compared. It is on the basis of these comparisons that control (by adjusting inputs) is exercised. The systems approach therefore emphasizes the need for precisely-stated objectives (i.e. precise standards of **quantity**, **quality**, and **time**), for imprecision and vagueness will result in difficulties of comparison and loose control. In addition, precise targets are a good motivator, for people work better if they know exactly what is expected of them.

Objectives are, however, of little value if they are not carefully planned and therefore *realistic*. If they are too difficult to attain, then:

1 the system will not achieve its planned output, which will have adverse repercussions on other systems in the business;
2 there will be conflict between the system controller and his subordinates;

3 people will become disheartened and give up trying to achieve them.

If they are too easy, on the other hand, then the system will not achieve its full potential, and resources will be under-utilized.

At the highest system level in the business – the enterprise as a whole – the objectives will be expressed in terms of the desired level of profit for the forthcoming planning period. To staff below this level this overall objective is not of immediate importance. Their concern is with the more detailed and specific objective of the subsystems to which they belong. The Sales Department is trying to achieve a planned level of sales within a given period of time, the Production Department a certain quantity and quality of output, and so on. Further down the organization are the individual sales sections or salesmen who are required to achieve certain monthly targets, individual production sections which are required to achieve their weekly planned production, and so on.

As a general rule, objectives are not stated below the supervisor level in the company hierarchy. It is not normally possible to specify precisely the quantity of work that a clerk in an office should produce in a day (though the *quality* of work can be specified). A clerk's output is governed by the amount of paperwork which is input into the system, and this can fluctuate greatly

CASE STUDY: OBJECTIVES IN A PRODUCTION CONTROL OFFICE

(The office referred to here is a department of the cigarette-making machine manufacturer referred to in the previous case study.)

The objectives that the Production Control Manager is expected to achieve are as follows:

1 The total inventory (i.e. stock) turnover ratio must not drop below 2.3 times per year (this ratio is calculated by dividing the annual cost of sales by the average value of the inventory). This objective ensures that stock levels are kept within reasonable limits.
2 Inventory expenditure must be kept within the monthly cash flow budget.
3 Requisitioning must be planned so that the parts required for the build programme arrive in stores at least four weeks prior to the first day of the build month. This objective ensures that the production of made-in parts by the workshops, and the ordering of bought-in parts and materials by Purchasing, is carried out in good time for the build programme. Objective 3 conflicts with objective 1, and to achieve both requires careful scheduling of work through the shops and of requisitions placed with the Purchasing Department.
4 Work-centre loading must be balanced. Each work-centre is allocated work according to the parts required to build the machines, and this workload should ideally balance with its capacity. (Note: a work-centre consists of a group of workers and machines undertaking a particular part of the production process.)

These overall departmental objectives generate the more detailed objectives that the supervisors of the sections within the department are expected to achieve. Objectives 1, 2, and 3, for example, generate the Inventory Control Supervisor's key tasks, as follows:

(a) The value of each category of inventory must be kept within specified limits.
(b) Any stock which has been held with no transactions for two years should be sold as scrap.
(c) The amount of slow-moving inventory should be held below a specified figure.
(d) The number of stock-outs should be below a specified figure.
(e) All orders must be placed in sufficient time for the materials and parts to be available by the first day of the month prior to the build month.

To monitor the achievement of objectives, the Production Control Manager receives the following information, all of which is generated from computer files:

1 Stock levels by value of each type of part (for Objective 1).
2 Month-end inventory breakdown showing stock usage (for Objective 1).
3 Month-end evaluations of the main categories of inventory (for Objective 1 and 2).
4 Number of orders placed late (for Objective 3).
5 Regular reports of late contract issues (for Objective 3).
6 Month-end breakdown of work-in-progress showing the jobs going through the workshops and the work-centre loadings (for Objective 4).

The adjustments that the Production Control Manager can make in the event of under-achievement of objectives are as follows:

1 Instruct the Inventory Control Supervisor to amend ordering rules so that order quantities and frequencies are adjusted accordingly (for Objectives 1 and 2).
2 Identify reasons for late ordering, and adjust e.g. staffing levels, or the information system for forecasting order requirements (for Objective 3).
3 If work-centres are working below capacity, then give instructions for jobs to be issued ahead of schedule; if they are too heavily loaded, then off-load work to outside contractors (for Objective 4).

In practice, however, the Production Control Manager rarely has to issue directions to the Inventory Control Supervisor, for the latter, by controlling *his* subsystem (the inventory control system) so that his key tasks, (a) to (e) above, are achieved, automatically ensures the achievement of the overall departmental objectives 1, 2, and 3. It is the exception, rather than the rule, for the Production Control Manager to have to step in.

from day to day. In a bank branch, for example, the objective of the clerks is to process all transactions by the end of the day, and if on a particular day there are a large number of transactions then the objective is achieved by working overtime.

System Control

The control of a system involves **measuring** the output, **comparing** this with the planned output (the objectives), and **deciding** and **effecting** input adjustments in the event of under-achievement. This process is carried out by means of the **control loop**, shown in diagrammatic form in Figures 2.2, 2.3, 2.4, and 2.6.

A control loop consists of the following parts:

1 A feedback arm, which is an information system for collecting data on the output and presenting it in a meaningful form to the controller. Modern information systems normally automatically compare the actual output with the planned output, informing the controller only of variances.
2 A controller, who decides what input adjustments, if any, are needed.
3 An adjust arm, which is a system for putting into

effect the controller's decisions – normally by communicating directives issued by the controller to his subordinates.

By concentrating attention on objectives, the systems approach encourages *self-control by subordinates*. The Production Control Manager's task described in the above case study typifies that of any manager:

1 To plan the objectives of all of the subsystems that comprise his department so that the achievement of each, when combined, results in the achievement of his overall objectives.
2 To ensure that the subsystems are organized so that their objectives can be achieved in an economical way. This involves the provision of adequate numbers of suitably trained staff, and adequate equipment, information, and other inputs.
3 To intervene subsequently in the running of subsystems *only if*:

(a) overall departmental objectives are not being achieved, in which case input adjustments must be made.
(b) changes occur, e.g. in overall departmental objectives, in which case the organization of subsystems and

the planning of their objectives may have to be modified (see next section).

The leadership style which is most consistent with this approach is the democratic style. Subsystem objectives, and the inputs needed to achieve those objectives, should be planned by a process of consultation between superior and subordinate. In this way those who have to achieve the objectives have a say in both the planning of those objectives and in planning their subsystem inputs (the resources placed at their disposal). *How* the planned objectives are achieved (i.e. how the subsystem processing is organized) can be left to the discretion of the subordinate (though the methods used must obviously conform with company policy regarding honesty, working conditions, and so on).

The advantages of this approach are that

(a) More brains are involved in the planning process, which may result in new ideas and better plans
(b) Involvement in the planning process results in a commitment to achieve the plan
(c) The responsibility given to subordinates to use their initiative in achieving the objectives results in improved motivation and innovation
(d) Freedom from having to intervene constantly in the running of subsystems increases the potential span of control of the superior, leading to a better use of business resources and greater flexibility in the grouping of subsystems (see next section). It also gives the superior more time for decision-making on important matters.

This process of planning objectives and inputs in consultation with subordinates should begin right at the top of the organization (the Managing Director consulting with the functional managers in order to determine their objectives and inputs) and work down to the supervisor or foreman level. The various inputs will be evaluated in financial terms, and as a result of this process realistic budgets which comprise both the input costs and the planned objectives can be set for the enterprise as a whole, for the major functions, and for the departments and sections within each function. Control can then be exercised by comparing actual expenditure and achievement against the budget (see Chapter 8).

This approach is not normally considered to be workable at the lowest level of the organization, where often the only practical leadership style is author-itarian. The typical clerk has little or no say in what his objectives should be, and he works under the watchful eye of his boss to ensure that he follows the laid-down methods. However, some companies have tried to extend the consultative approach down to this level, by giving work-groups responsibility for determining for themselves how their work should be organized, with notable results in some cases.

System Boundaries

The boundary of a system is the dividing line between it and its environment: it is defined by specifying all of the inputs to the system received from its environment and all of the outputs transmitted from the system to its environment. Many systems have natural and obvious boundaries: the tribal system considered earlier is one example, a business enterprise is another. There would be little practical value in attempting a formal definition of boundaries in such cases, for what is part of the tribal system (or business enterprise) and what is part of its environment is obvious to all concerned. At the subsystem level, however, the boundaries are often neither natural nor obvious, and it is at this level that there is much to be gained by formally analysing the boundaries with a view to organizing the subsystems in a way which enables the business as a whole to optimize its performance.

There is a natural tendency for the controller of a subsystem within a business to concern himself only with the performance of his own subsystem, and to ignore the effects that decisions he makes may have on the rest of the organization. For example, a factory manager, in order to maximize his output, may adjust his inputs in ways which are detrimental to the overall performance of the business; he may hold excessive quantities of stock (to avoid production hold-ups), or he may employ more staff than are needed. To counteract this tendency it is necessary to adopt what is known as the **total systems approach**, which involves designing subsystems and grouping them together into larger systems in such a way that the larger system controllers can plan the inputs and outputs of these subsystems so that overall performance is optimized. This approach to organizational design is explained in more detail in Chapter 3.

The computerization of data processing and other administrative functions is causing the total systems approach to assume increasing importance. A computer enables vast quantities of data on many business activities to be summarised rapidly into a meaningful form and brought together to a single control point. The information thus obtained enables a manager to exercise effective control over a wider span of business operations than was previously possible, and new and more effective groupings of subsystems are emerging to take advantage of this enhanced control capability.

One example of such a grouping is the materials management function. This made its appearance in the late 1960s, and has since been adopted by an increasing number of companies, especially in America. It includes purchasing, storekeeping, production control, and distribution, all under the control of a materials manager (see Figure 1.3). In traditionally-organized companies these departments are not grouped together in this way and tend to operate independently of one another, so that the distribution system (for example) attempts to optimize its performance without regard to the effects that this will have on other systems. Thus it will tend to transport parts and goods by the cheapest, and therefore slowest, means possible, with the result that warehouses and other depots suffer increased costs as they need to keep high levels of stock to avoid stock-outs. By grouping these subsystems under a single control point the organization can minimize its total materials handling and conversion costs and improve its service to customers. This overall optimization will normally result in the sub-optimization of some subsystems: in the case of distribution, for example, some multi-national organizations have found that total materials-handling costs are minimized if the most expensive form of transport, air-freighting, is used.

3
Designing
the
Organization

The most important physical resource of a business is labour, and it is in connection with this resource that the term **organization** is mainly used. It refers to:

1 The division of labour – the purpose of this is to enable the various business operations to be carried out in an efficient way.

2 The structure of authority – the purpose of this is to enable the operations to be properly co-ordinated and controlled.

Organizations must be designed with these two purposes in mind. So far as division of labour is concerned, the main objective of organizational design is to promote operating efficiency and a smooth workflow. So far as the structure of authority is concerned the main objective is to promote effective control and a good flow of information to the control points.

This chapter builds on the principles discussed in Chapter 2 to show how organizations should be designed so that these objectives are achieved.

The Main Steps

A rose bush, if allowed to develop in an uncontrolled way, soon channels its efforts into haphazard and largely unproductive growth. New branches seem to spring up everywhere, vying with each other for the available resources of sap and light, and the gardener's objective – the production of roses – is not satisfactorily achieved.

A business often follows a similar pattern of development. Sooner or later the point is reached when its organization needs to be critically examined and restructured to enable it to achieve the owners' objectives more effectively. For most businesses this point comes when the decision is made to computerize their data-processing operations. Although computerization can be (and often is) carried out in a piecemeal fashion (department by department, each being considered in isolation from the rest of the organization), for the business to achieve its full potential a review of the total organization should be made with a view to using the great power of the computer to integrate and optimize the operations of the business as a whole.

The main steps in carrying out such a review are as follows:

1 Identify the *general objectives* of the business. This step in the design process has been dealt with on page 7 and in case study 'Medtech' that follows.

2 Identify the *main operations* that the business must carry out in order to achieve these objectives. These operations will form a sequence (e.g. advertising – receipt of customer's order – processing of customer's order, etc.) and will generate a flow of work through the organization. This sequence of operations comprises the operating system of the business. It

processes the prime inputs (which might be raw materials, parts, etc. in the case of a manufacturer, or data inputs in the case of a bank or insurance company) and produces the prime outputs (finished goods, services, etc.).

3 Design the various subsystems of the operating system. The key design consideration here is *efficiency* − the methods of work, the workflow, and the staffing levels should be fixed so that operations are carried out in the most cost-effective way.

4 Identify for each operation the control *decisions* that have to be made, and the *information* needed for these decisions. An example of some operations, decisions, and associated information requirements is given in Table 4.1. (page 55).

5 Design information subsystems to provide these information requirements.

6 Group the subsystems designed in 3 and 5 above into larger systems in ways which best promote the flow of information and the process of decision-making; similarly group the larger systems, and translate the resulting network of control points linked by information flows into a restructured organization.

We are concerned in this chapter with the actual design process, namely (A) designing the operating systems, (B) designing the information systems, (C) grouping the systems. These parts of the process are discussed in the sections below. A further section of the chapter deals with other aspects of organizational design, and finally the systems approach to organizational planning is compared with the traditional 'classical' approach.

ASSIGNMENT GROUP WORK

Discuss and determine the solution to Assignment 2(i) & (ii), page 191.

(A) Designing the Operating Systems

The basic operations of the business are carried out by **primary workgroups**. A primary workgroup may consist of as few as three or four people or as many as twenty or thirty, under a supervisor, chargehand, or foreman. These workgroups, with their associated equipment, form the building bricks, or operating systems, from which the organization is constructed. The size of the primary workgroups is determined pri-

marily by the span-of-control limitations of the supervisors and foremen who control them.

Work study, and Organization and Methods (O & M) are concerned with the design of operating systems. Work study is applied mainly in the factory, its aim being to determine the best methods of processing physical inputs (such as raw materials and parts) and with fixing target outputs, and O & M is applied mainly in the office. (Systems analysis can be regarded as an offshoot of O & M which concentrates on the computerization of office procedures. Properly applied, however, it has a much wider scope: to treat the organization as an interconnected network of subsystems, none of which can be analysed and designed in isolation from the rest; *see* the remaining sections of this chapter).

At the individual operating-system level, the techniques of work study, O & M, and systems analysis coalesce into a single broad design approach. Each begins by examining the outputs of the system under review, asking the question, 'What is being achieved?' and following this up by asking, 'What *ought* to be achieved?' Having critically examined and established the purpose of the system by this questioning technique they then proceed to carry out a similar critical analysis of the processing methods used and the inputs required. In the case of an office this analysis will indicate which procedures should be computerized and which should be done manually or mechanically. The critical examination technique and the method of developing new procedures are examined in detail in Chapter 9.

The principles underlying work study and O & M were developed in the 1880s by Frederick Taylor and form the basis of what is known as 'scientific management'. It is an approach which emphasizes the need to analyse scientifically the operations that have to be carried out and to group them in ways which simplify work to the greatest extent and which lead to the most efficient flow of work.

A rather different approach to the organization of work has come from the human relations movement. This emphasizes the need to satisfy human social and psychological needs at work, and to group operations in ways which provide satisfying work.

Both of these approaches should play a part in the design of operating systems, and a description of their applications, and of their advantages and limitations, is given in Chapter 9. As is explained in that chapter, they can lead to quite different operating system configurations. The example is given there of a sales office handling the paperwork for a number of sales areas. Under the scientific management approach there might be a section dealing with enquiries and quotations, a section dealing with the receipt and processing of customers orders, a credit control section, and so on. Under the human relations approach the work might be grouped by sales area, the clerks attached to each area doing *all* the paperwork connected with customers in that area – order-processing, credit control, invoicing, etc. The former approach has the advantages claimed for scientific management – increased efficiency because of the high degree of specialization, reduced training, etc., whereas the latter approach gives each workgroup a more varied and interesting job covering a complete cycle of work and it enables the group to identify with the task of serving the particular customers in its sales area.

(B) Designing the Information Systems

This is the biggest part of the organizational design task, and it is considered separately in the next chapter. It is sufficient to note here that the design of these systems is the specialist task of the systems analyst. The procedure is to identify the decisions that have to be made by those responsible for planning and controlling the operations of the business, to determine the information needed to make these decisions, and to design the information systems that will provide this information.

These systems will provide a **flow** of information through the organization. The way in which information flows in a present-day business is illustrated in Figure 2.5. As is shown in the next section, in order to integrate decision-making and coordinate activities throughout the organization the decision-centres should be grouped around these flows. This results in particular groupings of supervisors under departmental managers, departmental managers under functional managers, and so on, and in this way a hierarchical structure of control is built up.

However, one of the results of the micro-electronics revolution is likely to be a shift away from this type of hierarchical control structure. The way in which information will flow in the business of the future is shown in Figure 4.1. (page 59). Integration of decision-making and coordination of activities will be achieved by means of a total computerization of all information collection, processing, and presentation, each decision-centre receiving the information it needs directly from the central computer (see page   ). The 'span of control' of this computer will be extremely wide, and this will result in a very 'flat' organization structure.

(C) Grouping the Systems

As explained in Section (A), the elemental operations in the flow of work should be grouped into operating systems in ways which promote efficiency and a good workflow, and which lead to satisfying work. As we move up through the organization above the primary workgroup level so the emphasis shifts from workflow to information flow. Operating systems should be grouped into larger systems according to the information needs of their control points (decision-centres), *not* according to the operations that have to be performed.

For an example of this type of grouping, the reader should refer to the sales order processing subsystem and the installation subsystem described in the case study 'Pinecrafts' (Appendix II, paragraphs 2, 3 and 9, page 188). These two subsystems are quite different in character. The sales order subsystem is at the beginning of the flow of work, whereas the installation subsystem is at the end, being similar in nature to and following immediately after the finishing subsystem. However, the installers' work-programme is decided from the sales orders, and the information that is passed to the customer when an order is processed is determined from the programmes. The systems approach, by concentrating on the information flows, shows that these two operating systems, although in themselves quite diverse and unconnected, should be grouped in the one larger system (sales).

Thus the information flows should dictate the basic configuration of decision-centres in the organization, and it is this configuration which determines the way in which organizational activities should be grouped. In order to achieve the maximum integration of decision-making and the most economical use of managerial and supervisory staff, as many activities as possible should be grouped together under a single controller, but human span-of-control limitations will limit the extent to which this can be done. The decision-centre configuration and human span-of-control limitations therefore combine to determine the arrangement and boundaries of the subsystems within the overall organization.

At the lowest level in the organization the operating systems that are closely linked by information flows should be grouped into larger systems, each controlled by a single controller (manager). He will have an overall view of the needs and capabilities of the subsystems within the larger system that he controls, and he will therefore be able to plan and organize their inputs and outputs so that the overall performance of the larger system is optimized. (For an example of this type of optimization see the notes on Materials Management on page 37.)

These larger systems should be further grouped in accordance with the same principles, and the process continued until a single **master system** is built up, which is the organization as a whole, whose controller is the Managing Director.

It is at this master system level that the outputs and inputs for the business as a whole are planned, and this overall planning process must be carried out within the context of the needs and capabilities of the systems that comprise the organization's environment: primarily the market which demands its outputs and the market which supplies its inputs. The information systems that feed this level of control must collect and process data not only from within the organization but also from its environment.

The final step in the task of designing the organization is to translate this hierarchy of subsystems and control points into a hierarchy of posts. An organization chart of the restructured organization will look similar to one drawn of the old, but a closer inspection will reveal that sections and departments have been grouped in different ways, and the way in which authority is distributed in the organization will be seen to be quite different.

Examples of Co-ordination Failure

If information is not flowing properly between decision-centres, there will be a lack of co-ordination in decision-making. The main results of this include:

1 Inconsistent objectives − as when the Production Department produces goods which fail to match the specifications required by the Sales Department.
2 Problems of timing − as when delivery dates promised by the Sales Department cannot be met by the Production Department.
3 Lack of awareness of changed needs − as when forms are completed in one department which are no longer needed by the user department.
4 Shirking of responsibilities − as when a job gets left because no one feels responsible for it.
5 Bottlenecks in the flow of work − as when hold-ups are caused by one section failing to carry out its part of the task.

Further Aspects of Organizational Design

1 Conversion of Subsystems to Master Systems: Divisionalization. Some organizations grow to such a large size that problems of planning and control arise at the master system level. For many organizations these problems came to a head during the 1960s as a result of the takeovers and mergers that occurred at that time. The extended lines of communication in these mushrooming organizations and the centralization of decision-making on the head office resulted in the various business units on other sites becoming unresponsive to the needs of their environment, standardized procedures being imposed from the centre which were often inappropriate to the local situation, poor communications, and low morale (see the case study 'Betapacers Inc.' on page 47).

The solution that has been widely adopted is **divisionalization**: under this the master system (the total organization) is divided into a number of smaller master systems (divisions), the controller of each having authority to plan and organize his own inputs and outputs (within the framework of overall organizational policies). He becomes, in effect (and often in name), the Managing Director of his division. In the case of a trading organization, divisionalization will normally be on a geographical basis (by sales area); in the case of a manufacturing organization it will be according to product. Each division will have its own Sales Department, Purchasing Department, Accounts Department, and so on.

2 Overlapping Systems: Centralization of Operations. Greater efficiency may be attained at the operating system level if certain operations (such as typing, word processing, data processing, purchasing) are carried out centrally by specialist departments. Such a department carries out some of the processing needed by the user departments to convert their inputs to outputs, and is, in effect, a subsystem which is shared by the user departments.

Operations will normally be centralized if

(a) they are common to a number of departments, and
(b) they involve expensive equipment or specialist staff which, if provided departmentally instead of centrally, would be under-utilized and would result in wasteful duplication of resources.

Besides giving a better use of resources, centralization leads to easier handling of peak work loads, easier coverage of staff absences, and more effective control (by a specialist supervisor) of the operations involved. The disadvantages of centralization include greater bureaucracy ('red-tape'), standardized procedures which may not suit every situation, inflexibility in responding to the changed needs of user departments, and delays in dealing with urgent work.

3 Overlapping Systems: Functional Authority.

Two systems will also overlap if the controller of one exercises authority over the way in which certain specialized operations are carried out in the other. This is called **functional** or advisory authority, for it allows functional specialists within the organization to ensure that operations carried out in a number of systems are performed in the most effective way and in accordance with company policies. The controller of the system in which the operation is carried out exercises *direct* authority over it: he is responsible for planning and monitoring its outputs, but he has authority to adjust only some of the inputs. Other inputs − some of the equipment and methods used, and possibly some of the staff − will be under the control of the specialist adviser.

Functional authority may be illustrated as follows:

(a) The Office Manager may have authority to decide the clerical procedures, the forms, and the office equipment used in other departments.
(b) The way in which staff are recruited, trained, promoted, reprimanded, etc. must conform with the rules and procedures laid down by the Personnel Manager (who may intervene in the event of a dispute).
(c) If some purchasing is decentralized (i.e. carried out

by departments instead of centrally), then the purchasing procedures to be followed will be decided by the Purchasing Manager, who may also be responsible for recruiting, training, and placing the staff who are to carry out the purchasing operations.
(d) If the 'Pinecrafts' installers are under the direct authority of the Sales Manager (as suggested on page 40), then the Production Manager should exercise functional authority over their working methods.

Functional authority of one post over another can be represented on an organization chart by means of a broken line joining the posts.

4 Overlapping Systems: Co-ordinating Authority.

Another way in which systems can overlap is if controller X is the coordinator of a project: he plans and monitors the output, but the processing is carried out by specialists from systems W, Y, Z, etc. Controller X is the project team leader, controllers W, Y, Z, . . . exercise functional authority over some inputs and the methods used. This type of authority is commonly found in colleges, where 'course co-ordinators' integrate the teaching activities of subject specialists so that course objectives are achieved.

5 Communications.

The lines on an organization chart show the formal (planned) relationships between posts. These relationships are made operational by communications:

(a) Communication upwards from subordinate to superior of feedback information
(b) Communication downwards from superior to subordinate of directives to put decisions into effect, and also of general information about the business
(c) Communication horizontally between controllers of related systems to ensure co-ordination of decision-making.

In addition to these there will be the informal (unplanned) relationships leading to informal communications which bypass these official channels − communications which take place in the canteen or other communal areas between staff who are not formally related on the organization chart. It is only in poorly-designed organizations that these form an important means of getting the right information to the right people (for an example .ee the case study 'Betapacers Inc.' at the end of this chapter).

In all organizations, however, communications are a

major problem. Formally-instituted procedures for encouraging communications both between related posts and, where necessary, between posts that are not related on the organization chart, are essential to ensure that decision-makers and staff receive the information they need. Committees provide for such procedures.

(a) **Management committees** – whose members comprise controllers from related systems – meet at regular intervals to ensure that decision-making is properly co-ordinated across the organization. Such committees may exist at several levels in the organization. At the master system level is the Board of Directors, a committee consisting of the Managing Director, non-executive (outside) directors with specialist knowledge of important aspects of the organization's environment, and executive directors who head the major functions (such as marketing, materials management, and finance). At meetings of this committee relevant information on the organization's environment and on its needs and capabilities is brought together in order to decide its inputs and outputs for the period ahead. From this committee emanate the strategic plans and the overall objectives of the organization.

At lower levels in the organization there may be committees to co-ordinate departmental decision-making. Such committees are necessary to ensure that related parts of the organization work harmoniously towards the achievement of the overall objectives, and they may consist of managers from a number of different functions who bring to bear on the decision-making process information from a wide area of the organization.

(b) **Consultative committees** (dealt with in detail in Chapter 11) exist to promote discussion between managers and staff representatives from a wide range of levels in the organization on decisions affecting staff welfare and interests. Important changes in conditions of work and employment should be fully discussed at such committees before final decisions are taken. Such committees are an important means of ensuring that staff are involved in and are in agreement with decisions affecting their interests.

(c) **'Ad hoc' committees** may be set up from time to time to deal with one-off problems. For example, they should be formed to facilitate consultation between management and staff if important changes in organization and methods of work are being considered. They enable staff representatives to air their views and participate in the decision-making process, and to ensure that those whom they represent are kept informed of developments (see the section and case study below).

Implementing Organizational Change

Organizations are made up of human beings, and changes in organization or methods of work must take full account of human needs. Any change of this nature constitutes a transition from the known to the unknown, and this is threatening to the individual's security. Organizations therefore face an inbuilt human resistance to change, and to overcome this it is necessary to remove the underlying threat by:

1 giving guarantees of employment to staff affected by the change (these include guarantees of job, pay, status, and job-satisfaction), and
2 adopting the democratic process of consultation between management and staff (or staff representatives) before instituting the change.

CASE STUDY: REORGANIZATION OF AN AIRLINE'S SUPPLIES FUNCTION

(This case study is included in this text because it illustrates many of the principles discussed above. It should be pointed out, however, that the reorganization of the airline referred to here was carried out on a piecemeal basis (department by department), not on the basis of a total systems approach.)

On 1st April 1972 the two major U.K. airlines, BEA and BOAC, merged to become British Airways. As a result of this merger the various functions of the two airlines – supplies, engineering, finance, etc. – were amalgamated, a feat which has taken a number of years to accomplish but which is resulting in a unified organization structure. In this study we trace the history of the amalgamation of the two supplies functions.

Supplies includes the tasks of purchasing, storing, and issuing spare parts, equipment, motor vehicles, uniforms, etc., as well as negotiating contracts for major cost items such as fuel. In BOAC all these tasks were carried out centrally by the Supplies Department; in BEA, however, the supplies function was decentralized, individual departments being responsible for ordering, storing, and issuing their own supplies (there was no Supplies Manager, though some of the high-cost items, such as fuel and aircraft simulators, were dealt with centrally by the Financial Director). A total of 650 supplies staff were employed in the two organizations.

The merger caused widespread apprehension amongst the staff of the two airlines, and in order to allay their fears and facilitate the various functional amalgamations that were necessary the new Board of Directors of British Airways gave the following undertakings:

1 No redundancies would arise as a result of the merger
2 The amalgamation of each function would be planned in consultation with staff representatives from both airlines.

The sense of security and of involvement in the planning process that these undertakings created in the staff was crucial to the ultimate success of the merger.

The amalgamation of the two supplies functions took place in two phases. Phase I, which commenced in mid-1973, was essentially a feasibility study. **A Supplies Review Committee** was set up, comprising fifteen senior management members and twenty supplies staff members, with the object of determining how, if at all, the functions might be merged. The supplies staff members were drawn from a number of grades from both organizations, and they were all trades union representatives (from a number of unions). The committee met once a month for a year, and between meetings each staff member discussed developments and proposals with the staff he represented.

Towards the end of 1974 the committee published a report embodying its recommendations. The two main recommendations were that:

1 *The negotiating of all contracts, the purchasing of high-cost items, and the storage and issuing of spare parts and uniforms should be undertaken centrally under a Head of Supplies*
2 *The purchasing and storage of all other supplies should be decentralized (carried out by individual departments), under the functional authority of the Head of Supplies, who should be responsible for the placement and development of departmental supplies staff.*

The rationale behind these recommendations was:

1 Eighty per cent of expenditure on supplies was accounted for by the relatively small number of high-cost items, (less than twenty per cent of all items), and to control this expenditure it was desirable that their purchasing be under the direct authority of the Head of Supplies
2 The purchasing of low-cost items (which comprised four-fifths of all items) should be carried out by user departments in order to minimize bureaucracy

and paperwork. The Head of Supplies should exercise functional authority over the supplies policies of user departments (to ensure standardized purchasing policies and procedures) and over the placement and development of supplies staff (to provide supplies staff throughout the organization with a good career structure).

Both the staff members of the committee – and the staff that they represented – and the senior management members were eager to see the proposals implemented, for they had been involved in the planning process. However, two problems arose:

1 In order for the Phase II of the amalgamation to commence, the British Airways Board had to approve the proposals. Although the Board was represented on the committee, some Board members felt uneasy about the proposals, which appeared to them to give too detailed a commitment on future staffing and organization policies. This led to some delay before the Board finally approved the committee's recommendations.

2 The middle managers in Supplies objected to the proposals. This difficulty arose primarily because they had been excluded from the staff-side of the committee, and they felt aggrieved that, while they would be responsible for implementing the proposals, they had not been involved in their formulation. However, due to the good relationship that existed on the personal level between this group and the senior management representative involved in the study, their co-operation was finally secured.

At the end of 1975, when the Board had finally given the go-ahead for the implementation of the Report, Phase II of the amalgamation process commenced. The Supplies Review Committee was reconvened and the following implementation dates fixed:

By April 1976 – the establishment of the central Supplies Department under the direct authority of the Head of Supplies

By April 1977 – the establishment of the departmental supplies functions under the functional authority of the Head of Supplies.

Under Phase II the committee had the task of making detailed recommendations for implementing the Report, and a number of subcommittees were set up to look into and advise on specific aspects of implementation. Each section of the supplies function – uniforms, contracts, catering equipment, etc. – was represented by a subcommittee, and in addition there were subcommittees dealing with matters of common concern, such as gradings. Typically, a subcommittee had six staff members (two of whom were drawn from the Review Committee) and four senior management members (two from the Review Committee).

Within the subcommittees a number of disputes developed, notably in the grading subcommittee over the proposed revised grading structure, and some of these disputes had to be referred to the main Review Committee for arbitration. However, by January 1977 all the implementation proposals were agreed.

The next task was to sell the detailed proposals to the general body of supplies staff, and so a team made up of the Head of Supplies, industrial relations personnel, and staff members of the Review Committee visited each supplies area to explain the proposals and to interview and appoint staff to new positions in the restructured organization. (This team was engaged virtually full-time on this task for about two months.) No difficulties were experienced at this stage (since staff had been fully consulted throughout the planning process), and immediately this task was completed the proposals were put into effect — about a year after the original target implementation dates.

EXERCISES

1 What are the advantages and disadvantages of allowing staff to participate in the planning process?

2 One of the proposals in the above case study was that the Head of Supplies should exercise functional authority over departmental supplies policies. What difficulties, if any, do you think this would create for the day-to-day supplies work of a department?

3 Phase I of the above study was extremely successful, but it created some unease at Board level and resentment at the middle management level. The result was delayed implementation and difficulties with the middle management group. How might these outcomes have been avoided?

Classical Organization Theory

What is known as the *classical* approach to organization was first formulated by Henri Fayol in his book *Administration Industrielle et Générale*, published in 1916. Although broadened and refined by later writers, the principles that he laid down still form the basis of a great deal of present-day thinking on organization. The classical school approaches organizational design from the top: *all* authority is vested in the Managing Director (acting for the Board), who, by virtue of his span-of-control limitations, is forced to *delegate* some of this authority to his immediate subordinates. Each of these subordinates is placed in charge of a specialized area of work (marketing, production, finance, etc.), but he in turn has to delegate some of *his* authority to specialist subordinates. The organization structure is developed by extending this process of delegation downwards to the operational level.

Disadvantages of the Classical Approach

1 A general consequence of this approach is that superiors delegate authority only when forced to do so by span-of-control limitations, with the result that decision-making tends to be carried out at too high a level in the organization. The disadvantages of this tendency are:

(a) Decisions are often made at a point in the organization which is far removed from the point of work, so that communications relating to that decision have to pass through several levels of authority, with delays, information-loss, and unnecessary work created at each level.

(b) Superiors spend time dealing with matters that should be left to the discretion of lower-paid subordinates, leaving themselves inadequate time for the overall planning and control of their area of responsibility.

(c) Subordinates gain reduced decision-making experience, and so are less well fitted for promotion to higher-level posts.

The systems approach, by tackling the problem of organizational design from the bottom up, ensures that a subordinate's area of authority and responsibility is limited only by his span-of-control limitations, not by the failure of his superior to delegate sufficiently.

2 The classical approach does not place emphasis on the need to exercise control by monitoring the achievement of objectives. Instead, it tends to encourage the more authoritarian approach of monitoring the processing itself, i.e. the way in which subordinates work. This tends to stifle initiative, which the systems approach avoids by emphasizing the need to allow subordinates as much discretion as possible in the way in which they achieve the planned objectives.

3 The delegation of authority according to specialism results in departments being grouped according to the type of work done. This can result in a lack of coordination, a defect avoided by the systems approach, with its emphasis on grouping departments according to decision-making needs.

4 The classical approach leads to an inflexible organization structure which cannot respond rapidly to environmental change. There are two reasons for this inflexibility:

(a) The organization is not structured around information flows, and so there may be considerable delays between the occurrence of a change and knowledge of it reaching the right people
(b) The 'top-down' approach to organizational planning results in a structure which cannot respond flexibly to technological change (e.g. computerization).

The systems approach, by concentrating on the information needs of decision-makers, and by attacking the problem of organization from the bottom up, leads to a structure that is better able to adapt to change.

CASE STUDY: BETAPACERS INC.

David left school in 1959 and began work as a technician in the hospital service. This job gave him invaluable experience with medical equipment (including pacemakers) and well-equipped him to become, in 1969, a sales representative for a small company selling medical equipment. Four years later he obtained the post of European Sales Manager of Betapacers Inc., a large American pacemaker manufacturer.

The job description of this post is given on page 8. In spite of the impressive title of the post, and the substantial responsibilities implied by the job description, David had no staff under him other than a typist borrowed for a few hours per day from an associated medical company in whose headquarters he had an office. He was the sole U.K. sales rep for Betapacers, and sales on the Continent were handled by a number of small companies which acted as agents for Betapacers. David's responsibilities towards these agents were mainly in connection with product-training and sales promotion visits.

David's immediate superior in the organization hierarchy was the Director of International Sales, a post based at the company's head office in America (see the organization chart in Figure 3.1). The geographical isolation of David from his superior and the rest of the company obviously created a communications problem. One way round this would have been to give David a great deal of autonomy in the way in which he marketed the company's products in the U.K. (i.e. to delegate to him as much authority and responsibility for this area of work as possible). Instead, however, David's superior exercised a very tight control, and David was constantly referring back to him for decisions on day-to-day matters (a telex message was sent almost every day). Also, no attempt was made to keep David informed of company changes that affected him. For example, over the five-year period that he worked for the company David had seven changes of boss. In

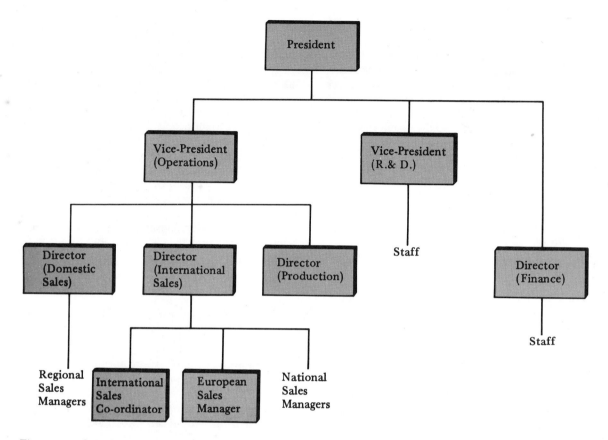

Figure 3.1   Organization chart of Betapacers Inc. (pre-summer 1976)

each case he received no warning of the impending change, learning of it only after the event.

This lack of delegation and poor communications had grave consequences for the company's U.K. operations. Competition in the U.K. pacemaker market was intense and growing — during David's five years with Betapacers the number of companies selling pacemakers had increased from 11 to 21, and the competition was based upon price rather than quality. Betapacers, however, based its U.K. marketing policy upon conditions in the American market, in which competition was not so intense or price-oriented. Hospitals there were prepared to pay the extra for quality products. David had no authority over the company's U.K. policies, and in spite of his urgings the company refused to reduce its prices in the U.K., believing it could increase its market-share through the superior quality of its products. As a result, its U.K. sales steadily declined. (Several years later the company did, in fact, cut its prices in this country, but by then it had virtually lost its foothold in the market.)

In the company's eyes the declining sales were caused by a lack of sales expertise on David's part, not by inappropriate marketing policies. It decided, therefore, to create above David's post the post of European Sales Director, which was to be filled by an American but based at the U.K. office. This took place in mid-1976, and was part of a larger reorganization. At this time the post of Director of Domestic Sales (responsible for the U.S. market) was eliminated, and the Director of International Sales became the Director of International and Domestic Sales (see Figure 3.2).

The American appointed to the post of European Sales Director came to England in September 1976, and took up residence near the U.K. office. His style of leadership proved to be extremely authoritarian: he proposed a radical reorganization of U.K. operations, but refused pointblank to enter into any discussion with David on the matter. David pointed out that he had a great deal of experience of the U.K. market, and said that he wished to take the proposals to a higher authority (namely the Director of International and Domestic Sales). At this point the European Sales Director threatened to fire him.

However, within two weeks of his arrival David's new boss was back in America. The Director of International and Domestic Sales had resigned, and he wanted to be back at base to ensure his succession to the post. He got the job, and the post of European Sales Director fell vacant. It was decided not to reappoint, and David was left on his own once more.

Because of his large area of responsibility (span of control), the new Director of International and Domestic Sales could not deal adequately with all his sub-

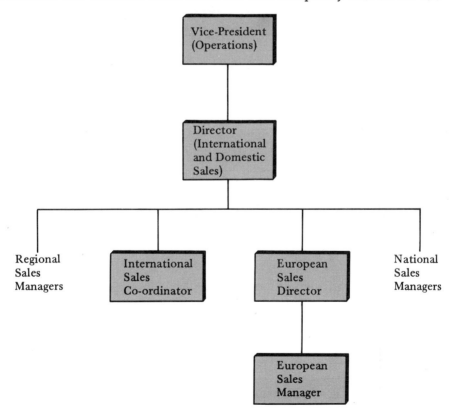

Figure 3.2   Re-organization of operations, Betapacers Inc. (summer 1976)

ordinates. The problem could have been solved by delegating more authority and responsibility downwards but instead it was decided that David should report directly to the next post up in company hierarchy, the Vice President (Operations). The incumbent of this post proved to be weak and ineffectual, and David found it impossible to get any decisions on the matters that he referred to him.

During his occasional visits to the American headquarters David had built up a good relationship with a colleague on the same level as himself in the company hierarchy, namely the International Sales Coordinator (who was responsible for the supply of products to Sales Managers in the various overseas markets). The informal relationship network now came to David's rescue, for this colleague had good personal relations with the Vice President, and David found that by communicating with him it was possible to obtain decisions from the Vice President. In the end, David routed all of his communications through the International Sales Coordinator.

During his years with Betapacers David had grown increasingly frustrated and demoralized. He was not consulted over any key issues that affected him, he was unable to influence in any significant way the company's marketing policies, and the steadily declining sales made him fear for his job. As his wife says, he was often 'unbearable to live with'. In the end he decided that he should leave and set up as an independent agent to market the company's products; his subsequent history is outlined in the case study on page 7.

EXERCISES

1 Identify and discuss the causes, results, and possible cures of the inadequate communications described in this case study.

2 Change often results in conflict. Discuss any changes that have taken place in your work situation, the conflicts that have resulted, and how these conflicts were resolved. How might the conflicts have been avoided?

3 Give an example of inadequate delegation of which you have knowledge, and discuss the reasons for it and the results of it.

4 How does the informal relationship network assist the work of your organization?

Part Two

Office
Procedures
and
Management Information

4
Information
for
Decision-Making

Failure to communicate the right information to the right people is reckoned to be 'the Number One management problem today'. It adversely affects not only decision-making but the whole morale of the organization. Although much information may flow through an organization via the informal communications network (the 'grapevine'), this is no substitute for properly planned information systems. In this chapter we examine the design of systems for producing and disseminating the information needed for decision-making. This is part (B) of the overall design task discussed in the last chapter.

The Need for Adequate and Relevant Information

Each manager in the organization should have access to information which is both adequate for and relevant to the decisions he has to make. To be adequate and relevant the information he receives must satisfy the following criteria:

1 It must pertain to, and cover completely, his sphere of interest. Extraneous information which does not impinge upon the decisions he has to make merely wastes time, obscures the vital information, clogs the information channels, and increases administrative costs. In one large organization over 250 copies were made of one original document as it passed down the management chain. As a result it took three weeks to reach the main user, a large number of other decision-makers read the document unnecessarily, and excessive clerical and photocopying costs were incurred.

On the other hand, incomplete information results in decision-makers having to work in the dark. Some years ago the accountant of one company let an important customer accumulate heavy debts. The salesman who dealt with this customer knew that he was in financial difficulties, but this vital piece of information was not passed on to the Accounts Department. Because the Accountant was not in possession of the full facts the company lost a great deal of money when the customer went into liquidation.

2 It must be in the right degree of detail for the decisions that have to be made. The decisions made at the top of the organization differ in character from those at the bottom, and the information requirements differ accordingly. It is at the top of the organization that the strategic plans and broad control decisions are made. A manager at this level has a wide area of interest and requires information covering the whole of that area; however, the amount of detail needed is slight − he needs to be able to see the wood, not the individual trees, and a large amount of irrelevant detail would obscure the salient features of the situation that faces him. A manager or supervisor nearer the bottom of the organization, on the other hand, is responsible for the much more detailed operational planning and control decisions relating to the point of work; his area of interest is relatively narrow, but the degree of detail needed is high. The examples in the next section illustrate the information needs of the various levels in the organization.

3 It should be timely, so that managers can react quickly to change. Information is relevant only if it reaches the manager *before* the decision that it relates to is made. For some decisions information has to be produced very speedily, and up-to-date information which is only 95% accurate may then be of greater value than information which is highly accurate but takes a long time to produce. In general, information which is produced quickly tends to be expensive, and for many of the decisions that are made highly up-to-date information is not required. For this reason some companies are installing computer output to microfilm (COM) equipment, which gives users a slightly dated but relatively cheap output, rather than putting into every department expensive on-line terminals giving immediate access to the computer (see page 99).

4 It should be accurate. Inaccurate information leads to poor decision-making; however, the cost of information rises as the accuracy increases, and the cost of achieving a high degree of accuracy must be balanced against the anticipated benefits. Errors can arise in the following ways:

(a) The data collection method may lead to **bias** (as in the case of a market research survey carried out by questioning shoppers in a town centre – those interviewed will be representative of people who shop in the town centre and who are prepared to talk to interviewers, but they are not representative of the population as a whole; however, this is usually the most cost-effective way of obtaining the data required)

(b) There may be **incorrect entry** of the data into the computer or other data processing equipment (the verification procedures described on pages 8ff enable this type of error to be minimised)

(c) In producing the information from the data **invalid assumptions** may have been made (as is often the case when the Costing Department apportions overheads to cost-centres according to a blanket formula).

5 It must be suitably presented. To make planning decisions a manager needs to be aware of relevant trends in his environment; to make control decisions he needs to know how the current performance figures of his department compare with the target figures, and with performance figures for previous periods. Much of this information is produced on a routine basis, and is most conveniently presented to management in the form of **reports**. These reports must be timely, they should be produced at appropriate intervals, and they should concentrate on information which is essential to the decision-making process (i.e. deviations from the plan or from the situation described in previous reports.) Information of this type is generally quantitative (numerical) in nature, and is best presented in the form of **tables**, **charts**, and **graphs**. (Research has shown that information is most easily assimilated if presented in a visual way.)

An example of a management report and its use is given in Figure 8.7 and the accompanying text (see page 135).

Examples of Information Needed for Decision-Making

1 Planning information needed by a retailing organization to select lines of merchandise:

(a) Trends in consumer behaviour, which can be obtained from published statistics, market research, and analyses of past sales. This will enable the top management to decide the general types of merchandise the organization should sell.
(b) What quantities of a particular line of merchandise can be sold at various price and quality levels. This information, again, can be obtained from published statistics, market research, and analyses of past sales, and it will enable the Chief Buyer to select the specific lines and quantities of merchandise to buy.
(c) Which manufacturer or supplier is offering the best value for money at the desired price and quality levels. This can be obtained from suppliers' quotations, and from analyses of past purchases. This will enable the buyers to select the supplier that offers the best combination of price, credit, delivery, etc.

2 Control information needed by a manufacturing organization to adjust production operations is illustrated by the following examples:

(a) A comparison between actual work-centre loading

figures and the forecasted figures may reveal significant discrepancies. This information will be received by the Production Controller, and it will indicate that inadequate forecasting is the cause of poor scheduling and loading of work in the factory. However, the provision of workload forecasts is outside his area of control, and so decisions for corrective action must be taken at a higher point in the organization.

(b) Production records will reveal to the Production Manager that the workloads of some sections are too high (resulting in excessive overtime), and that other sections are under-utilized (resulting in under-achievement of output targets). Production control problems will be seen to be the cause but, since that department lies outside his area of control, decisions for corrective action must be taken at a higher point.

(c) Costing information and production figures will show the Managing Director that production costs exceed the budgeted figure and that output targets are not being achieved. Having identified a broad problem area in the company he can issue directives for remedial action and allocate resources as necessary. The cause of the problem has been identified by information received further down the organization, and so appropriate measures can be taken (see the case study below).

Designing an Information System

The sequence of steps followed in the design of information systems is analagous to that used in operating system design (page 39). The first step is to establish the output required, and then the inputs and the processing needed to produce this output are determined.

1 Output. The information requirements of potential users must first be determined. The procedure is to list the business operations that users are responsible for, the decisions that have to be made in the control of the operations, and the information needed for these decisions. It is this information that the system must be capable of producing. Some examples of operations, decisions, and information requirements are shown in Table 4.1.

Operation	Decision	Information Required
Stockholding	When and what quantities to order	For each item the expected rate of usage, the lead time (delay between placing order and receiving goods), the cost of holding stock, the administration cost of placing an order
Production	When to schedule jobs through work-centres	Sales forecasts, current stock levels
Purchasing	Which supplier to use	Prices, quality, credit offered, delivery, reliability

Table 4.1 Some examples of operations, decisions, and information requirements.

2 Input. The data to be collected to produce this information output must be determined. The required data may already exist in the company's internal records (sales records, purchase records, representatives' reports, and the like) or in publications produced by outside bodies (government statistical publications, trade journals, and so on). Data such as this is known as **secondary data**. **Primary data** refers to data which has to be specially collected, either internally in the business (e.g. by a survey of employee attitudes), or outside the business (e.g. by market research surveys).

Systems analysts normally restrict their attention to

the collection and processing of secondary data from internal company records. (This type of data is constantly flowing through the business, and the production of management information from it can be organized on a routine basis.) In fact, 80% of the information produced for managers is derived from this type of data. However, most of the important decisions that have to be made concern *external* matters (primarily the market that supplies the business's inputs and the market that receives its outputs). It is clear, therefore, that present-day information systems are tending to process the wrong type of data and to produce inadequate information.

Businesses are now becoming aware of the need for a much more broadly-based approach to the provision of management information, and information specialists are beginning to make their appearance, their function being to ascertain the total information requirements of managers and to ensure that data from many sources, inside and outside the organization, is collected and brought together in optimally useful ways.

3 Processing. The final step in the design of an information system is to decide how the data should be processed to produce the required information. Computers are being increasingly used for this task, and systems analysts are primarily concerned with the design of computerized procedures. The way in which this is carried out is described in the case study below.

ASSIGNMENT GROUP WORK
Assignment 2, Part (iii) (page 191).

CASE STUDY: DESIGNING A WORKLOAD FORECASTING SYSTEM

One of the tasks of a Production Control Department is to plan the workload of each work-centre in the factory and to contract out work, as necessary, to outside firms. These plans must be based upon forecasts of the jobs that have to be done and of their work-content with respect to each work-centre.

In the mid-1970s the cigarette-making machine manufacturer referred to in the case studies in Chapter 2 was experiencing work-centre loading problems. Machines were being completed late due to overloads of work in some shops and to stock-outs of parts in the stores. The problem was caused by the inadequacy of the workload forecasts that were input to the workload planning system: they were produced manually, and were based solely on the layout document (the list of machines to be assembled and the parts required for each machine). No account was taken of the amount of stock held in the stores or on order. This information, however, is vital for planning the workloads, for if there are high stocks of certain parts, then those parts should be drawn from the stores and not manufactured in the shops; and if stocks of certain parts are low, then additional quantities should be manufactured to avoid stock-outs.

A systems analyst was called in and given the task of designing a more satisfactory workload forecasting system. The first step in such a task is to determine what the output of the system should be. In this case the required output was workload forecasts for each work-centre covering a period of up to a year ahead in fortnightly 'bites' (i.e. the amount of man-hours work per fortnight for the next 26 fortnights).

The second step is to determine the input data needed to produce this output. In this case it was the sales plan (specifying the machines to be built), the list of parts required for each machine, the work-content in man-hours for each work-centre in respect of each part, the stock held in stores (part numbers and quantities), and the stock on order (part numbers, quantities, and due-in-stores dates).

The third step is to decide how the input is to be processed to achieve the desired output. Systems analysts are normally concerned with designing computerized information systems, and this step will generally involve determining what files should be held on the computer and what input is needed to update these files. (If parts of the procedure are to be done manually, the analyst will also be concerned with these.) In this case it was decided that there should be one file for each of the above categories of input data, the variable data needed to update these files being the number of machines of each type to be built each month, any design modifications, receipts and issues of stock, orders placed for stock, and work-centre capacities (in man-hours).

Next, a cost/benefit analysis must be carried out to determine whether the anticipated benefits of changing over to the proposed system will outweigh the costs involved. This entails costing the existing system, estimating the costs of the proposed system, and valuing the expected benefits of the proposed system. It was found in this instance that the proposed system was 'cost effective' − it compared very favourably with the existing system.

The above series of steps constitute what is known as a *feasibility study*, the purpose of which is to ensure that any changes that are proposed are economically viable. In this example it involved the systems analyst in two months' work, at the end of which a report was written and the conclusions presented at a meeting with management. It was at this meeting that the decision to go ahead with the proposed system was made.

The remaining steps involve designing in detail the new system, writing the computer programs, and installing the system. In the example outlined here, this occupied two systems analysts and two programmers for six months. Each task that has to be carried out in the new system is specified by a step in a flowchart, and it is then translated into a computer program and tested by the programmers. When all the programs have been written they are put together and the whole package tested. The final step is to give a detailed presentation to the users of the new system, and then to run the new system in parallel with the old for a short while. When the new system is seen to be working smoothly, the old system is abandoned.

Integrated Information Systems

Most subsystems within a business depend, for their control, on information produced by other subsystems. In the past information has normally been produced and stored on a departmental basis, and the flow of information across the organization has been restricted by departmental boundaries. The example quoted at the start of this chapter − of the company which lost a great deal of money because of the failure by the Sales Department to pass vital information to the Accounts Department − graphically illustrates the outcome of this approach.

The systems approach stresses the need to establish a

'total' information system, in which information collection and processing is seen as an integrated activity which transcends departmental boundaries, the purpose being to provide all decision-makers throughout the organization with the information they need. One result of computerization is that an information system — such as the one described in the above case study — can be readily integrated with other computerized information systems. All the electronic files (such as the stock file referred to above) are held in the central 'database' (computer storage), and each information subsystem of the total system is able to draw upon any of these files for the data it needs. The case study on page 94 provides an illustration of such a system.

Setting Up an Integrated Information System

The task of designing an integrated information system involves the sequence of steps described for the individual information subsystem in the above case study, with the additional requirement that (a) the information needs of *all* decision-makers must be established, and (b) a common pool of data to meet *all* information needs must be set up.

The main steps are as follows:

1 Identify the information requirements of each decision-maker in the organization.
2 Establish uniform coding systems to replace the variety of systems that have been developed on a piece-meal basis in the various departments of the business. For example, part numbers in the catalogues produced by the Sales Department may not match those used in Stores — this sort of inconsistency must be eliminated. (What often happens in practice is that departments retain their long-established coding systems side-by-side with the new central coding system, communication between departments and the central system being achieved by a coding translator in the computer.)
3 On the basis of these uniform coding systems, set up a common pool of information, or database, from which the required management information can be drawn. This task involves the consolidation of the data held in departmental files in all parts of the organization.
4 Design procedures for updating these files from the data that is received by and generated by the business.

The principle here is that data should be collected as near to source as possible, and that an item of data required for a number of processes should be collected once only. For example, an order received from a customer may be keyed into a computer terminal in the sales office, and it is then used by the computer to generate the invoice, the despatch documentation, and the stock level adjustment.
5 Design the data processing procedures needed to generate the required information flows.

The establishment of an integrated information system involves several years' work by teams of systems analysts and computer programmers. The usual practice is to set up individual information subsystems (such as the workload forecasting system described in the above case study), and to integrate these gradually into a single master information system.

The Impact of the Micro-Electronics Revolution

The micro-electronics revolution is radically affecting the jobs of many decision-makers. Management information is becoming easier and cheaper to produce, much more plentiful, and much timelier. Computer terminals having constant access to data held on the central electronic files are becoming commonplace in many departments of large and medium-sized organizations, and the first electronic work stations are appearing. These 'intelligent' desk-top units give the manager instant access via a TV screen to information extracted from company files and to information from outside the organization received via the public view-data network (Telecom's Prestel System), as well as providing him with local data processing, text handling, and electronic mail facilities. (See Chapter 7 for details on all these facilities.)

The way in which information will flow in the integrated information systems that will appear in the near future is illustrated in Figure 4.1. For example, the Marketing Department will deposit in the database details of customer requirements. The Design Department will extract these details, together with relevant technical data about existing products, and use the combined information to draw up design modifications. These modifications will be extracted by the intelligent machine tools in the Production Depart-

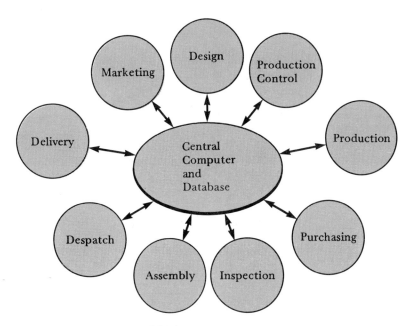

Figure 4.1   Information flows in an integrated business

ment, which will use them to control tool movements, and by the Quality Control Department to obtain performance figures and tolerances. Decision-making for the entire operation will be co-ordinated by the central computer, which will link up the work stations of individual managers. Acting under the control of these managers it will prepare the manufacturing schedules and allocate work to machines; it will notify Stores of parts to be looked out for the manufacturing programme, and Purchasing of parts to be ordered; it will calculate cost information for quotations, forward planning information for delivery dates . . . and so on.

The Science of Collecting and Analysing Data

A short while ago the writer was asked by a small antique-restoration firm to advise on its office procedures. The firm felt that it was becoming bogged down in paperwork – not the routine bookkeeping work that is the lot of every business, but the work of collecting and analysing data on the amount of work done on each restoration job in order to ascertain its costs. When the matter was looked into, it was found that in

almost all cases the customer was given an estimate of the price before the job was done, and when it was done he was invariably charged the estimate. The sole purpose of collecting and analysing cost data was to provide management with information on the accuracy of the estimating. This information was fed back to the partner who did the estimating so that he could improve his accuracy in the future.

It transpired that the cost of collecting and analysing this information exceeded its value to the business in terms of better estimating. (Significant and consistent under-estimating would in any case be eventually revealed by the state of the firm's cash flow, and over-estimating could result in orders drying up.) Furthermore, the data was collected by means of time sheets which were accurate only to the nearest fifteen minutes. Some parts of the restoration process have to be done in small 'bites' (for example, one job is glued, and while the glue is setting another job is polished, and so on), and the errors resulting from logging jobs in this way were substantial and unknown. Thus the management information that had been so expensively collected was of doubtful value.

The firm decided to adopt quite a different approach, namely that costs should be collected on

---

'DATA' AND 'INFORMATION'

The example on this page illustrates the distinction between data and information. The entries made on the time sheets constitute *data*. This data is analysed by totalling the times for each job and multiplying by the hourly rate to arrive at the total cost. The comparison of this cost with the estimated cost constitutes *information* which, when fed back to the estimator, enables him to achieve greater accuracy in the future.

---

only a 10% sample of jobs, and that for this sample the data collection procedure should be such as to ensure accurate cost figures. A job card was drawn up to accompany every tenth job, on which the time spent in the various sections should be logged. As a result of this approach the cost of the information was greatly reduced, while its accuracy was increased.

However, the information obtained by this method is subject to *uncertainty*. The 10% sample chosen by the firm might, by chance, consist of jobs on which the estimator had set too high a price, whereas many of the other 90% might be jobs on which he had set too low a price. The sample results would then be highly misleading. A great deal of management information is subject to uncertainty of this sort, and the uncertainty can only be reduced by collecting more data (by taking a larger sample), which may not be cost-effective.

The problem therefore arises, how can a business decide on the optimum amount of information to collect, and how can it deal with the uncertainty that arises from collecting anything less than the maximum amount of information? The science of deciding the *amount* of data to collect and the *method* of collection and of analysing the data and the uncertainty, is derived from a branch of mathematics known as probability theory. It is the science of statistics.

The remainder of this chapter is devoted to a brief outline of this science and of its applications to business information. It is hoped that this will provide a useful introduction to the subject for students taking professional courses, BEC Higher National Courses, the BEC National Award Business Studies Board Core

Modules, and the BEC National Applied Statistics Option Module. It is not required reading for the BEC Administration in Business Module.

Sampling

Situations often arise in business where the only economical way to determine the characteristics of a population is to take a sample. A population need not consist of people. In the antique-restoration example given above it consisted of jobs. In a quality control application it might be the population of lightbulbs produced by a certain process, the purpose of sampling in this case being to determine perhaps their lifetimes, or perhaps the proportion of defective bulbs. In an O & M application the population studied might be all the letters produced by a typing pool over a given period, in which case a sample might be taken to determine the average (or *mean*) time taken to type a letter. In a market research application the population would normally be people; it might consist of shoppers in a given area, the purpose of sampling perhaps being to determine preferences with regard to a certain type of good.

To illustrate the principles underlying the analysis of data obtained by sampling we shall suppose that we have been asked to investigate the time taken by clerks in a sales office to process customer order forms.

The steps involved in such an investigation are:

1 Select a sample of incoming orders
2 Time how long it takes to process each order in the sample
3 Analyse the sample results and draw conclusions about the population of orders being processed by the office.

In order to draw useful conclusions about the population of orders it is obvious that:

(a) **The sample of orders must be representative of the population**. If the sample were restricted to orders processed on Friday afternoons (for example), the processing times will not accurately reflect the time taken to process orders during the week as a whole — in other words, they will be *biased*. To be representative, the orders that comprise the sample should be processed on several different days, and at different times during the day.

(b) **The sample size must be sufficiently large**

for reliable conclusions to be drawn about the population. The time taken to process an order selected at random might be appreciably more (or appreciably less) than the mean order processing time, and if the sample consists of only a few orders the sample mean time (i.e. the average time taken to process the orders in the sample) may differ markedly from the population mean time (i.e. the average time that would be arrived at if *every* order were timed). If a large number of orders are included in the sample, however, individual variations in processing time will tend to cancel each other out, and the sample mean will not differ greatly from the population mean.

Because of these individual variations it is impossible to eliminate completely some discrepancy between the sample mean time and the mean time that would be obtained if the entire population of orders was surveyed. However, it *is* possible to calculate the likely effect of individual variations on the sample results, and thus to assess the reliability of the conclusions that are drawn about the population mean time. These calculations involve determining the **standard error** of the sample mean. The characteristics of the standard error are that there is a 67% chance (or **probability**) that the sample mean is within 1 standard error of the population mean; a 95% chance that the sample mean is within 2 standard errors of the population mean; a 99% chance that it is within 2.6 standard errors of the population mean; and a 99.8% chance that it is within 3 standard errors.

The size of the standard error is governed by the magnitude of the individual variations. If there are large variations in the times taken to process individual orders, then this can lead to a large difference between sample mean processing time and the population mean processing time, but if the individual variations are small, then the sample mean is likely to be close to the population mean. Also, the size of the standard error will decrease as the number of orders sampled is increased – the standard error is, in fact, inversely proportional to the square root of the sample size. It follows from both these facts that:

$$\text{standard error} = \frac{\text{magnitude of the individual variations}}{\sqrt{\text{sample size}}}$$

The magnitude of the individual variations in the processing times of the orders in the sample is calculated by averaging the squared differences (or **devia-** tions) between the individual processing times and the sample mean time. The average squared deviation thus calculated is called the **variance** (of the order processing times). To compensate for the squaring of the deviations it is necessary to take the square root of the variance, the number that results being known as the **standard deviation**. It is this number that indicates the magnitude of the individual variations.

The formula for the standard error is therefore:

$$\text{standard error} = \frac{\text{standard deviation}}{\sqrt{\text{sample size}}}$$

To illustrate the method, let us suppose that a sample of 25 orders is selected (the theory as stated above has to be modified slightly if the sample size is less than 25). The time taken to process each of these orders is measured, the resulting 25 times, in minutes, being as follows:

16, 11, 17, 14, 15, 15, 16, 16, 18, 13, 14, 15, 16, 18, 15, 12, 19, 14, 17, 11, 16, 15, 14, 13, 15.

The sample mean (i.e. the average of these numbers) is found by summing them and dividing by the sample size:

$$\text{Mean} = \frac{16 + 11 + 17 + \ldots}{25} = \frac{375}{25} = 15 \text{ minutes.}$$

The standard deviation is found by:
1 Determining the difference between each of the individual times and the mean:

$$16 - 15 = 1, 11 - 15 = -4, 17 - 15 = 2,$$
$$14 - 15 = -1, \text{ etc.}$$

2 Squaring these differences:

$$1 \times 1 = 1, (-4) \times (-4) = 16, 2 \times 2 = 4,$$
$$(-1) \times (-1) = 1, \text{ etc.}$$

3 Averaging these squared differences to find the variance:

$$\frac{1 + 16 + 4 + 1 + \ldots}{25} = \frac{100}{25} = 4$$

4 Taking the square root to find the standard deviation:

$$\text{standard deviation} = \sqrt{4} = 2 \text{ minutes.}$$

Knowing the standard deviation it is possible to calculate the standard error:

$$\text{standard error} = \frac{\text{standard deviation}}{\sqrt{\text{sample size}}}$$

$$\frac{2}{\sqrt{25}} = 0.4 \text{ minutes.}$$

This number gives the reliability of the sample mean as an estimate of the population mean (see the above text). It tells us that the sample mean time lies within:

(a) 0.4 minutes of the population mean time with a probability of 67%
(b) 2 × 0.4 = 0.8 minutes of the population mean time with a probability of 95%
(c) 2.6 × 0.4 = 1 minute of the population mean time with a probability of 99%
(d) 3 × 0.4 = 1.2 minutes of the population mean time with a probability of 99.8%.

The most commonly-used of these probability levels is 95%. At this level we can conclude that the sample mean lies within 0.8 minutes of the population mean or, put another way, we are 95% confident that the population mean is within 0.8 minutes of the sample mean time of 15 minutes (that is, it lies somewhere in the range 14.2 to 15.8 minutes).

There is a 5% chance that this conclusion is not correct, i.e. that the population mean is either less than 14.2 minutes or more than 15.8 minutes. If a higher degree of confidence in the estimated population mean time is required, then it is necessary to use the results in (c) or (d) above. For example, to be 99% confident of making a correct estimate, then use (c) − the population mean is estimated as lying within 1 minute of the sample mean time, i.e. between 14 and 16 minutes. It is a matter of commonsense that to increase the degree of confidence in our estimate, it is necessary to make the stated interval larger. Vague estimates are less likely to be proved false!

If a high degree of confidence is required *and* a precise estimate (i.e. a narrow interval) is asked for, then it is necessary to take a larger sample. To halve the size of the interval without altering the degree of confidence requires that the standard error must be halved, and this can only be achieved by doubling the square root of the sample size − and this means quadrupling the sample size. In this example, 100 orders instead of 25 must be timed to double the precision of the final estimate.

Statistical theory, therefore, not only enables the information worker to make very exact statements about a population from sample data, but it also permits him to determine how much data needs to be collected to achieve a given degree of precision in his estimates.

Sampling to Determine Proportions

A common application of sampling in business is to determine the proportions that various groups form of a population. For example, in a work study technique known as **activity sampling**, a sample of possible observations of the various activities engaged in by the staff of an office or workshop is taken in order to determine the proportions of the total workload that these activities form.

To illustrate, suppose that in an office there are six clerks engaged on the ten activities listed in the table below. The activity sampling technique involves observing what the clerks are doing at predetermined random times throughout the course of several days (this sample of times will normally be selected using a table of random numbers), and recording in tally form against the list of activities what each clerk is doing at each observation. If a sample of 100 times is selected, then, with six clerks, a total of 600 observations will result. The results might be as shown in the table.

For the activity 'mail', for example, the table shows that clerks were engaged on this for 0.17 (i.e. 17%) of the observations. It cannot, of course, be concluded from this that exactly 17% of the work of the office is concerned with this activity; as was explained in the previous section, there will be a discrepancy between the sample result and the population proportion (that is, the proportion that would be obtained if the activities were observed at every possible moment in time over the period of the survey).

In order to arrive at an estimate of the population proportion from the sample result it is necessary, as before, to calculate the standard error. When dealing with proportions the formula for the standard error is:

$$\text{standard error} = \sqrt{\frac{p(1-p)}{n}}$$

where p is the sample proportion and n is the total number of observations.

For the activity 'mail', for example, the standard error is

$$\sqrt{\frac{0.17(1-0.17)}{600}} = \sqrt{\frac{0.17 \times 0.83}{600}} = 0.015$$

Activity	Tally	Number of observations	Proportion (p)
Mail	𝍷𝍷𝍷 𝍷𝍷𝍷 𝍷𝍷𝍷 𝍷𝍷𝍷 𝍷𝍷𝍷 𝍷𝍷𝍷 𝍷𝍷𝍷 𝍷𝍷𝍷 𝍷𝍷𝍷 𝍷𝍷𝍷 𝍷𝍷𝍷 𝍷𝍷𝍷 𝍷𝍷𝍷 𝍷𝍷𝍷 𝍷𝍷𝍷 𝍷𝍷𝍷 𝍷𝍷𝍷 𝍷𝍷𝍷 𝍷𝍷𝍷 𝍷𝍷𝍷 //	102	$\frac{102}{600} = 0.17$
Filing		90	$\frac{90}{600} = 0.15$
Typing		120	$\frac{120}{600} = 0.20$
Reprography		48	0.08
Reception		42	0.07
Walking		36	0.06
Telephone		54	0.09
Idle		60	0.10
Miscellaneous		18	0.03
Absent		30	0.05
		600	1.00

Table 4.2 Activity sampling results

From this it follows that at the 95% confidence level the proportion of time spent on mail by the office staff lies within

$$2 \times 0.015 = 0.03$$

of the sample proportion, i.e. it lies in the interval 0.14 to 0.20. Thus we can conclude with 95% confidence that between 14% and 20% of the clerks' time is spent on dealing with mail.

Similar calculations can be carried out for the other activities listed in the table; however, it should be noted that the theory cannot be applied to any activity for which there are fewer than 5 observations.

As was pointed out in the previous section, if a more precise estimate is required, then it is necessary to increase the sample size – that is, the number of observations. For example, if an estimate which is accurate to within 1 percentage point is required, then 2 standard errors must equal 0.01 (instead of 0.03); to reduce the size of the standard error by a factor of three it is necessary to triple the square root of the sample size, and this implies that the number of observations must be increased by a factor of nine. The work of the office must therefore be recorded on 900 instead of 100 occasions, to give 6 × 900 = 5,400 observations in total.

Significance Tests

These are used to test whether the data obtained from a sample permits a given belief, or *hypothesis*, to be held about a population. An obvious area of application is quality control: by taking measurements of a sample of the output of a process it is possible to determine whether or not the process is behaving in the expected way.

To illustrate the method, suppose that a machine is set up to produce metal bars of mean length 200.0 mm, the standard deviation of the bars being 1.0 mm. To test the process a sample of 100 bars is taken, and the mean length is calculated and found to be 200.25 mm.

This is 0.25 mm more than the expected process mean (i.e. the result that would be expected if the length of every bar produced by the machine over a period were measured and the average calculated). There are two possible explanations for this discrepancy:

1 The process mean is no longer 200.0 mm
2 Variations in the lengths of individual bars in the sample have resulted in an unrepresentative sample mean. (As indicated in previous sections, *some* discrepancy between a sample mean and the population mean is to be expected).

The test involves determining whether or not (2) is a reasonable explanation of the sample result. The steps involved are as follows:

1 Decide on the confidence level to be used.   In quality control work two levels are normally adopted: 95% and 99.8%. The first is regarded as the **warning level** – the process should be monitored closely, but no immediate action taken; the second is the **action level** – the process should be stopped and the fault rectified.

2 Calculate the standard error of the sample mean.   In this example it is:

$$\frac{1.0}{\sqrt{100}} = \frac{1.0}{10} = 0.1 \text{ mm.}$$

3 Compare this with the discrepancy between the believed population mean and the actual sample mean.   In this case the discrepancy is

0.25mm, i.e. 2.5 standard errors $(\frac{0.25}{0.1} = 2.5)$. If the belief that the process mean is 200.0 mm is correct, then there is a 95% chance that the sample mean will lie within 2 standard errors of it – and therefore only a 5% chance that it will lie more than 2 standard errors away from it. The odds are therefore heavily against obtaining a discrepancy as large as the one we have in this example, *if the belief about the process mean is correct*. The reasonable conclusion is therefore that the belief is *not* correct, in other words that the machine is no longer producing bolts of mean length 200.0 mm.

4 Take appropriate action.   Stopping the process to correct a fault may be expensive – hold-ups may be caused further down the line – and the fact that there is a 5% chance that individual variations in lengths of bars in the sample *could* have caused the discrepancy is enough to make most factory managers hesitate before shutting down plant. As is indicated in (1) above, action is normally taken only if the test gives a significant result at the 99.8% confidence level. For this degree of confidence the discrepancy must exceed 3 standard errors – and in this example it does not. The process will therefore be kept running, but will be carefully monitored.

It is normal practice in statistical quality control to take small samples at fairly frequent intervals (rather than large samples infrequently). Although the standard error of the mean of a small sample is relatively large – so that the result obtained from an individual sample is of limited value – the advantage of this way of sampling is that the sample means can be plotted against a time axis on a quality control chart, and this will highlight any underlying trend in the results. Most faults develop progressively over a period of time, and the trend of the plotted points will reveal this progression.

Regression

This technique is used to determine the mathematical relationships that exist between the various inputs and outputs of a business. Examples of the sort of questions that regression deals with are:

- What is the relationship between the advertising expenditure of a company and the level of sales it achieves?
- What is the relationship between the price charged for a product and the quantity sold?
- What is the relationship between the resources devoted to training and the extent of labour turnover?

Knowledge of relationships such as these enables the decision-maker to predict what the effect of an adjustment in one input or output will have on others. In the case of the advertising/sales example, it enables him to determine the optimum level of expenditure on advertising, and in the case of the price/quantity example it assists in the determination of the profit-maximizing price.

The inputs and outputs of a business system will vary from one period of time to another, and so are known, in the terminology of mathematics, as **variables**. In a business situation there will rarely be an exact mathematical relationship between one variable and another and this means that any relationships that are worked out are subject to uncertainty. For example, other factors besides advertising expenditure will affect sales (the price charged, the quality, and the reliability of delivery are just three), and so it is impossible to predict with complete confidence what effect a change in the variable 'advertising expenditure' will have on the variable 'sales'. As is the case with sampling, it is only possible to produce by this technique a range of values for a variable at a given level of confidence.

The technique involves determining the mathematical equation – called the **regression equation** – that expresses the relationship between the variables under examination. Such equations are often quite complex, and are usually derived by the use of a computer and standard computer programs. It would be inappropriate to discuss the mathematics of regression in this text, but we can show how relationships between just two variables can be determined approximately by means of a type of graph known as a **scattergraph**. (In most regression problems more than two variables are involved, and the graphical method cannot then be used.)

The procedure involves using the horizontal axis of the graph to represent the values taken by one of the variables, and the vertical axis to represent the values taken by the other. An example is given in Figure 4.2, which shows the scattergraph of the sales achieved by a company over the period 1970 to 1981 plotted against its advertising expenditure for those years. The data plotted on the scattergraph is as follows. (The effects of inflation have been removed by converting all sales and expenditure figures to 1970 pounds.)

Year:	70	71	72	73	74	75	76	77	78	79	80	81
Adv. Exp. (£000):	19	23	24	26	22	10	10	13	14	15	20	17
Sales Rev. (£000):	460	480	500	480	440	260	330	330	390	410	400	400

Inserted on the scattergraph is the **line of best fit** – the line which best seems, to the eye, to follow the trend of the plotted points. (The insertion of this line is necessarily something of a guess – one reason why it is preferable to determine the regression equation mathematically.) This line can be extended a short distance beyond the range of the plotted points (see the dotted extension on the graph), but little confidence can be placed in an extension of the line far beyond the range of the plotted points, for the relationship that exists between the variables outside this range is unknown.

From the line of best fit the sales that can be expected from *any* given level of advertising expenditure within the range £8,000 to £28,000 can be predicted. For example, if £28,000 were spent on advertising, the expected sales would be £500,000. As indicated above, such a prediction is subject to uncertainty, and so strictly speaking a range of values rather than a single figure should be quoted as the expected sales. The scattering of the points about the line of best fit gives an indication of this range – about £460,000 to £540,000.

Time Series Analysis

To be able to predict future values of business inputs and outputs (called 'variables' – see above) would clearly be of enormous value to a business, and so a great deal of effort has been put into the development of statistical forecasting techniques. They involve the collection of a series of values of the variables under

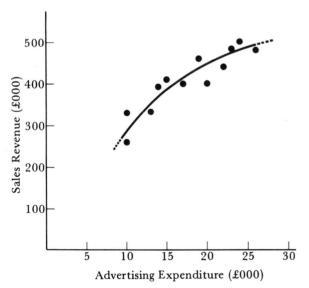

Figure 4.2 Scattergraph with line of best fit

examination over a period of time, and the calculation from this series of the relationship that exists between these variables and the variable *time*.

One commonly-used technique, based upon regression analysis, involves determining the mathematical relationship between the variables and *time*. Another is the method described below, which involves calculating the moving averages – which is simply a way of averaging out seasonal peaks and troughs and other irregularities in the data in order to discern the underlying trend – and then plotting the figures obtained on a graph and projecting them forward to obtain the required future figures.

The method involves four steps:

(a) Calculate the moving averages for the series.
(b) Determine the effects of seasonal variations.
(c) Determine the effects of any residual random fluctuations.
(d) Project the moving averages line forward on the graph to determine future values, and adjust these values to take account of the seasonal variations calculated in (b); (c) gives the effect that random events may have on the prediction.

To illustrate the technique, suppose that the quarterly sales figures (in thousands of pounds) over the period 1979 to 1981 are as shown in column 2 of Table 4.3, and that it is required to forecast the sales for the first quarter of 1982. An inspection of these figures in the Table shows that there are peaks in the winter and troughs in the summer, and these seasonal variations must be averaged out for the underlying trend to be discerned. A complete cycle of seasons is covered by four quarters, and so averages taken of successive sets of four will have the effect of offsetting the peaks of one season against the troughs of another. These are the moving averages (column 3), and they are entered in the Table against the midpoint of the period to which they relate.

(1) Quarter		(2) Quarterly figures	(3) Moving averages	(4) Trend	(5) Variation from trend	(6) Average variations	(7) Seasonal variations	(8) Residual fluctuations
1979	1	475						
	2	413						
	3	352	424	424	-72	-96	-98	+26
	4	458	423	424	+34	+59	+57	-23
1980	1	469	425	425	+44	+71	+69	-26
	2	422	425	440	-18	-26	-28	+10
	3	352	455	472	-120	-96	-98	-22
	4	579	489	495	+84	+59	+57	+27
1981	1	603	500	504	+99	+71	+69	+30
	2	467	507	501	-34	-26	-28	-5
	3	379	494					
	4	528						

Table 4.3 Time series calculations

Subsequent steps in the analysis require that the figures obtained in step (a) relate to specific quarters (not, as is the case with a moving average, to a point in time between two quarters), and to achieve this it is necessary to average successive pairs of moving averages. The results are the trend figures (column 4), and they are shown on the graph in Figure 4.3. By drawing the trend line through these points and extending it forward, the forecasted trend figures are obtained: for the first quarter of 1982 the forecasted figure is 490 (i.e. £490,000).

To determine the sizes of the seasonal peaks and troughs it is necessary to subtract the trend figures in column 4 from the quarterly figures in column 2. The

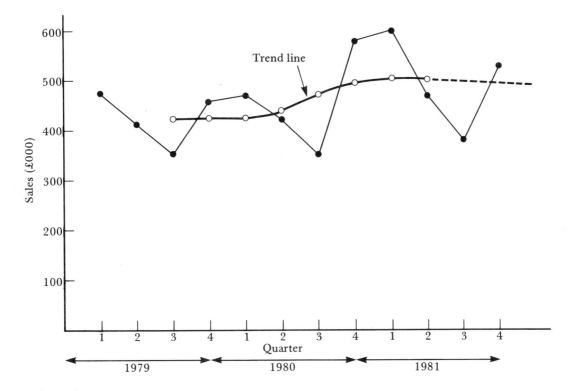

Figure 4.3 Time series graph

resulting variations from the trend are shown in column 5. The *average* variations for each quarter are then calculated (column 6).

These average variations indicate the sizes of the seasonal peaks and troughs. The peaks should exactly offset the troughs, i.e. these averages should add up to zero. In this example, in fact, they add up to +8. This discrepancy is apportioned among the average variations by subtracting 2 from each. The results are the seasonal variations (column 7).

The seasonal variation for the first quarter is +69. Adjusting the forecasted moving average for the first quarter of 1982 by this amount gives the forecasted sales:

490 + 69 = 599 (i.e. about £560,000).

The final step is to measure the residual fluctuations and so determine to what extent they will affect this figure. These fluctuations are found by subtracting the trend figures (column 4) *and* the seasonal variations (column 7) from the actual quarterly figures (column

1). The results are shown in column 8, and they show that random occurrences may increase or decrease the quarterly sales by up to 30 (i.e. £30,000). It follows that our forecast must be that the sales for the first quarter of 1982 will be £560,000 ± £30,000, i.e. they will lie in the range £530,000 to £590,000.

Spurious Relationships

Changes in the values of one variable may appear to correspond to changes in the values of another; but this does not necessarily imply that a relationship exists between the two. The incidence of cancer in the U.K. has grown apace with the consumption of tomatoes, but in the absence of any discernible cause-and-effect connection the relationship that apparently exists between these two variables must be regarded as *spurious*, or false.

It is not sufficient to analyse relationships and make predictions purely on a mathematical basis; the underlying causes of the changing values must be probed into. In the 1950s and early 1960s there was a strong and steady increase in the U.K. for consumer durables – washing machines, TVs, freezers, cars, and the like. The forecasters in some organizations projected the upward-moving line on the graph up to ten years ahead, and long-range plans were drawn up on the basis of their predictions of very high demand. The simple truth that was forgotten was that demand for such products was nearing its peak as the typical household acquired its washing machine, TV, etc., and that a levelling-off of the trend line was soon to occur. The result was that the planned capacity of many factories built during the late 1960s and early 1970s greatly exceeded the demand for their output.

This illustrates the fact that, if applied in a mechanical way, the mathematical analysis of relationships and time series can lead to conclusions that are

One manufacturer based his production plans on computerized forecasts of consumer demand. Although these forecasts usually proved quite reliable, at every 13th month they were much too high. It transpired that the predictions were based upon sales figures taken over a period when the government had presented two budgets 13 months apart, and the computer had projected the two pre-budget buying sprees forward as a form of seasonal variation!

quite false. Used properly, the mathematics adds precision to predictions which are based upon a careful investigation of the causes of movements in variables.

5
The
Work
of
the Office

The *office* is any area within the business where administrative procedures are carried out. Its work, which involves data processing and information management, is examined in this chapter. The equipment and systems that are available to facilitate this work are described in Chapters 6 and 7.

Information Processing

The various tasks that are carried out in the office are shown in Figure 6.1 (page 90). They fall into two broad categories:

1 Data processing, typified by the bookkeeping, form-filling and checking, and similar activities carried out by clerks. These activities entail the bulk collection and processing of the routine data associated with business operations: receipt and processing of customer orders; receipt, issue, and ordering of stock; production planning; calculation and payment of wages; and so forth. Data is normally expressed by means of *numbers*, and the data processing procedures, being formal and rigidly-defined, are ideally suited to computerization.

2 Information management, typified by information retrieval, information communication (by voice, letter or report, diagram), diary management, and other activities carried out by secretaries, personal assistants, and managers. These activities entail the accessing and distribution of information associated with business control: obtaining information, preparing letters, making telephone calls, arranging and attending meetings, etc. Information is normally expressed by means of *voice*, *text*, or *image* (diagrams etc.), and the information management procedures, being informal and highly variable, are only now, with the advent of microprocessor-based equipment, becoming computerized.

The micro-electronics revolution is causing the distinction between data processing and information management to become increasingly blurred. To illustrate: one public corporation has a large and varying population of employees, many of whom are casual labourers. Keeping track of these for payment and security purposes involves a great deal of file handling and high clerical costs. This is a data processing problem, and to solve it the employee data has been transferred to computer file, file handling for these purposes now being carried out automatically. However, if it is required to send standard letters to all or some of the employees, then this is an information management problem, although similar equipment and the same employee files are used. The letter is typed into a word processor, held in its internal memory, and merged with the employee details drawn from the central computer file to produce automatically the individually-typed letters.

In the electronic office that is beginning to appear, the same equipment (the hardware) is being used for both data processing and information management; it is the program instructions (the software) which differ. Because it is becoming increasingly difficult and meaningless to draw a distinction between the two types of activity, the term **information processing** has been coined to describe both.

The Need for Data Processing

There are three reasons why a business needs to collect and process data:

1 Some of the data inputs to the business are prime inputs – an example being customer orders – and the receipt and processing of these is an essential stage in the flow of work. This type of data input has to be processed for the same reason that raw materials have to be processed in a workshop: if this were not done the business would very soon come to a halt.

2 Some of the data inputs *model* the prime inputs – for example the entries in the receipt and issues columns of stock record cards (see Figure 5.10) represent, or model, what is happening to the prime input, the physical items of stock. The purpose of processing this type of data input is to enable the business to control the operations that are carried out on the prime input. In a very small business, or in the home, the operations on many prime inputs can be controlled in an informal way without recourse to formal data models.

3 Some of the data is required to produce the information needed by management for decision-making. Much of this information will be produced from the data needed for (1) and (2) above; for some information the data will have to be specially collected (see the notes on primary and secondary data on page 35).

The Need for Information Management

There are three reasons why a business needs to manage information:

1 Decision-makers need to *access information* produced by the internal data processing procedures and by external bodies.

2 It is necessary to *prepare documents* (such as letters), *send messages* (e.g. by mail or phone), and *arrange travel to meetings* in order to communicate information, facilitate the decision-making process, and communicate decisions.

3 Decision-makers need *personal information management procedures*, such as in- and out-trays and personal filing cabinets to hold in an immediately accessible form the information currently being used, and diaries and planning charts are needed to facilitate personal work-planning and follow-up.

Flowcharts

The activities in the flow of work through a system can be charted by means of a **flowchart**. There are a number of flowchart symbols; however, for our purposes it is sufficient to note the four main symbols illustrated in Figure 5.1.

A simplified flowchart showing the major activities in the flow of work through a manufacturing business is shown in Figure 5.2. Each of these major activities can be broken down into a sequence of subsidiary activities and similarly charted. Flowcharts showing the steps in the activity 'pay the supplier' and the activities 'receive order from customer', 'despatch

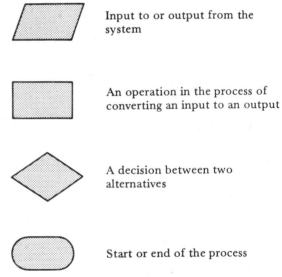

Input to or output from the system

An operation in the process of converting an input to an output

A decision between two alternatives

Start or end of the process

Figure 5.1   The main flowchart symbols

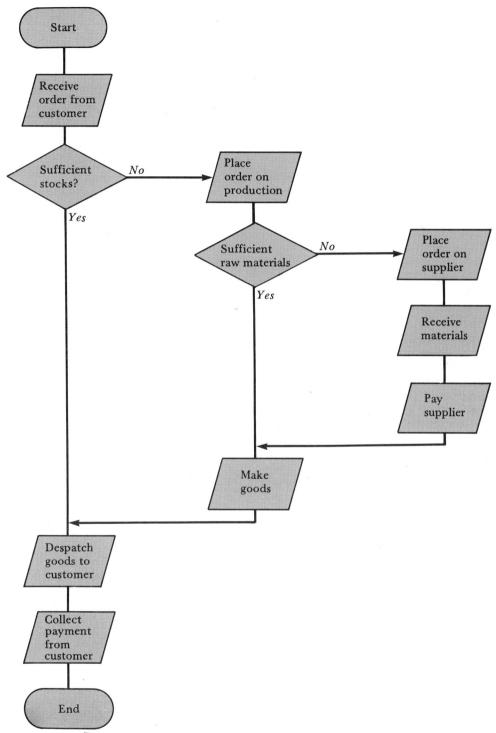

Figure 5.2   Flow of work in a manufacturing business

goods', and 'collect payment from customer' are drawn in Figures 5.3 and 5.4.

Examples of Data Processing Functions

Figures 5.3 and 5.4 illustrate the three data processing functions referred to in the section 'The Need for Data Processing' above:

1 The purpose of the paying procedure is to produce one of the prime outputs of the business, namely the cheque authorizing the business's bank to pay the supplier. In a very simple buying transaction (such as purchasing goods in a shop) such payments will be made at the time when the goods are received.

2 In most buying transactions in business, payment is made some time after receipt of the materials or goods, and so a data model of the transaction is required.
   The supplier's model consists of:
(a) The **receipt note**, signed by the customer, showing that the goods have been received
(b) The **invoice**, itemizing the goods received by the customer, together with the prices, and extended to show the total price
(c) The **sales ledger**, showing payments received from the customer and payments due
(d) The **statement**, requesting settlement of all payments due.
   The customer's model consists of:
(a) The **goods received note** (G.R.N.), recording the goods received from the supplier
(b) The **purchase ledger**, showing payments already made and payments outstanding.
   Before the customer issues the cheque (Figure 5.3), the details on the invoice will be reconciled (checked) with those on the G.R.N., and the details on the statement will be reconciled with those in the purchase ledger.

3 Sales and purchases data might be extracted from any of the above documents and analysed to produce management information. For example, total values of goods bought or sold might be produced on a monthly basis according to various categories (type of product, type of customer, etc.), and the information used to compare actual expenditure or sales in these categories with the planned expenditure or sales, or to determine the trend in purchases or sales.

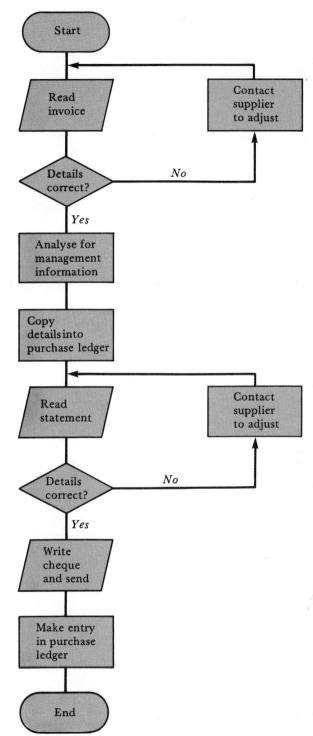

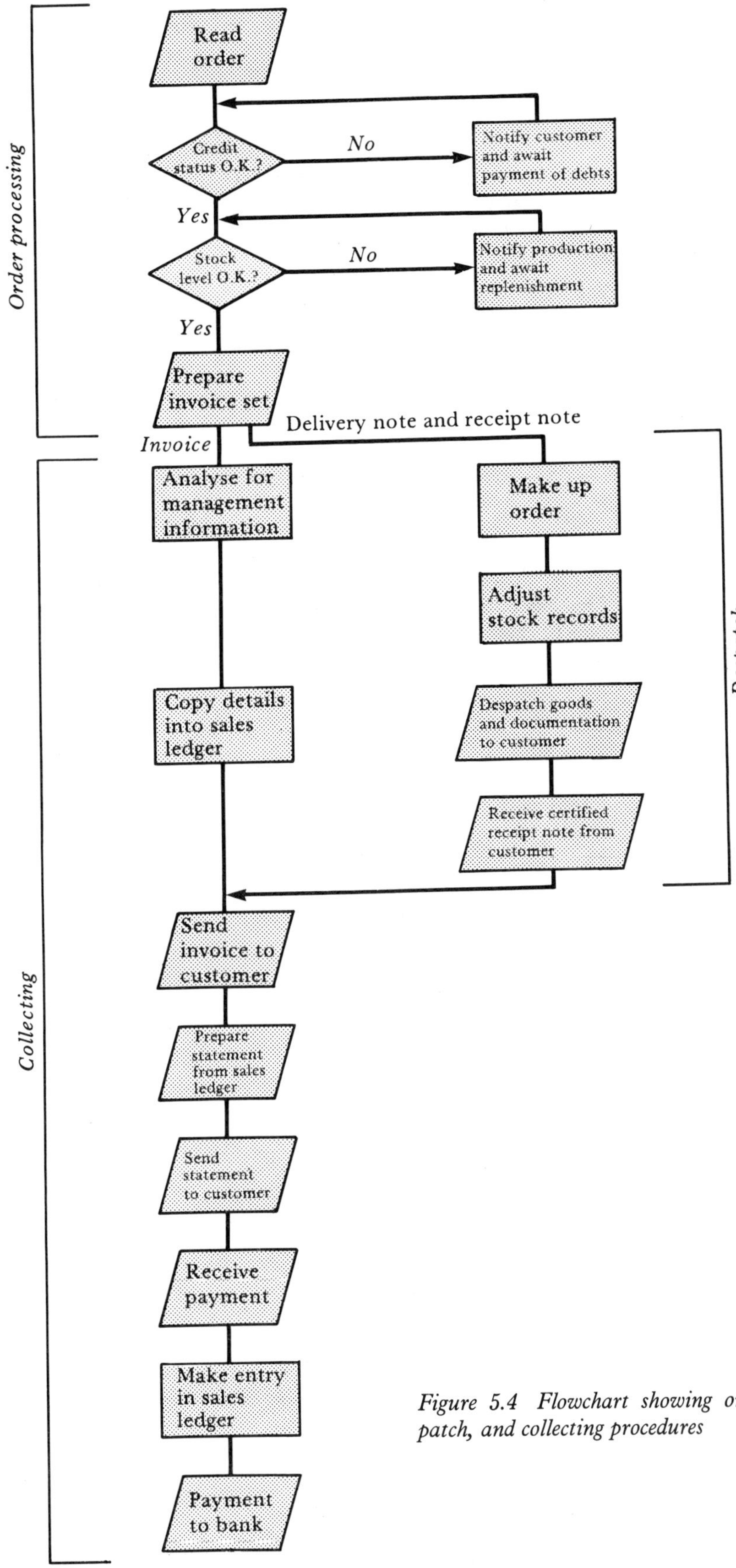

Order processing

- Read order
- Credit status O.K.? — No → Notify customer and await payment of debts
- Yes
- Stock level O.K.? — No → Notify production and await replenishment
- Yes
- Prepare invoice set

Invoice / Delivery note and receipt note

Despatch

- Make up order
- Adjust stock records
- Despatch goods and documentation to customer
- Receive certified receipt note from customer

Collecting

- Analyse for management information
- Copy details into sales ledger
- Send invoice to customer
- Prepare statement from sales ledger
- Send statement to customer
- Receive payment
- Make entry in sales ledger
- Payment to bank

Figure 5.4 Flowchart showing order processing, despatch, and collecting procedures

Process Charts

If the procedure shown on the flowchart is to be computerized, then computer programmers will be given the task of translating the flowchart steps − which will have been specified by a systems analyst − into a list of instructions, or program, specifying the operations that the computer must perform to process the data (see Chapter 7). Many office procedures are not carried out by computer, and so instead of a computer program some other method of showing the (manual) operations that have to be undertaken is useful. One such method is the **process chart** used by work study and O & M analysts.

There are five process chart symbols, shown in Figure 5.5. These symbols can be used to show what the clerk or operative does − the chart in this case being referred to as a **man-type process chart** (see Figure 5.12 for an example). The type of chart shown in Figures 5, 6, 7, & 11 below is a **material-type process chart** − the symbols in this case are used to show what is done to the document or material being processed.

Example of an Office Procedure

The example considered below is the first part of the paying procedure charted in Figure 5.3. The steps are:

* read the invoice;
* decide whether it matches the record of goods ordered and received and whether the prices charged and the invoice calculations are correct;
* if it fails this test, contact the supplier in order to adjust;
* analyse to provide management information.

We shall describe firstly two manual methods, and secondly a computerized method.

Under the manual methods the details on the invoice are reconciled with the goods ordered and received by comparing the invoice with a copy of the purchase order and with the goods received note, and the calculations are checked by calculator. The task of reconciling the invoice with the purchase order and the G.R.N. can be carried out either by the paying section of the Accounts Department (in which case a copy of

Symbol		Example	
		Material-type chart	**Man-type chart**
◯	Operation	Document is prepared	Clerk enters data on document
▢	Inspection	Document is checked	Clerk reads document
▷	Transport	Document is passed to another section	Clerk walks to filing cabinet
◻	Delay or temporary storage	Document waits in in-tray	Clerk delayed
▽	Storage	Document is filed	Clerk files document

Figure 5.5   Process chart symbols

the G.R.N. and of the purchase order must be sent from the section that received the goods to the paying section), or by the receiving section (in which case the invoice must be passed to that section for the reconciliation operation). The former method is most appropriate if the purchasing, receipt, and storage of goods are centralized operations carried out by specialist departments; the latter method is most appropriate if these activities are decentralized. It is the latter method which is described in the case study below.

CASE STUDY: INVOICE RECONCILIATION; THE PRODUCTION OF MANAGEMENT INFORMATION

This procedure was observed in mid-1979 in the paying section of the Accounts Department of a clothing manufacturer. The detailed steps described below are peculiar to this manufacturer (who has since computerized the procedure).

The procedure begins with the receipt of an invoice from a supplier. A small pre-printed sticker (about three inches square) is attached to the invoice, and the following details are recorded on it: the date, the invoice number, the VAT, the total value, and the company's product-code. Details from the invoice are also copied into an Invoice Register.

Invoices are then passed in batches to two comptometer operators, who carry out on a centralized basis numerical checks and calculations for the whole Accounts Department. They check the suppliers' invoice calculations, initialling the pre-printed sticker to show that the checks have been carried out, and they note any errors on the invoices. The invoices are then returned to the paying section, who record the fact that the calculations have been checked in the Invoice Register (against the original invoice entries).

The invoices are then sent to the departments that received the goods for authorization of payment — the departments check the invoices against their internal records of goods ordered and received, and sign the sticker if the invoice details tally with the receipt details. If there are any discrepancies, these are noted on the invoice.

The invoices are then returned to the paying section, who record their authorization-status in the Invoice Register (against the original entries), and phone the suppliers if invoices are faulty. Some suppliers rectify faults by sending a revised invoice, in which case the above procedure is repeated; many, however, will give verbal authorization for alterations over the phone, in which case the alterations are noted on the invoice sticker, and the invoice proceeds through the remainder of the procedure.

Next, the invoices are sorted into product-code order and batched, each batch containing the invoices for one product code only. The batch totals are then calculated and entered on a form that accompanies each batch through the remainder of the paying procedure. (The invoice amounts are entered onto the purchase ledger cards by means of a keyboard accounting machine, which automatically produces batch totals; by checking these against the batch totals on the forms any keyboarding errors by the machine operator are picked up.) The batch totals are also entered in a Bought Ledger Day Book in the appropriate product code column. At the end of the month the total value of purchases for each product code are calculated and the results passed to management.

A material-type process chart of this procedure is shown in Figure 5.6.

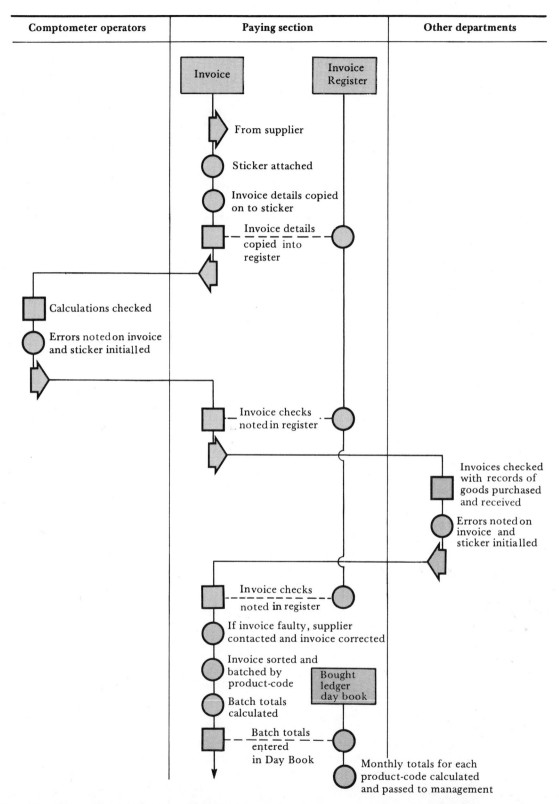

Comptometer operators	Paying section	Other departments

Invoice

Invoice Register

From supplier

Sticker attached

Invoice details copied on to sticker

Invoice details copied into register

Calculations checked

Errors noted on invoice and sticker initialled

Invoice checks noted in register

Invoices checked with records of goods purchased and received

Errors noted on invoice and sticker initialled

Invoice checks noted in register

If invoice faulty, supplier contacted and invoice corrected

Invoice sorted and batched by product-code

Batch totals calculated

Bought ledger day book

Batch totals entered in Day Book

Monthly totals for each product-code calculated and passed to management

Figure 5.6   Case study procedure: material-type process chart

Alternative Invoice Reconciliation Procedures

In the above case study the purpose of the invoice sticker is to enable the various sections which handle the invoice to record their output. The Invoice Register is kept as a record of 'work-in-progress'; it shows where the invoice is in the procedure. If the work of checking the calculations and reconciling the invoices were done centrally by the paying section neither the sticker nor the register would be necessary. The procedure in this case is shown in Figure 5.7.

If the procedure is computerized with on-line terminals in user departments, all these tasks are carried out automatically. Purchasing decisions will have originally been entered on a terminal in the Purchasing Department and stored on the computer purchase record file. Details of goods received will be keyed into the terminal located in the receiving department, automatically reconciled by the computer with the corresponding purchases on the purchase record file, and stored on that file. Details from the suppliers' invoices will be keyed in via a terminal in the Accounts Department; the computer will automatically check the invoice calculations, reconcile the invoice details with the data on the purchase record file, enter the amounts on the purchase ledger file, and produce monthly analyses for management.

The Flow of Data

If data processing is carried out manually, then forms and documents must be used at all stages, and data will flow through the business by means of movements of forms. Figure 5.8 shows some of the main movements of forms between a firm and its customers and suppliers, and internally between its main subsystems.

If the business is computerized, then forms move between it and its customers and suppliers as in the manual system (we are a number of years off the day when this type of communication will be carried out electronically); but data flows internally by electronic means. Much departmental data storage on record cards and in conventional files is replaced by a central database held on the computer's electronic files, and data will flow mainly between department and computer (as indicated in Figure 4.1) rather than between department and department. The case study on page 92 illustrates the impact that electronic data processing and the creation of a central database have on data flows and on the work of a business.

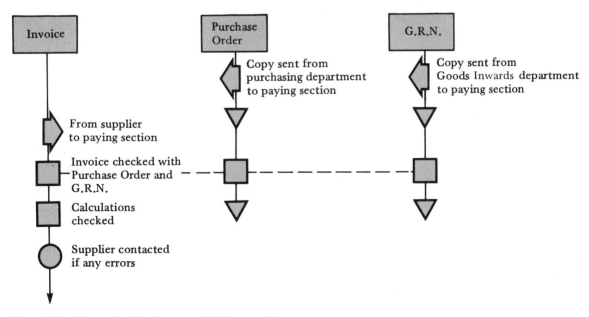

Figure 5.7   Alternative invoice reconciliation procedure

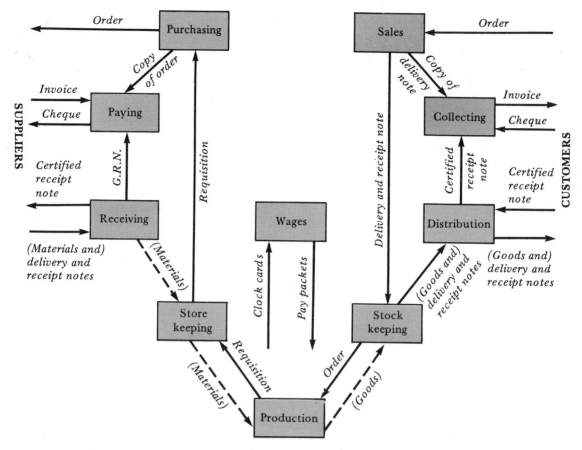

Figure 5.8   The movement of forms in a business (simplified)

Some Business Forms

The main forms that travel between a firm and its customers and suppliers are listed in Table 5.1. For completeness we have included in the table the **Purchase Requisition**, sent internally by departments to the Purchasing Department, to inform the latter of their purchasing requirements.

Two example forms are shown in Figures 5.9 and 5.10. These are the invoice and the stock record card that might be used by Pinecrafts (Appendix II). Further forms are illustrated in Appendix I.

Some Manual Office Procedures

Figure 5.11 shows a material-type process chart of the

procedure used in the Purchasing Department of a (non-computerized) business to order materials and goods for other user departments. Figure 5.12 shows a man-type process chart of the procedure used to receive goods in the Goods Inwards Department, and the procedure used in the Stores to enter the goods received on to the stock record cards. These charts should be read in conjunction with the descriptions of the forms given in Table 5.1, in the section 'Examples of Data Processing Functions' on page 72, and in the 'Administrative Procedures' section of the Pinecrafts case study (page 188).

The Design and Control of Forms

Although paper is expected to be a thing of the past in

Form	Sent by	Sent to	Purpose
Purchase Requisition	Dept requiring goods	Purchasing Dept	To inform Purchasing Dept of requirements
Quotation Request	Customer (Purchasing Dept)	Supplier (Sales Dept)	To determine prices and conditions of sale
Quotation	Supplier (Sales Dept)	Customer (Purchasing Dept)	An offer to supply the required goods at the stated price, subject to certain terms and conditions
Order	Customer (Purchasing Dept)	Supplier (Sales Dept)	To request supply of goods at stated price and conditions
Delivery Note & Receipt Note	Supplier (Sales Dept)	Customer (Goods Inwards Dept)	To notify supplier's Despatch Dept of the goods to be despatched, to notify customer of contents of packages. The receipt note, when certified (signed) by customer, is proof of receipt; it is returned with driver
Shortage Note	Customer (Goods Inwards Dept)	Supplier (Sales Dept)	To notify supplier of shortages in or damage to goods received
Invoice	Supplier (Sales or Accounts Depts)	Customer (Accounts Dept)	To notify customer of payment due and amount of VAT
Credit Note	Supplier (Sales or Accounts Depts)	Customer (Accounts Dept)	To adjust invoice in favour of customer (e.g. in event of a shortage)
Statement	Supplier (Accounts Dept)	Customer (Account Dept)	To request payment of all amounts owing
Cheque and Remittance Advice	Customer (Accounts Dept)	Supplier (Accounts Dept)	To pay amount due

Table 5.1 *Forms used in transactions between supplier and customer*

many offices ten years from now, present-day office routines (in particular data processing routines) depend upon the use of forms. They are the means by which data is recorded and communicated and action stimulated. Well-designed forms assist the work of the office in the following ways:

1 Fixed data is preprinted, variable data only having to be entered on the forms
2 They indicate to the office worker what data has to be entered on the form and what operations have to be carried out on that data
3 The user is presented with the data he requires in a standard format, and this permits easy assimilation.

Organizations tend to create forms on an ad hoc and piecemeal basis: a department sees a need for a form, and so creates a form to fill that need. This approach results in unnecessary duplication and storage of data and information, for much of the data to be entered on one form may exist already on other forms used elsewhere. A more rational approach is to set up, under the Office Manager or the O & M Department, centralized **forms control**, the purpose of which is to create a properly integrated system of forms.

The features of such a system are as follows:

1 No form is produced without the approval of the Office Manager or the O & M Department. Many

Invoice/Sales Order

Code No./Delivery Date_____   Order Date_____

Pinecrafts Ltd.
(Address and VAT No. here)

To_____

_____

_____

(APPROPRIATE PRINTED MATERIAL ON THE VARIOUS COPIES HERE)

Quantity	Description	Part No.	Unit Price	Total Price

Special Parts and Instructions

(TERMS, ETC. PRINTED HERE)

VAT

TOTAL

Figure 5.9   Invoice set for Pinecrafts. The top copy (shown here) is the combined sales order and invoice. For notes on this and the other copies see page 81

Part No _____		Description _____				
Reorder Level _____		Reorder Quantity_____				
ORDERED		RECEIVED		ISSUED		BALANCE
Date	Quantity	Date	Quantity	Date	Quantity	

Figure 5.10   Stock record card for Pinecrafts

forms will be designed by the O & M Department on the basis of a proper analysis of the needs of user departments.

2 Only forms which promote efficiency are retained, these being designed to avoid unnecessary copying and duplication of information.

3 Forms are designed to a common house style. For example, title, reference number, date, etc. should appear in identical locations on all forms, standard sizes are used, standard colour codes indicate destinations (e.g. white = primary user, green = Accounts, yellow = Audit, etc.) and the design is carried out by experts with a view to quick and easy completion and reading of forms.

4 Forms are produced centrally using the most suitable paper and printing methods.

A useful first step in setting up an integrated system of forms is to construct an **X-chart**. This shows the extent to which data is being duplicated on the forms and documents currently in use. The forms in use are listed across the top of the chart, the data appearing on the forms being listed down the side. An X-chart showing some of the forms and documents required for the Pinecrafts case study (Appendix II) is given in Figure 5.13.

There is clearly a great deal of duplication in the forms listed in this chart. This can be overcome by combining the sales order, works order, receipt note, and invoice into a single multi-part set, printed on no-carbon-required (N.C.R.) paper (copies are produced by chemicals impregnated in the paper, obviating the need to interleave carbon paper. The way in which this system of forms might operate is described below; the background to this description is the 'Administrative Procedures' section of the Pinecrafts case study (page 188).

The general design of the set is shown in Figure 5.9. The top copy forms the combined sales order/invoice, as indicated in the Figure. Other copies will be appropriately titled and will have appropriate printed material in the places indicated in the Figure. The price information should not appear on the works

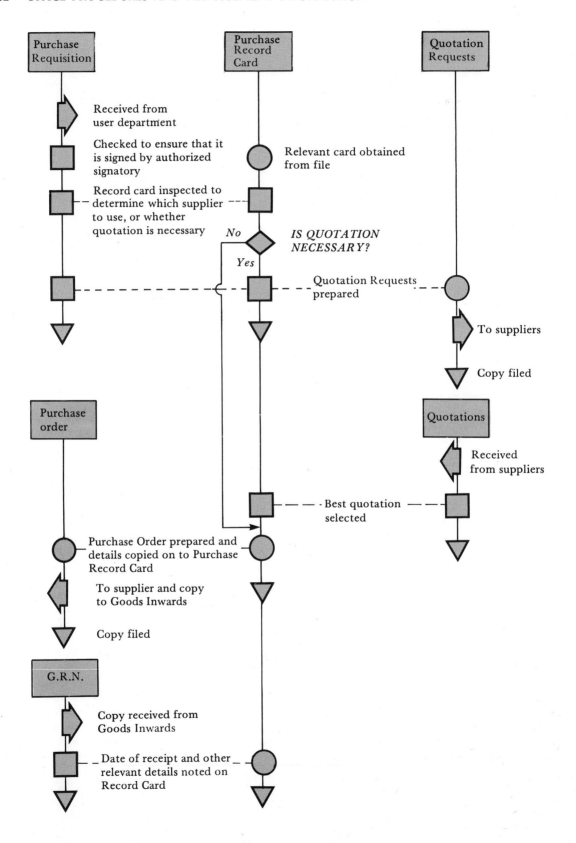

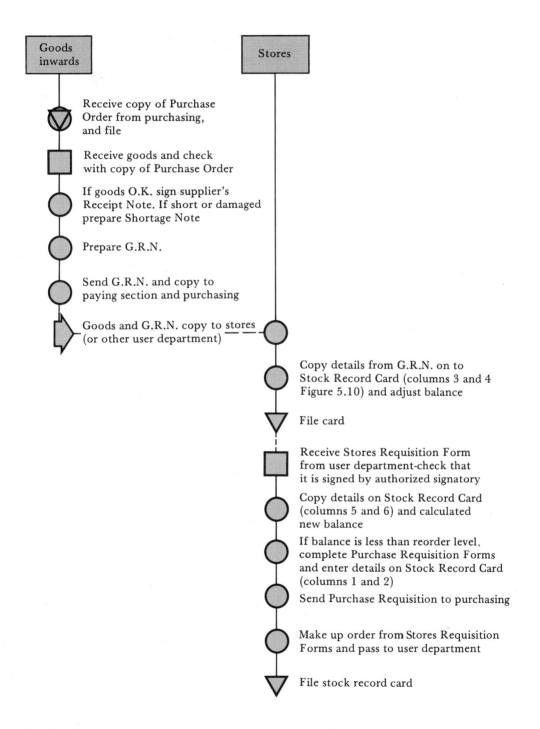

Figure 5.12   Receiving and storekeeping procedures: man-type process chart

FORM / DATA	Quotation	Sales order	Installers diary	Works order	Receipt note	Invoice	Sales ledger
Date	X	X		X	X	X	X
Reference/ Delivery date	X	X	X	X	X	X	X
Customer details	X	X	X		X	X	X
Product details	X	X		X	X	X	
Price	X	X				X	X

Figure 5.13   X-chart: part of the Pinecrafts documentation system

order/receipt note copy of this set, and so a scramble pattern may be printed over the 'Unit Price' and 'Total Price' sections of this copy, or alternatively these areas may be de-sensitized in the production process. It is envisaged that fitted kitchens will be produced and installed by Pinecrafts at the rate of one per working day, and so the delivery date could form the code number of the job, as indicated in the Figure.

The combined sales order/invoice will be held in the Sales Department in code number order and will ultimately be handed to the customer by the installers at the time of installation. If a quotation is required, then this can be produced by means of a suitably masked photocopy of the set (in this case the code number and the order date will not be entered until a firm order has been received from the customer).

The second copy of the set will be handed or sent to the customer at the time that the order is placed. The third copy will be sent to the General Office for book-keeping, credit control, and audit purposes, and again it will be held in code number order. The fourth copy will be on card, and it will form the works order: it will be passed to the Production Department, where again it will be held in code number order. (Since this number is the delivery date, the order of the cards corresponds to the order in which jobs should be scheduled through the workshops.) The card will accompany the job through despatch and delivery, and it will form the receipt note − it will be signed by the

customer when installation is complete, and returned by the installers to the clerk who deals with credit control. This clerk will again hold the card in code number (delivery date) order; when the account is settled the card will be removed from the credit control file and passed to the Sales Department. The cards remaining in the file will form the basis of the credit control system − cards representing overdue accounts will be at the end of the file.

When the forms and copies needed have been determined, by an analysis of departmental requirements and by constructing an X-chart, the forms themselves can be designed. Some guidelines to forms design are as follows.

1 Before beginning the task of designing a form, determine who is to complete it, bearing in mind that routine paperwork should be handled as low down the organization as possible. The form of wording and instructions printed on the form must be appropriate to the level of staff using the form.

2 A second preliminary step is to determine how the data is to be entered on the form and the method of processing. If the form is to be completed in a workshop then it should be printed on stiff paper or card; if the data is to be entered by machine (typewriter, word processor, or computer terminal) then the line and character spacing on the form must match that of the machine, and the use of continuous stationery may be

desirable (this enables the automatic feeding of forms through machines). The way in which any copies are to be produced, and the most appropriate size of form – bearing in mind the machine size, file sizes, and sizes of other forms – should also be determined at this stage.

3 List the essential information that is to appear on the form, and put it into the most logical sequence, bearing in mind the sequence in which such information appears on other forms used by the organization.

4 Draw up the form in accordance with the above sequence on a **spacing chart** (similar in appearance to graph paper) with a grid size that matches the line and character spacing of the machine which is to enter the data. These charts can be obtained from office equipment suppliers; they are not necessary if the form being designed is to be completed by hand. The number of spaces required for each item of data must be calculated and allowed for in the design, as well as any margins required at the edge of the form. Note that any instructions should appear at the top rather than the bottom of the form, so that they are read before the form is completed. If these instructions are lengthy, they should be typed on a separate sheet of paper for subsequent insertion by the printer.

The remaining step in the forms control process is to arrange for the production of the forms by the most suitable methods. In traditional office systems, the production of forms and the insertion of data are quite distinct operations. With many of the larger computer-based systems, however, it is now more economical to hold the form design in the electronic memory of the computer and to print it concurrently with the data. The advantages of this method of form production are:

1 the need to hold a stock of forms is eliminated, and
2 the spaces allowed on the form for data can be varied according to the amount of data to be entered.

Forms design and control is a continuing process, for departmental needs are continually changing. A frequent response to a major change is to add additional forms to those already in use, so that systems gradually become more complex and administratively expensive. A more appropriate response is to adapt the total system of forms by reviewing all those forms affected by the change and redesigning them as necessary.

ASSIGNMENT GROUP WORK
Assignment 3 (i), (ii), and (iii) (page 191).

Data Classification

The number of items of data flowing through a business is very large, and to enable these items to be sorted, stored, and retrieved from storage it is necessary to *classify* them (group them into classes). Classification can be thought of as a way of providing each item of data with an *address*.

Invoices for purchases made might be classified and stored according to supplier name, so that they can be quickly located when needed for statement reconciliation; this is an example of **group** classification, for it enables all items bearing the group characteristic (in this case the name of the supplier) to be distinguished from those which lack that characteristic. The Pinecrafts sales documentation described in the above section is classified according to the planned delivery date: this is an example of **particular** classification, for it enables one item (in this case an individual job) to be distinguished from all other items.

An individual item of data may be classified in more than one way. For example, an individual purchase may appear;

1 under supplier name in the purchase invoice file
2 under product code number in the purchase record card index and the stock record card index
3 in delivery date sequence in the G.R.N. file.

A major advantage of the computer is its ability to update automatically a number of files, such as the electronic equivalents of these, on the basis of a single data entry.

The classifications given in the previous paragraph illustrate the main classification methods, which are:

1 Alphabetical
2 Numerical
3 Chronological.

The alphabetical system is widely-used, being particularly convenient if the number of classes is small. For a large number of classes, however, the numerical system is normally preferred, the advantages being that it can be expanded indefinitely, it can encompass a large number of subdivisions (as in the

Dewey decimal system used for non-fiction books in libraries), and it is easier to store and retrieve documents by number rather than by name. It is, moreover, the most convenient classification system for computer data processing.

Telephone numbers provide a good example of numerical classification and its use by a computerised system. Subscribers are classified according to locality, each class being assigned an STD code number. Within each locality the individual subscriber is assigned a unique telephone code number. This coding system minimizes the amount of data that has to be dialled or keyed into the telephone system and processed by it: typically four digits for the STD group code and five digits for the particular number.

The disadvantage of classifying by numerical code is that a reference device is needed if the user wishes to determine the code number of an item. In the case of the telephone number, this is the STD code book for the locality codes and the area telephone directory for the individual's number. The disadvantage of reference books is that as items cannot be added or deleted, periodic reprinting is necessary. In the office this disadvantage can be avoided by the use of card indexes or visible strip indexes, the cards or strips being held in alphabetical order and added to or removed as necessary.

Quality

'Quality', when applied to data processing, refers primarily to numerical accuracy: the accuracy with which data is entered on to forms or computer terminals, and the correctness of calculations. When applied to information management it embraces such matters as the quality and appearance of letters and other documents, literary style, and the adequacy and relevance of information.

Quality costs money, and unnecessarily high quality represents wasted resources. In any office task the standard of quality aimed for should be determined by comparing the *cost* of achieving that quality standard with its *value* to the organization. Figure 5.14 illustrates what effect increasing the quality has on costs and benefits. Above point B the cost exceeds the value. For example, in the case of invoices received by a company for low-value amounts the cost of reconciliation with the orders placed and goods received may exceed

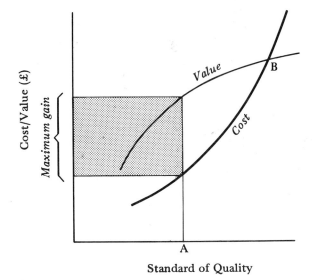

Figure 5.14   The quality of office work: its cost and its value

the benefits gained. A more cost-effective alternative would be to make a quick scrutiny of each invoice to ensure that it is addressed to the organization, is for goods normally purchased, and is for approximately the right amount.

The optimum quality is at point A: here, the marginal value of the quality standard aimed for is equal to the marginal cost, and the difference between the value and the cost is maximized. The location of point A varies with the application. Figure 5.15 illustrates the two extreme qualities of response to a letter received by the organization. Quality P would be most appropriate if the letter were from the Inland Revenue – it creates the impression of lack of resources and low profitability. At the other end of the scale, Quality Q is most suitable if prestige is important and a good impression needs to be created, for example when writing to a potential customer.

Accuracy is the most important aspect of quality in the office. In many situations (such as the invoice reconciliation example given above and the estimating example given on page 59) a 100% check on accuracy is not cost-effective. **Sampling** may then be used: a proportion of the work is checked and any errors found are recorded; if the error-rate exceeds given limits, then the cause is identified and corrective measures

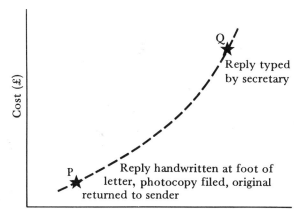

Figure 5.15 Quality of response to a letter

taken (see the notes on statistical quality control on page 63). Sampling may be used to monitor the overall quality of work, or the quality achieved by each individual in the office.

In integrated data processing, an item of data is entered into the computer once only and is then used for all subsequent processing. In this case a 100% check on the accuracy of data entry may be cost-effective (the subsequent processing, if carried out by computer, is error-free). Such checks involve two data entry clerks keying in the same set of data. The machine holds the data entered by the first clerk and matches it with that being entered by the second. If a mismatch occurs the machine indicates this (often by locking the mechanism), and the second clerk inspects the data and selects the correct entry.

The process of isolating and correcting errors in data is called **data verification**. The above 100% check method is obviously expensive; more sophisticated, cheaper, and virtually fool-proof alternatives are **check digit verification** (CDV) for fixed data (described below), and the various batch checks for variable data (described in the next section).

Check digit verification operates by incorporating a built-in check in fixed data such as code numbers. Common examples are document reference numbers and bank account numbers, where incorrect entry of the number will result in data on the document or cheque being posted to the wrong storage address, with possibly disastrous consequences.

CDV involves cumbersome verification calculations, and is therefore only suitable for use in computer-based systems. It works like this: code numbers are assigned to items or documents in the usual way (by sequential numbering), and an extra digit is added to the end of each code number so that a new number is created with the property that, if each digit is weighted in the way shown below, then the sum of the weighted digits is divisible by 11. An error in entering this number into the computer terminal will destroy this property, and this will be picked up immediately by the machine and the operator informed.

Suppose that the initial code number is 387064. To determine the digit (which we will call χ) to be added to the end of this number, the digits are weighted in turn by factors of 1, 2, 3, . . . , and the results added:

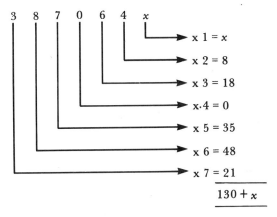

The lowest number above 130 that is divisible by 11 is 132, and so χ, the check digit, is equal to 2. Hence the new number is 3870642. As an exercise the student should confirm that the ISBN number of this book (see rear cover), when weighted in this way, is divisible by 11.

Batching Work

Although much of the work received by an office flows in in a steady stream, it is often best processed on a batch-basis. Batching is sometimes necessary because the economics of computer operation may demand batch data entry and processing (see page 103); another important reason is that batching breaks the work up into manageable lots for verification purposes. An example of batching is given in the case study on page

75; the purchase invoices were batched by product-code.

Verification procedures that are commonly carried out on batches of forms are as follows:

1 Batch total checking. Each batch is accompanied through the processing cycle by a control slip, on which is entered the batch total. (This may be the total value of a batch of invoices, as in the case study on page 75, or the total hours worked of a batch of clock-cards, or whatever total is appropriate to the data being processed.) When the data on the forms is entered into a machine (or operated on in some other way) a check is made that the sum of the entries agrees with the batch total shown on the control slip. If the totals do not agree, then either a document has been overlooked or lost, or an error has occurred in entering or copying the data, or, in the case of manual data processing, a mistake has been made in the calculations.

Provided the batch size is not too large, the isolation and correction of such an error are not normally difficult. The procedure might be:

(a) Check that no documents are missing by counting

(b) Calculate the difference between the two batch totals − if this difference is divisible by 9, then digits in the data have been transposed (entered in the wrong sequence); this is the most common source of error
(c) If neither of the above checks reveal the error, then check the individual entries and, in the case of manual data processing, the calculations.

2 Range checking. This entails scrutinizing the batch values and picking out for detailed checking any that are unreasonably high or low.

3 Sequence checking. This is used if the serial numbers of the documents on the batch form a continuous sequence. The highest and lowest numbers of the sequence are entered on the control slip, and this provides a way of checking the order and completeness of the batch at any point in the processing cycle.

If data is processed by machine, then batch totals will automatically be calculated after data entry and displayed for checking with the control slip accompanying the source documents. Unreasonably high or low batch values may also be highlighted.

6
Office Systems I: The Equipment

The past twenty years have seen office costs increase from 40% to over 60% of total business costs. The reason is not hard to find: the amount of money spent on equipment to support the office worker is less than one tenth of that spent on his blue collar colleague in the factory. Whereas the productivity of workers in general has more than doubled over this period, that of the office worker has remained virtually static.

The next twenty years will see a reversal of this trend. The micro-electronics revolution will transform every type of office activity. In this chapter we examine the office equipment that is now available, and in Chapter 7 we show how developments in the computing and telecommunications fields are leading to the integrated office, in which each item of equipment is linked electronically to, and is an integral part of, the larger office system.

Office Activities

Salaries are the biggest component of office costs. The chief cause of the increase in these costs has been the huge rise in the managerial and professional salary bill – this now accounts for 70% of the total office wage bill. It is the managerial and professional sector of business, therefore, which will be most greatly affected by the micro-electronics revolution.

Figure 6.1 shows the activities that are carried out by office workers, and the approximate proportion of time spent on each (these proportions obviously vary from office to office and from business to business; Figure 6.1 gives only a general indication). Office systems and equipment have been developed to assist all of these activities, and are described later in this chapter. This equipment will greatly reduce the time spent by managers and professionals on routine activities (such as filing and retrieval), thereby enabling them to spend a larger proportion of their time on the more important non-routine activities associated with decision-making (such as reading).

Artificial Intelligence

In sharp contrast to the rise in the office wage bill, computer costs have been declining at the rate of 20% per annum per unit of performance over the past decade. The cost of microprocessor-based devices is now falling even faster – at 35% p.a. per unit of performance. An inevitable consequence is the appearance, in every type of office equipment, of low-cost artificial intelligence to supplement, and even supplant, expensive human intelligence. The power of the computer is being distributed about the office in microprocessor-based descendents of the typewriter, printer, calculator, and TV set, and it is also becoming available, on

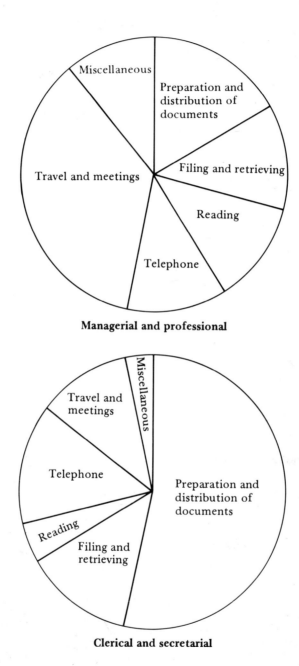

Figure 6.1   Office activities: where the wage bill goes (Area of segment indicates wage-slice)

tap, in the communications networks linking these machines. ('Intelligence' as applied to machines refers not to creative thinking but to inbuilt computing power, cf. page 4.)

We are at the moment at a transitional stage, where side by side in the same office may be found non-intelligent manual/mechanical devices, non-intelligent peripherals connected to an intelligent mainframe computer, and microprocessor-based devices possessing their own inbuilt intelligence. All three types of device are described in this chapter. In the type of office towards which we are moving (which is described at the end of Chapter 7), all devices will possess inbuilt intelligence, and they will be linked electronically to the larger intelligence and database of the organization's own mainframe computer, or alternatively (or as well as) into the external computing and information storage facilities provided by, for example, the **teletex** communications network being implemented by British Telecom (the telecommunications arm of the Post Office).

The Development of Office Systems

Four stages can be discerned in the historical development of office systems:

1 Manual/mechanical systems. This first stage represents the application of principles which originated in factories during the industrial revolution and the scientific management movement which followed it: the mechanization of individual office operations, notably document preparation, through the introduction of the typewriter one hundred years ago, and calculations, through the introduction of adding machines at about the same time, also the simplification of manual office tasks through the application of work study techniques.

The main features of manual/mechanical office systems are:

(a) Data processing is decentralized, being carried out locally in offices throughout the organization.
(b) Each item of data has to be entered many times. For example, a buying transaction will be entered on a number of documents by clerks in the supplier's organization: on the order form, on the stock record card, on the invoice, and in the purchases ledger, amongst others.

(c) The individual office tends to develop systems in a piecemeal way to suit its particular needs rather than the needs of the larger organization. This does not make for an efficient flow of information through the organization and it inhibits managerial control.
(d) Manual/mechanical office systems are expensive in terms of labour, and the processing of data is slow and prone to error. However, these systems are very flexible, and, unlike modern centralized data processing installations, they can respond very quickly to meet the changing needs of the local situation.

2 Punched card systems. In this second stage in the evolution of office systems the individual data processing operations were linked up through the use of punched card equipment, so that items of data, recorded on standard punched cards, could be fed into punched card sorting, calculating, printing, and other machines. This introduced the principle of once-only entry of data into the system, all subsequent processing being automatic (although human operators were required to feed the cards into the various machines). It also brought about the centralization of data processing on the punched card operations room, and it imposed a certain uniformity on the associated office procedures. However, punched card equipment is expensive, and although invented at the end of the last century it was not applied on any scale until the 1940s. It is now virtually obsolete, apart from the (diminishing) use of punched card data-entry equipment for computers, and it is not described in this text.

3 Computer systems. The first electronic computers were developed in the 1940s, and were applied to business data processing in the 1950s. Since that time their cost, size, and performance characteristics have steadily improved, and today a computer of some sort is an economical proposition for almost every business. A small business computer system, including the software, can now be purchased for the cost of little more than one year's salary of one office worker. Being 'solid-state' devices (i.e. having no moving parts) they do not suffer from the relatively slow speed, high cost, and limited life of the earlier mechanical office equipment. (However, many computer peripherals (attachments), notably external memory and printing devices, are still mechanically driven and suffer from these disadvantages.)

The widespread adoption of large computers by

business organizations has brought to its logical conclusion the trend that punched card systems introduced: the centralization of local data processing functions on the Data Processing Department, and the replacement of piecemeal manual/mechanical systems by integrated automatic systems designed to meet overall organizational needs.

4 Microprocessor-based office systems. With the micro-electronics revolution of the late 1960s and the 1970s came the emergence of small, cheap computers of great power, and the spread of computing power to all types of office equipment. With this has come a trend away from the complete centralization of data processing. The principle of integrated data processing still holds, for the central computer still performs the major data processing tasks and maintains the company database, but the operation of this facility, and the execution of subsidiary data processing tasks, are steadily moving into the hands of user departments. With this has come a return to the flexibility inherent in the earlier manual/mechanical systems and the ability to satisfy local needs more effectively.

Of even greater significance has been the impact of the micro-electronics revolution on office activities other than data processing. Of paramount importance in this connection has been the appearance of the word processor. This is essentially a computer dedicated to the production of letters and other documents, and with important additional information management capabilities, and this, linked to the central computer as well as to external computer networks such as Prestel, is revolutionizing the total information processing task. The ability of machines such as this to communicate electronically with other compatible machines has ushered in the era of electronic mail and with it the gradual decline of paper as the universal medium of office work.

Microprocessor-based systems will affect almost every office activity (see Figure 6.1). The productivity of office workers in the preparation of documents is increased by around 50% with word processors; filing and retrieval can be largely automated with electronic filing systems and computer-controlled microfilm systems; telephone communications are made more efficient by the use of such automatic facilities as store-and-forward and retry-if-busy; computer-based teleconferencing facilities cut down travel and meetings. Details of all these facilities are given later in this chapter.

Although these systems can cut costs through manpower savings, this is incidental to their main function: to enhance the quality of office work through faster and more accurate data processing, through improved production and distribution of information, and through the improved control over business operations that results.

CASE STUDY: THE DEVELOPMENT OF OFFICE SYSTEMS IN A PURCHASING DEPARTMENT

The Purchasing Department referred to is that of the cigarette-making machine manufacturer spoken of in previous case studies.

1 PRESENT MANUAL/MECHANICAL AND PUNCHED CARD SYSTEMS.

At the time of writing this study, the requisitioning and purchasing procedure is carried out using manual/mechanical and punched card systems. Requisitions for items to be purchased are produced in two ways:

(a) The Production Control Department writes out by hand the part numbers, quantities, and due-in-stores dates of the bought-in parts required for the manufacturing programme on cards, which are passed to the Data Processing Department. Here, the data-entry clerks produce punched cards from these (using card punches), one card for each part number requisitioned. At the beginning of each week these are stacked into a punched card sorter, which sorts them into part number order, and then into a punched card printer, which produces the requisition print-out. (The same punched cards are also used as computer input to update the Order Requirements File.) The print-out is then passed back to Production Control for authorization, and then on to the Purchasing Department.

(b) For other requisitions, manually-typed lists are produced by the requisitioning departments, authorized, and passed to Purchasing. Like the Bought-In Parts Requisition, these contain the item code numbers, the quantities, and the due-in-stores dates.

In the Purchasing Department each requisition list is passed to the buyer responsible for ordering the type of part shown. The ordering procedure is as follows. If the item to be purchased is new, then the buyer must find a suitable supplier. For new items that are similar to existing items, the normal preferred suppliers may be used; otherwise two or three possible suppliers will be contacted for quotations, and the most favourable selected (the decision will depend upon price, quality, delivery, etc.). It is sometimes necessary to order a proportion of the items prior to obtaining quotes, in order to avoid production hold-ups.

If the item to be purchased is a repeat, then reference is made to the record card for that item held in the card index on the buyer's desk. This gives the preferred supplier and any other suppliers, the last purchase price, and other relevant price information. The buyer notes by hand the supplier to be used and the price to be paid on the requisition list, which, when all the items it contains have been marked in this way, is passed out to the typists for the production of the purchase orders.

2 PROPOSED COMPUTER SYSTEM – FIRST PHASE (NON-INTEGRATED).

The first phase of the computerization of the purchasing procedure is being implemented at the time of writing. In this phase the procedure is *not* integrated with other computerized procedures in the company. An additional file (the Purchase Record File) will be created, to hold data at present stored manually on the record cards. A number of computer terminals, with screens and printers, will be housed in the Purchasing Department – the plan is to assign one to each buyer. The requisition lists will be produced by the present methods, and will be distributed to the appropriate buyers. The ordering procedure, however, will be as follows.

The buyer will take each item on his lists in sequence and will key the part number into his terminal. The computer will respond by displaying on his screen the data held under that number on the Purchase Record File. This data will include the description of the item, the preferred supplier, any other suppliers, the price history, when the price was last confirmed, packing and carriage information, and other product information such as the economical order quantity and price breaks (i.e. at what quantities discounts are given). The buyer will key in his purchasing decision, and the computer will store that decision with the other purchasing decisions, printing the purchase orders automatically on demand at the end of the day. Prior to printing, it will sort orders by supplier, so that all orders for the same supplier will be printed on the same purchase order form. For urgent orders, the buyer can request an immediate print-out.

To update the Purchase Record File the buyers will have to key in the relevant information on the orders placed. Update information on deliveries will also have to be keyed in from information received from the Goods Inwards Department.

3 PROPOSED COMPUTER SYSTEM – SECOND PHASE (INTEGRATED).

Further extension of computerization throughout the company will result in the various systems developed for individual departments being integrated, so that automatic update of all files is obtained from a single data-entry, and so that each department has limited access (according to its needs) to other departments' files. In the case of the requisitioning and purchasing procedures, departments will key in their requisitions (via their terminals) on to a Purchase Requisition File. The computer, in response to a command keyed in by a buyer in the Purchasing Department, will display on his screen each requisition relating to the products which he is responsible for ordering, together with the product information (listed in the previous section) which it automatically selects from the Purchase Record File. It will store his decisions and print the purchase orders as in the first phase of computerization, but updating of the Purchase Record File with information on the orders placed will now be automatic.

Information on deliveries and inspections will be keyed into the computer via the terminal in the Goods Inwards Department, and this information will be used for automatic update of the Purchase Record File. In addition the work of invoice reconciliation will be carried out automatically by the computer on behalf of the Financial Accounts Department – it will match the invoice details held on the Invoice File with the order and delivery information held on the Purchase Record File, and signal any discrepancies.

EXERCISE

Refer to the case study on invoice reconciliation and the production of management information (page 75). Construct a flow chart of the procedure and outline the way it would be carried out by an integrated computer system. State what computer files will be needed.

The Manifestation of Information

The remainder of this chapter and Chapter 7 is devoted to a description of the technology of data and information processing. As was pointed out at the beginning of Chapter 5, developments in this technology are causing the distinction between data and information to disappear, the term 'information processing' being used to cover all types of office activity, including data processing. From now on in the text we shall use the term **information** to include data.

Information manifests itself in a variety of forms:

1 In numerical form, as *data* (code numbers, prices, quantities, etc.)
2 In written verbal form, as *text* (letters, reports, etc.)
3 In spoken verbal form, as *voice* (telephone calls, meetings, etc.)
4 In pictorial form, as *image* (diagrams, photographs, etc.)

Office equipment, described below, is concerned

with processing all these manifestations of information.

The Elements of an Office System

The purpose of an office system is to perform a sequence of operations on an information input to produce a desired information output. Its constituent parts are shown in Figure 6.2.

The subsystems of this system include the recording system, the processing (computing and editing) system, the temporary storage system, the long-term mass storage system, and the communications system. In manual/mechanical offices the equipment for these subsystems is 'stand-alone' – each piece of equipment operates independently of the other pieces. In computer-based offices these subsystems are (or should be) tightly integrated, so that the input, output,

and storage devices are peripherals linked electronically to the computer's central processing unit (which carries out all control, processing, and temporary storage functions).

The integration of these subsystems in the computer-based office results in a certain inflexibility of operation. It is usually impossible to interrogate the mass-storage subsystem about an item of information independently of the central processing unit – the interrogation procedure entails accessing the computer via a terminal, and this may involve overcoming bureaucratic hurdles (particularly if data processing is handled centrally), delays, and certainly expense – but this disadvantage is more than offset by the great advantages of computerization (see page 110). Recent developments in computer-based systems, e.g. Viewdata and COM (mass storage of computer output on microfilm), have gone a long way towards eliminating even this drawback.

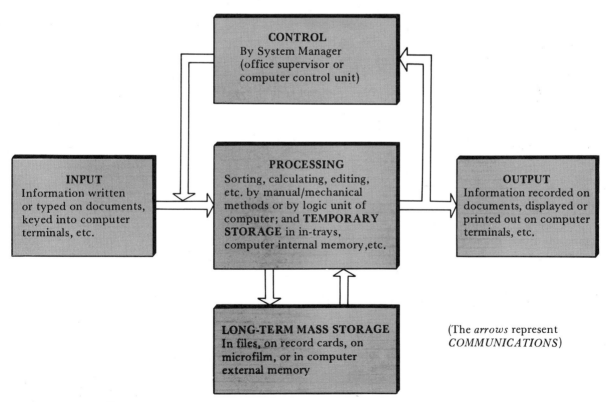

Figure 6.2 An office system

System Elements (1): Input/Output

We have grouped the input and output elements of the office system together, for the same device usually performs both functions (typewriters, for example, are used to both input data on to forms and to output letters).

1 Writing systems (for data and text). Handwriting still has an important place in the office. In fact, one of the most cost-effective ways of dealing with correspondence (if quality is not important) is to write the reply at the foot of the incoming letter or memo, file a photocopy, and return the original to the sender. One American company which adopted this system for the bulk of its correspondence achieved enormous savings in secretarial staff with no reduction in executive effectiveness.

A simple and useful device to assist manual data processing in small businesses is the **posting board**. This is a large board (about 70 cm by 50 cm) on which a number of documents can be accurately positioned by the use of metal pegs at the side (the pegs fit into holes punched at the edges of the documents). The documents are normally carbon-backed, and this allows entries to be recorded simultaneously on each document. On a wages run, for example, entries will be recorded simultaneously on the paycheques, the wages slips, and the wage sheet.

With the distribution of computer data processing facilities to user departments has come the appearance of the **electronic writing pad**, designed to permit handwritten entry of data into the computer by keyboard-inexperienced personnel. In some versions of this device the characters (capital letters or numerals) have to be written in defined squares on a pressure-sensitive surface. The electronic gadgetry connected to the sensors beneath the surface recognizes the characters and converts them to binary digital form for entry to the computer. In the latest version of the pad it is not pressure that is detected, but low frequency signals emitted by the point of a special pen, and the electronics is capable of recognizing ordinary handwriting written on any area of the surface.

Some optical character readers (see below) are able to scan and read handwritten text (capital letters and numerals only) and convert it to computer or word processor input.

2 Keyboard-based systems (for data and text). The manual **typewriter** was introduced 100 years ago and is still one of the commonest items of office equipment. A surprisingly high proportion of offices in this country have not even progressed to the electric typewriter — though perhaps they will leapfrog this stage of office mechanization and adopt the more sophisticated **electronic typewriter**. At present this type of machine costs some 50% more than the conventional office electric typewriter, but this differential is expected to largely disappear in the early 1980s.

The electronic typewriter differs from conventional electrics in that it is microprocessor-controlled, and the keyboard-to-letterplate connection is achieved by electronic impulses, not by mechanical linkages. These features enable it to store a small amount of text prior to printing (so that typing errors can be corrected on a one-line electronic display before the text is transferred to paper), and they permit the incorporation of facilities such as automatic carriage return, centering of headings, and justification of right-hand margins. They also give it the potential ability to communicate electronically with other electronic equipment.

The latest electronic typewriter from IBM can store several pages of text prior to printing (which allows fairly extensive text editing prior to printing), it incorporates features such as storage of forms layout (to speed the completion of forms), and it costs £1,470.

At several times the price of the electronic typewriter comes the much more sophisticated **word processor**. A typical machine today costs in the region of £5,000, though prices can be expected to halve over the next three or four years. A typist requires several months' experience on such a machine before she is able to use its advanced facilities effectively, and running costs are much higher than for conventional typewriters. However, these machines give a very high quality of output, and a much faster throughput of work. Average productivity increases are 50% for stand-alone word processing systems, and 100% for shared-facility systems (see below). In some applications productivity increases of 300% have been achieved.

Besides offering the basic electronic facilities available on electronic typewriters, word processors normally incorporate the following features:

(a) a screen capable of displaying several dozen lines of text;
(b) a large electronic memory (usually disc-based) capable of holding several hundred pages of text;

(c) the ability to rearrange text in the memory on command from the operator;

(d) automatic substitution of a particular word or phrase throughout the text by another;

(e) storage of standard paragraphs of text and insertion, as required, in letters or other documents;

(f) merging of lists of names and addresses with standard letters to produce automatically individually-typed letters to selected addresses (this can be done while the machine is unattended, e.g. at night);

(g) storage of forms layout in the memory, so that information is entered automatically in the appropriate spaces;

(h) page-length control and automatic pagination (page numbering);

(i) simple data processing capabilities, e.g. automatic addition of numbers in a table, and insertion, deletion, or rearrangement of entries (such as names and addresses) in a file;

(j) high quality and speed of printed output – highest speeds are achieved by the use of an inkjet printer (as against conventional impact printing); note that the printing device is a separate unit, and in a word processing pool a small number of printers only will be installed as a shared facility;

(k) graphics facilities for the production of histograms and other charts.

Word processors have the greatest impact on productivity in situations where a great deal of standard material is handled, a good example being solicitors' offices, where productivity increases can exceed 100%. In one-off document situations a productivity increase of only 10% might be achieved. The procedure in this case is for the author's dictated input to be transferred by the operator into the memory of the machine (typing errors do not matter at this stage – if she is not making errors, she is not typing fast enough!); a draft is printed out for amendment by the author (typing errors are ignored); this is returned to the operator, who amends the text stored in the machine's memory, proofreads (on the screen) for typing errors and amends these, and instructs the machine to print the finished result.

The small office will probably move into word-processing by acquiring a single **stand-alone** word processor. This consists of a keyboard, screen, processor (i.e. computing device), a disc drive for the electronic storage of text, and a printer. In large offices word-processing will often be organized on a

A WORD PROCESSING APPLICATION

Word processors have a role to play in almost every office situation. Take a hotel, for example. To produce quotations, acknowledgments of bookings, and so on, the standard text is called up on the screen and variables (names, addresses, dates, prices, etc.) are inserted at the appropriate places. By pressing the 'run' key the operator instructs the machine to type out the finished document – and while it is doing this she can be inserting the variable material in the next piece of standard text on the screen.

For menus, a variety of type-faces can be used, and headings can be automatically centred. Additional dishes can be inserted as necessary in the standard menu, and any other alterations, such as price changes, can be carried out on the screen. Standard translations of foreign dishes can be retrieved from the machine's memory and inserted.

For mailing promotions, the word processor will store customer details in its memory, and it will produce mailing lists by sorting these according to date of last booking, type of booking, or other relevant variables. In this way it is able to select suitable customers for a particular mailing, and automatically produce standard letters with a personal touch (each will be individually addressed and may refer to personal details such as date of last stay), together with labels for envelopes.

Besides all these facilities, the word processor is able to record bookings and produce booking lists, show vacancies, and the latest models can even handle the hotel's accounts.

shared facility basis: a number of workstations (keyboards and screens) will share common processing, disc storage, and printing facilities. The advantage of this arrangement over a number of independent stand-alone systems is:

(a) workstations (keyboards and screens) can be added to the common word-processing facilities at a cost of only £1,500 each, and
(b) the large amount of disc-handling that has to be done by operators of stand-alone systems is eliminated by the use of more sophisticated disc-drives, resulting in marked increases in productivity.

Note that extensive electronic dictionaries (of up to 200,000 words) are being compiled for storage in central computer memory; connecting the word processor to this will permit automatic correction of typing and spelling errors. Word processors are already available with more limited inbuilt dictionaries (up to 50,000 words).

Like the electronic typewriter, the word processor has the ability to communicate with other compatible machines, and many are provided with facilities (such as suitable input/output ports) to allow this. This ability is of major importance, for the large internal memory permits a complete message or series of messages to be stored electronically, transmitted at high speed (and low cost) to word processors or other machines at distant locations, and read by the recipient on a screen, without ever being transferred to paper.

Connected to the organization's computer a (compatible) word processor has access to powerful data processing facilities as well as to the common database. It becomes, in effect, a rather expensive **computer terminal**. A more common type of terminal is the **teletypewriter** (or teletype), a non-intelligent device consisting of a keyboard which transmits electronic impulses to the computer and a printer or screen on which the output of the keyboard, as well as that of the computer, is displayed.

Mention should be made here of **line printers**, so called because they produce printed output a line at a time (rather than a character at a time). The quality of reproduction, although not high, is perfectly adequate for normal computer printout, and the speed is very high.

One of the latest developments in computer output technology is the **page printer**. This prints output a *page* at a time, and could produce the volume of text in this book in about 30 seconds. The quality, unlike that of line printers, is high. One type of page printer works by creating on special paper an electrical impression of the characters to be printed. The surface is then sprayed with ink, which adheres to the electrically charged areas but is washed off the rest. Only the largest organizations have a need for such a device or, indeed, the financial resources to buy it (around £150,000).

3 Optical systems (data and text). The **cathode ray tube** (CRT) is becoming an increasingly important information-output device. It converts a stream of electrons to ordinary light, and is an efficient and inexpensive way of translating the electronic language of a computing device to human-readable form. It can also be used as a means of producing images for other purposes (e.g. for printing onto microfilm or paper), but this application is being superseded by the use of the laser-based device described below. CRTs manifest themselves as computer output terminals (**visual display units**), as word processor screens, and as viewdata terminals.

Viewdata systems (described on page 112) can use any suitably-adapted TV set as a terminal, but for office use microprocessor-controlled intelligent sets are now available. They have large screen sizes (i.e. normal domestic size, as distinct from the rather smaller word processor displays), high quality definition, colour, full-sized keyboards, and some built-in information processing capabilities. These machines are intended mainly for executive use, but they can perform all the usual data processing and word processing functions by utilizing the software (programs) available on the organization's central computer.

It is now possible to convert ordinary typescript, on paper or on microfilm, into an electronic signal by means of **optical character readers** (OCR's). The most cost-effective way to use a word processor, for example, is in conjunction with a bank of ordinary typewriters: the draft copy produced by the latter is fed into the memory of the word processor by the OCR, and is subsequently amended and corrected for final printing by the word processor operator. (This way of organizing typing work, however, creates human problems, for the individual worker does not perform a 'complete' task.)

Although the term 'electronic office' has been coined to describe the emerging office of the 1980s, in view of the increasing use being made of **laser light technology** and of **microfilm** this is not altogether appropriate. A laser light beam is a much more efficient information carrier than is an electric current or radio signal: 40,000 A4 pages of text per second can be transmitted by laser over an optic fibre system. Information carried by laser can be converted into an electronic signal, and vice versa, and so laser-based systems are a means of inputting and outputting data to and from computers and other office equipment.

Computer output can be laser-printed on to microfilm at high speed and low cost (speeds of up to 30 frames a second are possible, the processing cost being less than 0.1p per frame of film). Thus COM (**computer output microfilm**) is a viable way of storing computer output, retrieval for computer use being possible by means of an OCR. Advantages of this system include the ability to bypass the computer to retrieve information (thus reducing the number of computer terminals required), and the ability to access the record simply and quickly, to read it means of a simple projector, and to produce hardcopy using the microfilm as a master. Also, it is now possible to erase a frame and replace it by another, thus permitting the updating of information held on microfilm. However, access speeds are far too slow for normal computer data processing applications and it is, therefore, an additional, rather than an alternative, method of storing information; though for the archival storage of 'old' information, for which high access speeds are not required, it is a viable alternative to magnetic storage media. (For a description of microfilm systems see the section 'Mass Storage' below.)

Computer laser output can also be used for **phototypesetting** (the production of masters for copying and printing purposes). The latest printer copiers (described below) use this technology, and produce copies at the rate of around 120 per minute at a cost of 1½p or less each.

4 Imaging systems (data, text, and image). **Facsimile** devices were developed at the turn of the century to transmit images (such as photographs) by telephone line to distant locations. (A page of text is an image, and so can be transmitted by these devices.) The image to be transmitted is scanned by a photoelectric cell which converts the blacks, greys, and whites into electrical signals. A facsimile transmitter will also act as a receiver, and will decode incoming signals and print them as image on special paper.

Facsimile machines are grouped according to the quality of scanning and reproduction: Group 1 give the highest authenticity of reproduction, the transmission time for an A4 size document being 6 minutes; Group 2 has a time of 3 minutes; and Group 3, which reproduces in black and white without grey tones, has a time of 1 minute. Group 3 machines are, in fact, digital machines (that is, they convert the image into a string of O's and 1's), and they are therefore potentially able to communicate with other electronic office equipment, which is almost invariably digitial. It is, moreover, perfectly adequate for the transmission of data and text (which contains no greys), and the latest Group 3 machines have transmission times of under 30 seconds, which is very economical on telephone line time (very much cheaper than Telex − see the section 'Communications' below).

Also available for the conversion of images on paper to electronic digital form are **optical character/facsimile readers** of the type referred to in the previous section. These give much faster transmission times than conventional equipment. The use of these readers, and of Group 3 facsimile machines, permits the input of images into computers.

The reproduction of images on to paper is termed **copying** if a specially-prepared master is not required or **duplicating** if a special stencil or master is needed. (In the case of the electronic output from a computer or word processor, a master of some sort must be prepared for either of these processes.) The cost per copy of reproduction by the former type of machine is relatively high, but the absence of the need to produce a special master makes it the most economical form of reproduction if only a few copies are needed.

Copying machines include photocopiers (which use a photographic process), thermographic machines (which use a heat process), and electrostatic machines (which include the well-known Xerox machines).

Duplicating machines are of three types, namely:

(a) **Spirit duplicating machines**, so-called because a chemical spirit or solvent is used in the process. The master consists of a reverse image of the material to be duplicated, and it is produced by placing a special carbon sheet behind the master sheet prior to writing or typing the material. The carbon is transferred to the back of the master, which is then attached (back uppermost) to the drum of the machine. The drum is rotated (manually or by motor), and the spirit transfers the dye from the carbon impression on the master to the copy paper. This is the cheapest and simplest duplicating process, and a variety of colours can be produced by the use of coloured carbon sheets. However, the quality is not high, and only 50 copies or so can be produced before the dye begins to become exhausted. The speed of reproduction is around 100 copies a minute.

(b) **Stencil duplicating machines**, so-called because the master consists of holes typed in the wax surface of a stencil. The master is fixed to the drum of the machine, and as the drum rotates ink oozes through the holes onto the copy paper. The quality of reproduction is superior to that obtained by the spirit process, several thousand copies can be produced from one master, and the speed of reproduction is about 200 copies a minute. However, the initial cost of the master and of setting up the machine for a run is higher, and the process is economical only if the number of copies required exceeds 50.

(c) **Offset duplicating machines**, so-called because the image is first transferred from the master onto the rotating drum, from which it is 'offset' onto the copy paper. Masters can be prepared either by typing directly, using a carbon ribbon, on to special paper or metal plate, or by photographically transferring material prepared on ordinary paper on to paper or plate. Up to 5,000 copies can be produced from a paper plate, between 20,000 and 50,000 from a metal plate. The speed of reproduction is between 100 and 150 copies a minute, and the quality is very good (offset litho is the normal process used in printing). It is, however, the most expensive duplicating process.

Microprocessor-controlled **intelligent copier printers** (ICPs) are now available which can accept input in electronic form and then produce the masters and run off and collate the required number of copies automatically. These devices are able to perform a number of functions normally associated with word processors, such as storing material electronically prior to printout, and automatic formatting (layout) of the material on the printed page.

5 Voice systems. The spoken word has always been a major method of inputting and outputting information, and its use will not diminish in the future. It is a highly interactive communication medium (it provides for immediate response), and its use satisfies human social needs. The use of the **telephone** to assist this process is, of course, long-established, and will remain for the foreseeable future.

The use of the telephone has, at present, two major drawbacks:

(a) 70% of business calls fail because the recipient is unavailable or the number is engaged
(b) The recipient suffers an 'interruption factor' of three minutes (the average length of time needed after the termination of the call to pick up the threads and resume his interrupted work).

The micro-electronics revolution is, inevitably, going to affect even this: automatic message storage and forwarding facilities (**store-and-forward**) and automatic redialling if the number is engaged (**retry-if-busy**) facilities are becoming available, and will in the mid-1980s be available as a service on the public telephone network. Also, microprocessor-controlled handsets are available with facilities such as storage of commonly-used numbers for automatic dialling.

The telephone can also be used to input voice to a **central dictation system**. Such systems normally use tape cassettes as the storage medium − the latest micro-cassettes will allow up to an hour's recording time on each side and can be used in recorders as small as 6 cm by 11 cm, which makes them ideal for dictation in out-of-office environments. Modern dictation systems are microprocessor-controlled, and include facilities such as automatic printing of self-adhesive cassette labels with detailed information about each job on the cassette.

Voice is likely to replace the keyboard in the future as the main means of data entry to electronic equipment. **Speech recognition systems** are already quite highly developed, and equipment is available which will accept a limited range of verbal commands (about 200). Considerable effort is currently being put into developing systems for matching the characteristics of a large vocabulary of words spoken into a terminal with those held in the electronic dictionary of the central computer to permit the direct entry of spoken text into the system. Speech synthesizing equipment is also well-developed, and so verbal communication between man and machine may soon be possible. Speech recognition does of course mean that the production of printed text from the spoken word will be an automatic process.

6 Punched card and paper tape systems (data and

text). The use of these systems to input and output data is still widespread, although it can be expected to decline sharply during the 1980s. The computer manufacturers continue to provide for this type of data entry only because so many users are reluctant to give up their outdated, but expensive, punched card and paper tape equipment.

Punched cards are about 19 cm by 8 cm, and data is recorded as a pattern of holes arranged in vertical columns. Each alphabetical character can be represented by a pair of holes punched in a column. There are 12 possible hole positions in a column, and a hole will be punched in one of the first 3 positions and in one of the last 9: the letter 'A' is represented by a hole in the first position and a hole in the fourth position, 'B' by a hole in the first and a hole in the fifth, 'J' by a hole in the second and a hole in the fourth, and so on. A numerical digit (0 to 9) is represented by a single hole punched in one of the last ten positions. A mechanism within the punched card reader senses the position of each hole or pair of holes in a column and so reads the card.

Most punched cards have 80 columns (allowing entry of 80 characters or digits), and these may be grouped into 'fields', each category of data being assigned to a specific field. For example, if customer orders are recorded on punched cards, then the first field, covering perhaps the first 8 columns, will hold the customer account number, the second field will hold the code number of the item ordered, the third field the quantity, and the fourth the unit price. If a customer orders a number of different items, then these must be recorded on separate cards.

Data is recorded in a similar way on **paper tape**, each character or digit being represented by a pattern of holes across the width of the tape. Paper tape is very much more economical and compact than punched cards but, being in a continuous strip, it is not as flexible as the punched card system – individual items cannot be added to, or extracted from it, and the sequence cannot be altered.

Punched cards and paper tape are normally used in batch processing applications. Prior to the computer (or other machine) run, a large volume of data is entered on cards or tape (using a card punch or tape punch). These are then read by the machine at a very high speed, thus minimizing the use of machine time and, if communication is via the telephone system, telephone line time.

System Elements (2): Communication

Communication has to take place between the various parts of the office system, or between one office and another. It involves either *transportation* – moving documents from one individual's out-tray to another's in-tray – or *telecommunications* – transmitting voice, data, text, or image from one machine to another.

1 Transportation. At its simplest, transportation is accomplished by the originator of the document taking it to the user; but unless the distances involved are small, and the matter is urgent, this is an uneconomic method. Many organizations operate a **messenger service** for transporting documents between departments, with collections and deliveries at fixed times. One organization even has a robot messenger which trundles along a magnetically-charted route!

A number of **document conveyor systems** are available which operate by linking floors or departments by continuously-moving belts. Documents fed into the system at one point are automatically ejected upon reaching their destination. In some systems up to 30 channels run in parallel, each travelling to a different destination; in others, departments share a common channel, mechanical or electronic devices being used to ensure that documents are ejected at the required point.

The G.P.O. postal service will normally be used for external transportation. If the organization has a messenger service or document conveyor system there should be a **mail room** to which all outgoing mail is sent prior to posting. Centralized mail-handling brings the usual benefits that accrue from centralization (specialist staff and equipment, the latter including collating, addressing, and franking machines), and it also permits a number of communications from different departments to a single addressee (such as a branch office) to be sent in a single package. If there is no messenger service or conveyor system, it may be more efficient for each department to handle its own outgoing mail, especially if the quantities involved are small.

2 Telecommunications. The great advantage of telecommunications over transportation methods is the speed of transmission: messages can be communicated instantaneously to suitable receiving machines in any part of the world. The main telecommunications facilities presently available are described below; the advanced systems that are currently being developed and implemented by British Telecom are outlined in Chapter 7.

The most familiar piece of telecommunications equipment is the **telephone**, described in a previous section. Patented by Alexander Bell in 1876, it is the one item of present-day equipment that we can still expect to be in offices in the year 2000. Besides being used for voice transmissions, the telephone network is also used for communicating data, text, and image (see below).

For data communications, a variety of Post Office **Datel** services are available, utilizing the ordinary public telegraph or telephone lines, or special high frequency lines for high transmission rates. These services enable terminals in remote locations to communicate with central computing facilities, such as the facilities offered by computer bureaux. The transmission rate over ordinary lines is equivalent to several A4 pages of text a minute.

So far as text is concerned, the most important telecommunications method available today is **telex**. Teletypewriters are used to transmit and receive telex messages. Transmission is via telephone lines, contact between any two teletypes being established by dialling in the usual way. The message is typed in to the transmitting teletype by the operator; in order to minimize telephone line time the message can be recorded prior to transmission on paper tape (teletypes normally incorporate paper tape punches and readers). The receiving teletype is activated automatically by the transmitting teletype, and prints the message.

The majority of large organizations are telex users. There are, in fact, over a million users world-wide, the number in the U.K. alone now exceeding 80,000 and likely to level off at around 200,000 in the late 1980s. Telex is, however, relatively slow (transmission rate is about 66 words per minute) and therefore relatively expensive on line time. It will probably be superseded eventually by **teletex**, a more advanced system being developed by British Telecom for introduction in 1985 (see page 112).

For image, the most important telecommunication method is **facsimile**, described on page 99. Facsimile transmissions can be sent over ordinary telephone lines, but, unlike telex, the equipment of one user may not be compatible with that of another (owing to differing transmission/reception rates), and no directory of facsimile users exists. It is, however, faster (and therefore cheaper) than telex, and it can transmit text as well as image.

Although facsimile is dwarfed by telex as a text-communication method, current developments are likely to make it much more attractive as an alternative to telex in the future. British Telecom is planning to introduce a directory of facsimile users, based upon a transmission/reception time of 40 seconds for a document (a time which will be adopted as a standard by the various manufacturers, thus ensuring machine-compatibility). It is also planning a subscriber facsimile service. This will make use of telephone lines at night (thus taking advantage of cheap rates) − documents will be scanned during the day, stored on magnetic tape, and automatically transmitted at night − and it will incorporate retry-if-busy facilities to overcome problems of engaged receiving devices.

System Elements (3): Processing (Computing and Editing)

The processing (or analysis) of information includes such tasks as sorting, merging, and calculating (data), and editing (text). Three examples of analysis are:

1 The production of purchase orders (referred to in the case study earlier in this chapter) − this involves merging materials and parts requirements with suppliers' names, sorting into supplier order so that orders for the same supplier appear on a single order form, and calculating the total order value;
2 The production of analyses of purchases for management information − this involves sorting purchases by product code, and adding the entries under each code to produce monthly totals;
3 The replacement of one string of characters in a document by another.

Equipment for sorting and merging documents includes simple **pigeon-holes** (such as those commonly used for sorting mail), and containers housed in rotating devices which allow the worker to remain seated.

Electronic calculators provide the simplest and most cost-effective way of carrying out calculations on small amounts of data. These range from models with only basic functions to intelligent programmable calculators costing up to two or three hundred pounds.

The latter will accept plug-in modules containing calculation programs for a number of fields including statistics, navigation, and structural engineering, and they are capable of producing a hard-copy printout of data and of statistical diagrams. The user can write his own programs if he so desires, and one model has a permanent memory which will store programs and data when the machine is switched off.

The **computer** is, today, the most cost-effective way of carrying out sorting, merging, and calculating routines on large volumes of data. It operates automatically and at very high speed, and improves the productivity of the office in terms of both quantity and quality of output. The micro-electronics revolution has had a major impact on computing, and **microcomputers** suitable for small business use are available at a cost of two or three thousand pounds, plus a similar amount for software (programs). These generally incorporate keyboard, screen, and printer, and occupy the area of a desk-top. Many small business systems are modular – they can be expanded as necessary to accommodate growth in data processing requirements. (A small business system is illustrated in Appendix I.)

The word processor can be regarded as a microcomputer dedicated to text rather than data processing. Many word processors incorporate quite powerful sorting, merging, and calculating functions, and the distinction between word processing and conventional computer data processing equipment is becoming steadily more blurred. Mainframe and mini computers (described below) can be used to support word processing applications by the provision of suitable software.

A large organization will probably require a powerful **mainframe computer** or a rather smaller **minicomputer**, the former costing upwards of £100,000, a typical price for the latter being around £50,000. Input and output facilities are provided by means of **peripherals** (remote devices connected by wire to the computer) – teletypewriters, visual display units, printers, and so on.

The control, processing, and temporary storage functions are carried out by the **control unit**, **arithmetic logic unit** (ALU), and **internal memory** respectively; collectively these comprise the **central processing unit** (CPU) of the computer. The CPU also contains an **operating system**, which enables the computer to run a number of programs simultaneously. The programs currently being run will be held in the external mass storage system (see next section), but will be switched in turn in and out of the internal memory for very short periods of time (measured in milliseconds). While a program is in the internal memory the computer will perform at very high speed a sequence of computing operations: in this way it will support a number of users running different programs (on separate terminals), the switching and operating speeds being so fast that each user will, under normal operating conditions, experience virtually no delay between the input of commands or data into his terminal and the computer's response. This facility is known as **time-sharing**, or **shared logic**; it is not available on most microcomputers, which can handle only one user and program at a time.

Much computer data processing is carried out in an **interactive** manner: the user communicates directly with the computer via his terminal by keying in commands and data and receiving an immediate response. For some applications, however, processing is carried out on a batch-basis: data is keyed in over a period of time, but it is processed in a single computer 'run'. Examples of batch processing include payroll and the production of management information. In the former a large number of individual clockcard details are fed in prior to the run; in the latter a large volume of data accumulated in computer files over a certain period is analysed and summarized.

Batch processing permits data to be keyed into an **off-line** data entry device (i.e. a device which is not connected to the computer), punched cards or paper tape being produced for subsequent high speed input to the computer. This minimizes the use made of computer time and, in the case of terminals sited in remote locations, the use made of telephone line time. (This facility does not apply, and is not relevant, to microcomputers.)

Computing facilities can be hired on a time-sharing basis from a **computer bureau**. There is a growing demand for this type of service, and there are currently about 250 bureaux in this country. The user pays a rental based on the amount of computer time used. Terminals are installed on his premises, linked by telephone line to the bureau's computers. The bureau will normally carry out systems analysis for the user, and, if necessary, will write tailor-made programs – although the usual (and cheapest) practice is for the user to adapt his systems to fit in with the standard program packages offered by the bureau.

The advantages of using a bureau are:

1 It enables the user to gain experience of computer-based systems without committing himself to the purchase of expensive hardware and to the employment of computer personnel

2 The user is able to take advantage of its expertise in specialist applications such as network analysis

3 It provides the user who already possesses his own in-house computer system with an economical way of acquiring additional capacity and software

4 It provides a 24-hour support service

5 The bureau, not the user, has to face the problem of equipment obsolescence resulting from rapid technological change.

The disadvantages of using a bureau include:

1 The high cost of telephone line time and high rental charges for heavy users

2 Lack of flexibility for the user, who generally has to fit in with the requirements of the bureau's program packages and ways of working.

System Elements (4): Storage

There are three categories of information storage:

(a) **Temporary storage** of information required immediately at hand during processing

(b) **Current mass storage** providing for the rapid retrieval of information required for future processing

(c) **Archival mass storage** providing for low-cost storage of information which will be referred to only infrequently (if at all) in the future.

Information which is known to have no further use after processing should not be stored but destroyed. Information in current or archival mass storage should also be destroyed after its usefulness has lapsed, and this is normally achieved by reviewing records in rotation over a one- or two-year period. In certain circumstances it is worthwhile to store information which is likely to be of only short-term value separately from that which will need to be kept for a long period.

Information can be held on **documents**, on **microfilm**, or on **electronic** storage media. The storage systems available for these three types of media are outlined below.

1 Document storage systems. During temporary storage on a desk (in in- and out-trays) documents will be held **horizontally**. During mass storage documents bearing the same code (e.g. customer reference number, part number, supplier number, etc.) will be held together in a file jacket which will be housed with others in one of the following types of storage system:

(a) **Lateral** storage, in which the file jackets are stacked like books on shelves and withdrawn laterally. The equipment available ranges from open shelving to lockable cabinets in which files are held in pockets suspended from rails. In the latter system, each jacket is assigned a specific pocket, minimizing the possibility of misfiling (replacing the jacket in the wrong location).

(b) **Vertical** storage, in which the files are stacked in cabinet drawers and withdrawn vertically; again, the files will normally be held in suspended pockets. Vertical filing is more expensive on space than lateral filing, for room must be provided to allow the cabinet drawers to be opened to their fullest extent, and vertical extraction limits the height of the top drawer to about four feet.

(c) **Rotary** storage, in which the containers that house the files rotate horizontally or vertically, thus allowing the worker to insert and extract files from a seated position.

Data which is referred to or updated frequently may be held on **record cards**. Such cards are often used as **indexes** – they facilitate the location of records held in numerical or other sequence (an example being index cards in a library which hold details of non-fiction books in alphabetical order). Cards are commonly stored vertically in drawers; however, for frequent referral and updating the more expensive **visible-edge** card system is to be preferred – the cards are held horizontally in drawers, each attached to the drawer by a hinged spine and overlapping the card above so that its title is visible, access to any card being achieved by lifting and rotating on their spines those lying above it.

2 Microfilm storage systems. To reduce the amount of storage space required and to allow for fast retrieval, documents can be photographed and stored on microfilm – 35 mm film for quality work (such as technical drawings), 16 mm film for data and text. Individual photographs (or frames) can be held on continuous rolls in **cartridges** or **cassettes**, individually in **aperture cards**, or on a sheet of film known as **microfiche**. The standard microfiche size is A6 (105 × 148 mm), and this will hold over 200 frames – this book could be produced on a single microfiche, for a fraction of conventional printing costs. Similar to microfiche is the **microfilm jacket**, a transparent plastic holder of A6 size into which individual strips of film can be inserted.

Microfilm is becoming an increasingly popular way of storing information, the number of users increasing at the rate of 25% per annum. Filming of the original documents is a fast, automatic process, and during the process each frame is automatically coded for subsequent retrieval. Only 2% of the storage space occupied by the original documents is required. Individual frames can be located within seconds using modern computerized retrieval systems – the code number of the required frame is entered on a keyboard, and the frame is automatically retrieved and displayed on the screen of a microfilm reader. If required, enlarged paper copies of the frame can be produced automatically. The initial equipment cost is high, but in the case of a large organization this will be offset rapidly by the space and labour savings achieved.

3 Electronic storage systems. For data and text which are processed by computer or word processor, some form of electronic storage is necessary. For temporary storage the internal memory will be used, the device commonly used for this type of storage being the **silicon memory chip**. This is a solid-state device (it has no moving parts), and so it is virtually indestructible, but its capacity is too limited for mass storage use, and in any case it will only hold data while the power is switched on. Other types of solid-state device suitable for mass storage are currently being developed. One example is the **bubble memory**, which stores information in the form of magnetic 'bubbles' of subatomic size. Another type is an electron beam accessed memory which can hold the equivalent of 40,000 A4 sheets of text in a tube of material the size of a cotton-reel.

Internal memory is **random access memory** (RAM), for information can be retrieved from it in any order. This contrasts with tape-based external mass storage, described below, which allows sequential access only (the information must be scanned in the order in which it is recorded).

For the present, the only feasible mass storage media for information in electronic form are **magnetic tape** and **magnetic disc**. Of the two, tape is the most economical, but its use is limited by the fact that the information held on it must be scanned sequentially. With disc a tracking head gives virtually instantaneous access to information held at any point on the disc's surface. Tape is therefore useful for storing information which is to be read sequentially, e.g. customer details for the production of monthly statements; whereas disc has to be used for applications in which it is necessary to jump about files to retrieve information from different places (i.e. random access), e.g. product details for the production of invoices. Typical mainframe computer systems use both tape and disc; small business microcomputer systems and word processors are normally disc-based. (Cheaper tape-based systems suffer from long access times and are unsuitable for many business applications.) The small **floppy discs** that are used with microcomputers will hold up to 130 A4 pages of information; the large discs used in mainframe systems hold ten times this amount.

At the present time images are normally stored in hardcopy or microfilm form. In the future, however, electronic storage of images will assume increasing importance, and higher capacity devices than are currently used will then become necessary (since image will occupy some 10 times the amount of space used by data and text). **Videodisc**, a by-product of laser technology, offers a possible solution – a single disc will store the equivalent of 400,000 A4 pages of text.

System Elements (5): Control

The supervision and organization of the sequence of operations needed to convert an information input to the desired output is undertaken by a human supervisor in the case of a manual/mechanical office system, and by the control unit of the CPU in the case of a computerized system. In the latter case the sequence of operations must be defined by means of a **program** of very precise instructions.

To illustrate the work of the control unit, consider the following simple program:

1. INPUT X
2. LET Y = 2X
3. PRINT Y

This sequence of instructions will cause the control unit to perform the following operations:

1 Route the value entered on the input device to the internal memory and instruct the memory to store it at a certain address (or location) which it assigns to the variable X.

2 Route the value held at the address of variable X to the arithmetic logic unit, and instruct this unit to multiply this value by two. The result of this calculation is routed to the internal memory and stored at the address assigned to the variable Y.

3 Route the value held at the address of variable Y to the output device and instruct this device to print or display it.

A brief description of computing technology and computer programming is given in the next chapter.

ASSIGNMENT GROUP WORK

Assignment 3 (iv) (page 191).

7

Office Systems II: The Emerging Technology of the Integrated Office

In this chapter we examine the *integrated office* − the office in which the various pieces of equipment communicate electronically with each other and with the organization's central computer and database, as well as with external networks such as Prestel. The integrated office has been born of the developing technologies of computing and telecommunications, and an account of these occupies a major part of this chapter.

Computing

The 'brain' of a computer − its central processing unit − can be regarded as an array of electrical switches, each connected to three wires − two incoming, one outgoing. One of the incoming wires turns the switch to ON or OFF, thus either permitting or preventing the flow of an electrical pulse through the switch from the other incoming wire to the outgoing wire.

Any item of numerical data can be represented by a sequence of ON and OFF switches. The number nine, for example, is a sequence of four switches in the positions ON-OFF-OFF-ON (see the table below). Any alphabetical character can be expressed as a number (e.g. A = 0, B = 1, etc.), and so it is possible to convert any item of information into a switch sequence for computer processing. (Image can be converted to a switch sequence by identifying any point as either black (ON) or white (OFF).)

Since a switch can be in only one of two positions, the data that is input to the computer must be in binary (two-digit) form, one digit converting to OFF, the other to ON. The computer itself will carry out the conversion process. The table below illustrates the principle:

Number	Binary Code	Switch Sequence
zero	0	OFF
one	1	ON
two	10	ON-OFF
three	11	ON-ON
four	100	ON-OFF-OFF
five	101	ON-OFF-ON
six	110	ON-ON-OFF
seven	111	ON-ON-ON
eight	1000	ON-OFF-OFF-OFF
nine	1001	ON-OFF-OFF-ON
etc.		

In most computers the switches are arranged in groups of eight, sixteen, or twenty-four. An eight-switch group can store a number comprising 8 **b**inary dig**its**, or **bits**, a sixteen-switch group can store a 16-bit number. Unused switches are left in the OFF position, so that in an eight-switch group the number nine will be represented as

OFF-OFF-OFF-OFF-ON-OFF-OFF-ON.

The disadvantage of an 8-bit group size is that the

computer works to a restricted number of significant figures, and this limits its accuracy when carrying out computations involving large numbers (its accuracy being equivalent to that of most pocket calculators). As computing power increases the 16-bit and 32-bit group sizes found on larger computers is likely to be extended to many microcomputers in the future. (For engineering and scientific applications requiring high degrees of accuracy a group size as large as 48 bits is often necessary; the 16-bit group size is ample for business applications.)

The central processing unit is built up of many thousands of individual switches with associated wiring. The internal memory of the typical microcomputer contains 16 thousand groups of switches, and models containing 64 thousand groups and upwards are becoming available. The great power and low cost of present-day computers is a result of the revolution that has taken place since World War II in switch technology.

In the 1940s and 50s each switch was a valve (similar in size and appearance to an electric light bulb), and the computers that were built from these occupied very large rooms and were extremely expensive. In the 1960s silicon transistors were developed, where a single transistor, or switch, was etched on to the surface of a silicon chip – the forerunner of today's microprocessors, and a much cheaper and more reliable form of switching than that provided by valve technology. Next, a way was found of etching two transistors, and then four, on to a chip, and every year since has seen a doubling of the number of transistors per chip, with a consequent fall in the cost per transistor (by about 40% per annum). Some chips being produced today contain 64,000 transistors, and chips containing 128,000 and 256,000 transistors will soon be available.

At present the various elements of microcomputers and other microprocessor-based devices are contained on individual chips – microprocessors that perform the computations and control the work, and memory for storing information. Single-chip processors incorporating all these elements are currently under development, and it seems likely that these will ultimately dominate the microprocessor market.

Computer Programming

Unlike other office machines, which are dedicated to specific tasks, the computer is capable of carrying out a great variety of tasks. However, in order to carry out a task it must be given a program of precise commands telling it what operations to carry out, written in a language it can understand. There are a number of programming languages; COBOL, for example, for business applications and FORTRAN for scientific applications. Mainframe and mini-computers will operate in whatever language is specified by the user. Many microcomputers, however, will operate only in an all-purpose language called BASIC – the language is etched on to the surface of a Read Only Memory (ROM) chip wired into the computer. (Some microcomputers will work in any language; the required language has to be loaded from tape into the internal random access memory chip each time the microcomputer is used.)

There are two types of command: **machine commands**, which are used by the operator to tell the computer what to do with the program, and **program commands**, which are used within the program and which specify the operations to be carried out when the program is run. Some commonly-used BASIC commands are given below.

Machine Commands
RUN – run the program and obey the program commands
LIST – print (or display) the program
SAVE – store the program in the external memory
LOAD – retrieve the program from the external memory

Program Commands
INPUT – transfer the data entered on the input device to the internal memory
PRINT – print (or display) the specified information on the output device
LET – assign a given value to the specified variable
IF . . . THEN – make the specified comparison, and if it is true then proceed to the specified line of the program
END – terminate the program.

Each program command should normally occupy a separate line of the program, and each line must be sequentially numbered. Unless otherwise instructed, the computer will read and obey the lines in strict numerical order, which may not necessarily be the order in which they were keyed into the input device. It is conventional to number the lines 10, 20, 30, etc. so that, if required, additional lines (e.g. 12, 14, 25) can be inserted later.

To illustrate computer programming we give below a simple program, written in BASIC, for producing a multiplication table. Note that the symbol for zero is $\emptyset$ (to avoid confusion with the letter 0), and the multiplication sign is * (to avoid confusion with the letter X). $ instructs the computer to treat the input as text instead of numerical data.

```
10    INPUT A
20    LET I = 0
30    LET I = I + 1
40    LET B = A * I
50    PRINT I; "X"; A; " = "; B
60    IF I < 12 THEN 30
70    PRINT "DO YOU WANT ANOTHER
      MULTIPLICATION TABLE?
      (YES/NO)"
80    INPUT C$
90    IF C$ = "YES" THEN 10
100   END
```

The first instruction given to the computer (line 10) is to route the value keyed into the input device to an address in its internal memory which is to be associated with the variable A. Upon reading this command the computer will print/display '?' on the output device and will not proceed until it receives a value. If, for example, the value 3 is keyed in, the computer will convert this to binary code (i.e. 11) and will store this number at the appropriate address.

The computer now moves on to the next line of the program, which instructs it to assign to the variable I the value zero. It therefore stores this value at an address in its memory which it associates with I.

Line 30 tells the computer to read the value stored at the address associated with I, add 1 to this value, and replace the old value of I in its memory by this new value. At address I the computer has therefore now stored the value 1.

Line 40 instructs the computer to read the value in its memory assigned to A, read the value assigned to I, multiply one by the other, and store the result at an address to be associated with the variable B. At address B the computer has therefore stored the value 3.

Line 50 instructs the computer to print/display the value assigned to I, followed immediately by the information within the quotation marks (i.e. a multiplication sign), followed by the value assigned to A, followed by '=', followed by the value assigned to B. The computer therefore prints

$$1 \text{ X } 3 = 3$$

Line 60 tells the computer to read the value of I and compare it with the number 12 (1100 in binary code). If I is less than 12 (as it is in this case), the computer returns to line 30, reads as instructed there the value of I (1), adds 1 to it, and stores the result (2) at address I (the old value being automatically erased). Next, it multiplies the value of A (3) by the value of I (2), and stores the result (6) at address B. It then prints 2 X 3 = 6 in accordance with line 50, and from line 60 it returns once more to line 30.

This routine is repeated until I reaches the value 12. When this happens, 12 X 3 = 36 is duly printed out, and at line 60 the computer does not return to 30 (since I is now *not* less than 12), but instead proceeds to the next instruction, line 70. It prints the information given there, and awaits the operator's response. The response (which is keyed into the input device) is stored at an address associated with a new variable C$ (see line 80).

Line 90 instructs the computer to compare what is stored at C$ with the word YES. If the two are the same, it returns to the start of the program, requests another value for A, and prints the appropriate multiplication table. If any response other than YES is keyed in, the computer proceeds to line 100 and terminates the program.

The speed with which the computer carries out the above operations is impressive. The internal operating speeds of the central processing unit are, in fact, measured in millionths of a second. Immediately the operator keys in the value of A the computer prints out the required multiplication table.

A Data Processing Example: Invoicing

To illustrate computer data processing we describe in this section the production of sales invoices. The output required from an invoicing system is a series of invoices, each of which contains the following information:

1 The customer's name and address
2 The type and quantity of goods ordered

3 The prices of the goods
4 The VAT and the invoice total.

The data in (1) and (3) are static and will be held in the computer's external memory in the customer file and the product file. The data in (2) is variable, and will be created each week (assuming weekly invoicing) from the sales data on the despatch file. The data in (4) is calculated from (2) and (3) during the invoicing program run.

Each customer and each product will have a code number, and their details will be addressed on the customer file and the product file by means of these numbers. Each entry on the despatch file will consist of the following numbers:

the code number of the customer
the code number of the goods ordered
the quantity ordered
the despatch date.

Entries will be stored according to customer code number, and all sales to one customer will be grouped together and will ultimately appear on a single invoice.

The invoicing program will instruct the computer to carry out the operations described below. Before commencing the run it is necessary to set up the invoice forms (printed on continuous stationery) in an on-line printer.

1 Read the first customer code number on the despatch file, read the name and address stored under that number in the customer file, and print both in the permitted area of the invoice form set up in the printer.
2 Read the first product code number and the quantity for that customer on the despatch file, and read the product details and the unit price stored under that number in the product file. Multiply the unit price by the quantity to obtain the total price for those goods, and print the quantity, description, unit price, and total price in the permitted area of the invoice form.
3 Repeat step (2) for all product-code numbers entered for the first customer on the despatch file, and when the last entry for that customer has been processed sum the total prices, calculate the VAT, and print the sum, the VAT, and the VAT-inclusive price on the invoice.
4 Feed the next invoice form into the printer, and carry out the above sequence of steps for the second customer code number appearing on the despatch file.

The procedure is repeated until the list of customer code numbers on the despatch file is exhausted.
5 The invoice program will probably instruct the computer to produce from the data being processed the total quantities purchased of each product (for stock control), and weekly sales figures by product and by market (for management information). The relevant files will be automatically updated with this information.

Business Applications of Computing

Some of the ways in which computer power manifests itself in the office were described in Chapter 6: in microcomputers, in word processors, in intelligent viewdata terminals, and so on. It is affecting every aspect of the work of the office:

1 *Accounting and other routine data processing*, such as payroll, invoicing, sales ledger, purchase ledger, and stock control (for details see Appendix I).

2 *The production of management information*, such as costing information, customer activity reports, stock analyses, and budget reports (for details see Appendix I).

3 *Database management*, permitting storage and rapid retrieval of information by any authorised user in the company (see pages 58 and 105).

4 *The building of mathematical models*, to aid decision-making (such as the regression models described in Chapter 4 and the operational research models described in Chapter 8). By means of these models one can calculate the effect upon output of variations in business inputs and determine the best course of action.

5 *The production of letters, and other word processing applications* (see page 97).

The benefits that accrue from the use of the computer in its various manifestations include:

1 *Economy* – a computer will undertake tasks previously requiring a number of specialized office machines, and it will reduce the amount of office

labour needed (or it will enable the existing labour force to be utilized more effectively, by improving the output produced)

2 Speed – the speed at which operations are carried out is measured in millionths of a second

3 Quality – the quality of every type of office work is improved:
(a) Data is processed more accurately
(b) Better management information is produced
(c) The appearance of letters is improved (using a word processor).

4 Compactness – a computer and its electronic files occupy a fraction of the space needed by manual/mechanical equipment and storage

5 Integration – the great power of the computer permits the integration of administrative procedures throughout the organization:

(a) Data processing can be integrated (see page 94)
(b) A common database can be established (see page 58)
(c) Decision-making can be integrated (see page 6)
(d) Office systems can be integrated (see below).

ASSIGNMENT GROUP WORK
Assignment 4 (page 192).

The Electronic Architecture of the Integrated Office

In every medium-sized or large organization a vast amount of information is constantly flowing from one point to another by a variety of means: documents, computer lines, telephone lines, telex, etc. There is obviously much to be gained by replacing all these disparate communication systems by a single network, and considerable effort is currently being devoted to the development of the 'integrated office', that is, the office in which the various pieces of equipment (word processors, copiers, telex terminals, etc.) are linked electronically to each other and to the organization's central computing facilities and database.

The type of electronic architecture that offers the most promise of supporting such an office is the **local area network**, essentially a cable laid around the premises with sockets at convenient points into which communicating equipment can be plugged. Current transmission speeds over such a network are equivalent to 150 A4 pages of text per second. A local area network requires no switching devices: instead, each machine connected to the network feeds information into it in electronic 'packages', each of which is prefaced by the coded address of its destination machine. The latter will recognize the address and pluck the package of information from the network.

The main alternative electronic architecture, and the one which is mostly used at the present time, consists essentially of cables radiating from the central computer to the various pieces of equipment. This architecture suffers from the disadvantage that all communications have to be routed through the central computer, which undertakes the necessary switching, and this creates a potential bottleneck which limits the volume of traffic that can be handled. Microprocessor-controlled private branch exchanges (PBXs) are being developed for switching such communications, but these suffer from the same potential limitations.

A local area network could be connected to external telecommunications networks such as Teletex and Prestel by means of a switching device (such as a PBX). This would enable the office to utilize on a time-sharing basis any computing facilities or information bases that may be available on such networks, as well as using their data transmission facilities (see below).

Electronic Ordering and Invoicing

Purchase orders sent on pieces of paper from customers to suppliers, and invoices sent by the same means from suppliers to customers, are already beginning to disappear. Some large retailing organizations are sending the computer tapes containing their order requirements to their suppliers, and the latter are then able to feed the data on the tapes directly into their computer systems. The supplier subsequently invoices the retailer in the same way – the invoices are contained on a reel of tape which is fed directly into the customer's computer, which then automatically carries out the reconciliation, purchases ledger, and payment functions. (Under the Finance Act 1980 electronic invoices are now acceptable to the tax authorities.)

It is but a short step from this to direct communication between customers' and suppliers' computers over the public telephone network, and British Telecom is currently implementing a new data communications system to facilitate this type of exchange (see below).

Telecommunications: Public Packet Switched Networks

Information transmissions to destinations outside the immediate business premises take place at present over the public telephone network or over leased lines by means of the telephone, Datel, telex, or facsimile (see page 102). This network is low-grade, and designed primarily for voice transmissions. For large amounts of information it is slow, and therefore costly. To handle the information transmission requirements of the computer age the public telecommunications authorities of the major European countries are installing public packet switched telecommunications networks.

The public packet switched network being implemented by British Telecom is *System X*. By 1985 this will link up the main areas of the country, and it will also be linked to the networks of other countries. The technology employed will be laser transmissions over optical fibres (see page 99). These can carry vast amounts of data at high speed, and usage costs will therefore be low.

The main features of public packet switched networks are as follows:

1 All types of information – whether voice, text, image, or data – are converted prior to transmission to binary digital form. The network is therefore indifferent to the type of communication being sent.

2 A message is sent as a 'packet' (or set of packets), which includes the coded address of its destination. Each packet contains, typically, 128 bits. There is no need for the transmitting machine to 'dial' the receiving machine, or, indeed, for there to be an open line all the way from one to the other. The network, which is intelligent (i.e. computer controlled), will recognize the coded address and will work out the best route for each packet, storing it if necessary for short periods at intersections ('nodes') in the network. The packets that comprise a particular transmission may each travel by a different route, but the network ensures that they are assembled in the correct sequence at the destination.

3 Like the conventional postal service, the user will be charged according to the volume of information sent, *not* according to the transmission distance.

4 Office equipment using the system will have to comply with a set of interface standards known as X25. These standards will enforce a certain level of compatibility between the machines of different manufacturers and will therefore facilitate communications between them.

Telecommunications: Value-Added Networks

Value-added network services (VANs) offer users not only data transmission services but also computing facilities, electronic storage, and access to information bases. In effect, these networks provide inter-organizational facilities comparable to the intra-organizational facilities provided by an in-house computer.

Of particular importance is *Teletex*, a world-wide text-communication system planned for implementation by the Public Telephone authorities during the 1980s, and already introduced in West Germany. This will operate on any type of network (including the telephone and the packet switched networks). As with telex (which it will probably ultimately replace), any user in the world will be able to communicate with any other user, but the rate of transmission will be some fifty times faster. Although intended primarily as a text communication service, it will handle any information which has been converted to binary digital form – including images transmitted by digital facsimile machines. Teletex is expected to provide an economical alternative to conventional mail for any business sending more than six letters per day to other business users.

Any word processor, electronic typewriter, facsimile transceiver, or other office machine can act as a teletex terminal provided it has the right interface and operating code characteristics. Teletex will offer users of such machines a number of value-added services, such as text editing, electronic storage and retrieval, and store-and-forward and multi-address mailing facilities. A small user with a word processor hooked into the system will have at his disposal many of the information processing facilities at present enjoyed only by large computer-based organizations.

Viewdata

Viewdata is the term used to describe an electronic filing system which arranges information in a way which permits easy access by network users. Information is stored in 'pages', or frames, of text, and any page can be accessed and displayed on the user's TV screen simply by keying in its code number.

An important feature of viewdata is its **menu system** – a comprehensive index which enables the user to locate any frame whose code number he does not know. The first page of the index displays the main subject headings. By keying in the appropriate code (a single digit between 0 and 9) the more detailed topic index relating to the selected subject is displayed. By repeating this operation once or twice more the desired frame is located.

Company viewdata systems, or systems provided by computer bureaux, will, in the future, form an important way of providing decision-makers with management information in a readily-accessible and comprehensible form. As with any electronic storage system, the text held on a frame can be updated easily by keying in new data. Bureaux are also offering customers facilities for the bulk updating of frames from information held on other stores. For example, information held in a manufacturer's frame store could be used for the bulk updating of his distributor's frames.

Manufacturers of viewdata systems are, at the moment, pointing the way forward in the development of business information processing. They are developing combined viewdata/data processing/word processing systems which, it seems, will form the basis of the multi-role electronic workstations that will be used in tomorrow's office (see below).

Prestel is the public viewdata service run by British Telecom. It contains many hundreds of thousands of pages of information, provided by a large number of organizations. British Telecom charge the information providers an annual rental plus a per frame fee, and it collects charges from users on behalf of the providers. Access to a frame of information costs the user, typically, 2p or 3p, though prices range from nothing to 50p or more.

Prestel is available over the public telephone network, and it will also be available on System X when it comes on-stream. Any telephone subscriber can make use of the service – all that is required is an ordinary TV set fitted with a suitable adaptor to connect it to the telephone network and, of course, a keypad. Besides the per frame fee, the user is charged for the use made of telephone line time (at ordinary local call rates), plus a 3p per minute charge for the use of Prestel computer

time. Unlike BBC/ITV television pictures, Prestel information is transmitted in digital form, and so can be recorded on ordinary tape or cassette, or stored in the internal memory of an intelligent viewdata terminal for later use.

The information available on Prestel ranges from government statistics, inter-company comparisons, and stock exchange information, to holiday information and food prices. The system is interactive, and messages can be sent between users. It is possible, for example, to make purchases over the Prestel network, to book hotel rooms, and to make travel arrangements, and use can be made of the computing facilities available on the Prestel computers. In addition, hardcopy of Prestel pages can be obtained by connecting a printer to the network, and this means that bills and other documents can be transmitted via the system.

Prestel also incorporates 'closed user' facilities to allow subscribers to rent space on the computers for access by designated users only. These facilities enable

---

WHICH? ON PRESTEL

Up-to-date information produced by many organizations is available on Prestel. *Which?* Reports published by the Consumer's Association can be found on frame groups 333 and 334. The main index to these reports is free of charge, and can be accessed by keying in 334-0. *Money Which?* costs 3p per frame (1981 prices), and includes the following:

Interest rates for borrowers	333-41
Interest rates for savers and investors	333-40
Average earnings index	333-426
Financial Times industrial ordinary share index	333-420
Retail price index	333-424
Mortgages:	
How much they cost	333-460-6
How much you can borrow	333-460-4
How do you get one	333-460-3
Which type to choose	333-460-2
Who will lend the money	333-460-5

the various branches of a company, for example, to obtain up-to-date information via the system on orders, stocks, and other matters relevant to their operations.

Prestel is, in fact, a value-added communications network which, although lacking some of the advanced features of the proposed Teletex system, is already in operation and is available to every telephone subscriber, both business and private.

The Integrated Office

In the integrated office that will emerge during the 1980s each piece of equipment will be linked electronically to, and will be an integral part of, the larger office system. The technology that will characterize this type of office is as follows:

1 An electronic communications network that will link the various items of equipment in the office with each other and with the larger public telecommunications networks. This will provide the passageway for 'electronic mail' between machine and machine and between manager and manager. This may take the form of voice, data, text, or image, and will provide information processing facilities such as store-and-forward, retry-if-busy, and information storage and retrieval. The communication of information by means of conventional paper-based systems will gradually disappear.

2 Electronic workstations provided for most managers and office workers. These will replace the conventional office desk plus typewriter plus in-tray plus filing cabinet. The most familiar manifestation of the electronic workstation is the word processor, designed for secretarial staff. For managerial staff much more sophisticated devices are becoming available, similar in appearance and function to word processors, but with added data processing facilities and large colour screens for displaying viewdata and other management information. Clerical staff, on the other hand, will probably use less sophisticated (and much cheaper) computer terminals (see below).

Communications between workstations will take place via the communications network referred to above, and the normal route for inter-organizational letters and memos will be by this means. A message keyed in at one workstation will be forwarded auto-matically to any other workstation in the system to which it is addressed. It will be stored at the receiving workstation and displayed on the screen on the recipient's command. Verbal messages sent by telephone over the network will be similarly stored at the recipient's workstation for action at a convenient time.

Access to Prestel will enable travel and other bookings to be made via the workstation, and the manager's diary will be created and held in the workstation's memory.

3 Shared facilities, such as printers and the central computer, will be available to each information worker via his workstation. This will provide him with rapid and easy access to the organization's database, as well as to the dictionary for automatic spelling correction, the 'electronic noticeboard' for company news, and other centrally-provided electronic services.

One such service will be computer-based conferencing systems, which will link up the workstations of all conference members for simultaneous interaction by voice, text, and image. These systems will also permit contributions by project team members to a continuing program of work without the necessity of regular meetings: all contributions will be held centrally and will be accessible at all times to all members of the team.

Clerical workers (such as those working in sales, purchasing, and accounts offices) will probably access the central computer and other shared equipment by means of ordinary on-line computer terminals.

4 Access to the information bases of other organizations will be available. These include government statistics already available to subscribers from the Central Statistical Office's databank, and more general information provided by the British Library Automated Information Service. Additionally, **electronic transactions** can be expected to take place between suppliers, customers, and banks.

The retail business provides a good example of this. The traditional cash register that has been for so long the central piece of shop equipment will be replaced, during the 1980s, by its newly-arrived descendant, the 'point-of-sale terminal'. This intelligent device scans the product code printed on each item purchased by the customer, looks up the price in its internal memory, tots up the bill, updates the stock records of the store, and compiles the reorder list. If linked to the banking system, it will automatically debit the customer's bank account and credit the store's account, the customer requiring no cash, only a bank card.

5 Speech recognition devices are currently under development, and these are expected to appear on the commercial scene towards the end of the 1980s. These are likely to bring about the demise of the keyboard. They operate by matching the characteristics of the words spoken into the equipment with those held in the electronic dictionary of the central computer. Such devices are already in use in Japan (whose spoken language is phonetically much simpler than our own), and they allow the direct entry of spoken text into the system. Speech synthesizing equipment is already well-developed, and it is anticipated that verbal communication between man and machine will soon be feasible.

The bed in which Forrester awoke was oval, springy, and gently warm. It woke him by purring faintly at him, soothingly and cheerfully. Then as he began to stir the purring sound stopped, and the surface beneath his body gently began to knead his muscles. Lights came on. There was a distant sound of lively music, like a gypsy trio. Forrester stretched, yawned, explored his teeth with his tongue, and sat up.

'Good morning, Man Forrester,' said the bed. 'It is eight-fifty hours, and you have an appointment at nine seventy-five. Would you like me to tell you your calls?'

'Not now,' said Forrester at once . . .

'I have just received another message for you, Man Forrester,' said the bed.

'Save it,' said Forrester. 'After I have a cup of coffee.'

'Do you wish me to send you a cup of coffee, Man Forrester?'

'You're a nag, you know that? I'll tell you what I want and when I want it.'

From *The Age of Pussyfoot*,
by Frederick Pohl,
published by Victor Gollancz.

Information Privacy

Electronic data processing systems are capable of storing, retrieving, comparing, sorting, and communicating vast quantities of information at very high speeds. The proliferation of these systems in public and private organizations is bringing about an 'information explosion'. Detailed information on almost any matter is becoming available in both the office and the home at the touch of a key.

This will bestow upon society enormous benefits. However, there is growing public concern over the ability of these systems to allow users to pry into information held on many aspects of individuals' lives. In Sweden, for example, the typical citizen is registered on over 100 computer files (medical records, tax records, insurance records, police records, etc.), and it is technically not difficult to merge the data on all these files on to a single master file. The technology enables the stored data to be sorted and selected extremely rapidly – for example, the names and addresses of all individuals possessing certain characteristics can be retrieved in a matter of moments. Furthermore, an operator located perhaps many hundreds of miles from the files can gain access to this information via a remote terminal.

The fear that this capability might be used for repressive purposes has made information privacy a live issue in Western democracies. Most European countries have passed data protection legislation to prevent users of data processing systems from abusing the privacy of information held on the ordinary individual. The legislation covers information held on both computerized and non-computerized systems, and it requires that:

1 information about an individual must be collected legally
2 the individual must be told what information is being collected and held, and who is holding it
3 the information held must be used solely for specified, legitimate purposes.

Responsibility for administering data protection laws normally rests with independent bodies known as Data Inspection Boards. These have extensive powers in applying the law.

In Britain, privacy is protected to some extent by the practice in government departments of not divulging information held on individuals to other departments or organizations. However, the Lindop Committee, in its Report on Data Protection (1978), felt that this protection is inadequate, and that comprehensive data protection laws should be passed.

Information Security

Organizations also wish to protect the privacy of information held on their files, the risk in this case being one of 'industrial espionage' by unauthorized users gaining access to files. This is a security problem, and it is made particularly acute by the distribution of computer data processing to user departments and the linking of organizations' computers to external tele-communications networks. It is not unknown for even schoolboys and students to crack the security of organizations' computer systems using terminals in schools and colleges.

The following measures are commonly used by organizations to prevent unauthorized access to files:

1 Checking personnel entering buildings or sensitive parts of buildings by means of identity cards
2 Locking terminals and providing authorized users only with keys
3 Programming the computer so that access is gained only if the user keys in the correct password. This pass-word contains the coded references of the files that the user is permitted access to, and the computer will not retrieve information from any other files. Where security is critical, the passwords can be changed weekly or daily.

Apart from the risk of access to files by unauthorized users operating remote terminals, organizations need to guard against theft of or damage to the discs or tapes on which the information is stored. It is normal practice to keep a second tape copy of all files, stored on a site remote from the computer room to ensure the safety of information in the event of fire or other disaster. All discs and tapes should, of course, be stored in secure areas to minimize the possibility of theft.

Part Three

The
Well-Regulated
Business

8
The Well-Controlled Business

Control lies at the heart of the administrative process. The work of the controller of a business system was examined in Chapter 2; it involves

(a) **Planning** – planning the outputs (objectives) of the system, and planning and organizing the inputs (resources) needed to achieve these outputs

(b) **Control** – comparing the achieved outputs with the planned outputs, and adjusting the inputs in the event of under-achievement.

This chapter describes some of the ways in which these two processes are carried out in the well-regulated business.

Decision-Making

Central to planning and control is **decision-making** – deciding what the outputs and inputs of the business should be, and what input adjustments should be made if the planned outputs are not being achieved. Decision-making consists of the following three steps:

1 *Collecting information* on the situation confronting the business – on its inputs, outputs, and environment

2 *Formulating alternatives* in the light of this information

3 *Choosing the best alternative.*

Over the past century, and especially over the past thirty years, a large number of quantitative techniques have been developed to assist the decision-making process. They include work measurement and costing (drawn from the work study and management accounting fields), sampling and time series analysis (drawn from the science of statistics), and various operational research techniques for choosing between alternatives. Apart from work measurement and costing, they all belong to a fairly broad branch of mathematics known as **quantitative analysis**.

The quantitative techniques that are described in this text are listed below; sampling and time series analysis are outlined in Chapter 4, work measurement and costing are dealt with at the appropriate point in this chapter, and decision theory, linear programming, and network analysis are dealt with as a group at the end of this chapter.

1 Information collection and analysis techniques. These include:

- statistical sampling for measuring output and determining the status of the environment
- work measurement for measuring output
- costing for measuring input
- time series analysis for forecasting the future situation from the present.

2 Decision-making techniques for choosing between alternatives. These include:

- decision theory for choosing between alternative strategies
- linear programming for choosing between alternative allocations of resources
- network analysis for deciding priorities.

Planning

Planning is the process of determining what the outputs and inputs of a business and its subsystems should be. It involves, essentially, asking and answering five basic questions:

> WHAT should we do?
> WHEN should we do it?
> WHERE should we do it?
> WHO should do it?
> HOW should we do it?

To each of these questions the general procedure referred to in the previous section must be applied – collect information, formulate alternatives, and choose the best – and so the planning process consists of a matrix of 15 questions, as follows. (This matrix is the basis of the questionning technique used by work study and O & M officers – see Chapter 9.)

This questioning process should be carried out repeatedly, first at the master system level, to determine the overall objectives and inputs of the business, then at the various subsystem levels to determine their objectives and inputs, and finally at the level of personal work planning.

At the master system and major subsystem levels in the business, planning is a time-consuming and complex activity, and distinct types of planning are employed for each of the WHAT-WHEN-WHERE-WHO-HOW questions. (More detailed planning, such as the planning of individual work procedures, adopts a formal questioning technique employing all five questions.) Some of these major types of planning are shown in Table 8.1. Organizational planning is dealt with in detail in Chapter 3, and job design and office planning are dealt with in Chapters 9 and 10. The other types of planning are outlined in the sections below.

> I keep six honest serving men,
> (They taught me all I know)
> Their names are What and Why and When,
> And How and Where and Who.
>
> (Rudyard Kipling, *The Elephant's Child*)

	Information	*Alternatives*	*Best Alternative*
WHAT?	Information on the present situation	What could be done?	What should be done?
WHEN?	,,	When could it be done?	When should it be done?
WHERE?	,,	Where could it be done?	Where should it be done?
WHO?	,,	Who could do it?	Who should do it?
HOW?	,,	How could it be done?	How should it be done?

	Objectives and Organization	Operations	Some techniques used
WHAT	Strategic Planning	Budgeting	Decision Theory Costing
WHEN	Strategic Planning	Scheduling	Network Analysis
WHERE	Organizational Planning Manpower Planning	Loading	Linear Programming
WHO	Organizational Planning Manpower Planning	Loading	Job Evaluation Work Measurement
HOW		Job Design Workplace Layout	Systems Analysis O & M Office Planning

Table 8.1   The Planning Process

Strategic Planning

This covers a period of over five years ahead, and involves the planning of overall long-term objectives, and of the resources to achieve those objectives. It is carried out by the top management, and it is a continuing process – each year the plan is 'rolled on' to cover the next five years. Like all planning, it consists of three phases: obtaining information, formulating alternatives, selecting the best alternative.

1 Obtaining information This is of two types:

(a) Information on the status of the organization's environment – the technology, the economy, its markets, competitors, and sources of supply (see Chapter 4 for notes on the collection of this information). By using time series analysis, forecasts can be made of the status of the environment over the planning period.
(b) Information on the strengths and weaknesses of the organization – its performance in terms of profitability, return on capital employed, etc., its market success (sales trends, market share, etc.), its resources of personnel, finance, and equipment, and its productivity (i.e. the efficiency with which it utilizes its resources).

2 Formulating alternatives Using the forecasts of the organization's environment and the assessment of its strengths and weaknesses the possible objectives that could be pursued in the future are determined. These alternatives should be stated in quantitative terms – the financial inputs needed and the outputs expected over the planning period (the investment required, the anticipated return on capital required, the degree of risk involved, etc.).

3 Choosing the best alternative The alternatives are compared and the best selected using, if possible, mathematical decision-making techniques (see page 136 ff).

CASE STUDY: STRATEGIC PLANNING AND ORGANIZATIONAL OBJECTIVES

The following is abstracted from a 70-page planning document covering the period October 1979 to December 1980 which details the objectives set for the British division of an international organization. It illustrates the principles of strategic planning, and gives examples of objectives which are specified in *time* terms.

The document begins with a statement of purpose, which is:

'1 To state clearly what the aims and objectives of the Division are
 2 To identify the necessary activities in order to best attain those objectives, and to define the level of activity to be aimed for
 3 To identify the competence in personnel and other resources needed to maintain the required level of activity
 4 To make an evaluation of our strengths and weaknesses, noting any gaps in our activities
 5 To estimate the additional resources needed in terms of personnel, finances, facilities and equipment
 6 To set measurable goals (in terms of quality, quantity, and timing) for activities so that progress can be realistically assessed.'

Following a short statement of the general objectives come the specific departmental objectives. The Directorate Department, for example, which is responsible for planning, is set four primary objectives, one of which is:

'To establish Divisional strategy, and to develop one-yearly, three-yearly and long-term plans for all Departments: to carry out a system of annual review and updating of strategy and planning.'

Later in the document come the very detailed secondary departmental objectives. The above primary objective generates a number of these, one of which is:

'To establish in cooperation with the Heads of Departments the 1981 plans, initiating activity in September 1980.
To seek, at the same time, to outline plans for the 3-year period 1981−3, and to seek to consider long-range and contingency implications in the planning process.
Plans to be presented, if possible, to the December meeting of the Council.'

Organizational Planning

This involves planning the organization so that the strategic plans are achieved − designing the structure of posts (see Chapter 3), and specifying the responsibilities (the job description) of each post. As indicated in Chapter 3, this type of planning is based upon the techniques of systems analysis, O&M, and work study. Mention should also be made of the technique of **job evaluation**, which enables posts to be placed in the correct rank order within the overall organization. The value of each post relative to other posts is assessed from the job description by awarding points for the experience, education, and initiative required, and the degree of responsibility and supervision exercised. The grading of the post, and hence its rate of pay, are determined by the total number of points awarded.

Following on from organizational planning is **manpower planning**, which is concerned with planning the supply of suitably trained personnel to fill the posts (for example, through training schemes).

Budgeting

Budgets are detailed short-term (usually one year) plans specifying for each department the output that should be achieved and the inputs (expressed in cost terms) that are available to it. The information on which budgets are based is:

1 The strategic plans, in particular the sales plan, for the forthcoming period − this determines the output that the company must achieve
2 The costs of each activity, as established by the Costing Department − the input costs are calculated from these.

The first stage of the budgeting process is the construction of budgets for the main functional areas of the business − marketing, production, etc. It is at this point in the total planning process that difficulties in implementing the overall strategic plan may be unearthed − for example, the planned level of sales may create problems for Production. When these problems have been resolved the functional budgets are broken down into the detailed departmental budgets. For the Production Department, for example, the departmental budget will specify the number of units of output to be achieved over the budget period, and the expected labour, material, and other costs that will be incurred to achieve this output.

When this process is complete the departmental budgets are amalgamated in a summarized form in a master budget, which specifies the overall expected performance of the company over the budget period. From this the forecasted profit and loss account and balance sheet are prepared, together with cash flow forecasts for the budget period. From these forecasts it can be seen whether the overall plans from which the budgets are derived are financially viable − if the forecasts are unfavourable the plans and then the budgets will have to be modified. Also, the cash flow forecasts enable the company to make arrangements for credit facilities, if these are needed, or to employ surplus cash.

Scheduling

Scheduling is the process of establishing priorities for the jobs that have to be done, and drawing up a detailed timetable on the basis of these priorities. The information needed for this process is the list of jobs to be done during the forthcoming period (as given, for example, in the sales plan), and the work content of each job.

Although this type of planning is normally associated with the work of the Production Department, in fact it is used in every department. Priorities for departmental, sectional, and individual tasks must be established, and entries made on planning charts or in diaries. In its simplest form scheduling involves showing, on a planning chart, a vertical list of workers' names, with the jobs allocated to each shown as horizontal bars covering planned periods of time.

For complex jobs or projects involving many interrelated activities the task of establishing priorities and constructing a timetable can be extremely complicated. The technique of **network analysis** is widely used in such situations, normally by applying a network analysis computer program to the project data. An example illustrating the use of this technique is given on page 140.

So far as offices are concerned, scheduling, if carried out properly, involves separating the work out into three types of activity, determining the work content of each, and amalgamating the three types into a single schedule:

1 The bulk of the work will be routine jobs that have to be completed by specified dates – e.g. the end of the week or month. These comprise the first element of any work schedules that are drawn up.
2 Some activities will be cyclical in nature – they will recur at predictable times in the month or the year and cause work peaks. These activities must also be built into the schedules, and routine jobs shuffled around so that as far as possible they do not coincide with these peaks.
3 A small proportion of the work will be unforeseen

jobs that arise at random times. Although unpredictable, the average amount of time spent on these can be determined and an allowance built into the schedules to accommodate them.

Even at the individual office worker level, scheduling must take place, if only informally. At any given moment there will be a number of jobs waiting to be done, and the question of priorities then arises. In deciding the order of work, three principles should be observed:

1 Work should be batched, as far as possible, so that jobs of the same type are done together. This minimizes the time spent changing over from one type of activity to another.

2 Jobs should be tackled in the order in which they arrive, unless there are clear reasons for doing otherwise. Thus incoming correspondence should be dealt with at the time of first reading – if at all possible it should not pass through an intermediate 'pending' stage.

3 If a conflict of priorities does arise, then the needs of everyone affected should be taken into account in determining the order of work. If managers or staff outside the department are affected, then the priority-decision will normally be taken at departmental manager or supervisor level. Priority-decisions affecting only a few individuals within the department can normally be taken at supervisor or clerk level. Routine work should normally be assigned the lowest priority, as it is normally not urgent and can be caught up on later.

Loading

Loading is the process of balancing the work between sections and individuals, with a view to minimizing bottlenecks and giving each a reasonable amount of work. It is normally carried out concurrently with scheduling, and like scheduling it is normally associated with the work of the Production Department, although it is applicable in every area of the business.

The information needed to carry out this type of planning is a list of jobs to be done and the work content of each, and the capacities of each work centre.

(A work centre might, for example, be a work group or a machine.) On the basis of this information the jobs are allocated to work centres, though the detailed allocation of tasks to individuals is often left to the discretion of the foreman or supervisor in charge of each work centre. A simple form of loading chart (a Gantt chart) is shown in Figure 8.1: the top thin line represents the planned loading, expressed as a percentage of the total capacity, the lower thick line records the actual output. Causes of significant discrepancies between the planned loading and the output can be indicated on the chart.

In many situations, particularly in offices, the amount of work to be handled by each section cannot be adjusted to match the capacity of the section. Instead the capacity of the section has to be adjusted

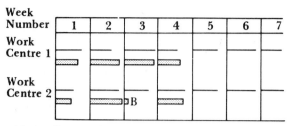

Notes: Present date = Week 5
B = Machine Breakdown

Fig. 8.1   Gantt chart showing work-centre loading

(by altering staffing levels) to meet the requirements of the work input. This is an organizational planning problem, and the way in which it might be tackled is illustrated in the case study on page 130.

CASE STUDY: COMPUTERIZED LOADING AND SCHEDULING

In a large manufacturing company the loading and scheduling of production operations is a complex task. It is carried out by the Production Control Department, usually with computer assistance.

03 MH28 MILLING-H

		WEEK NO	SCHED LOAD	CAPACITY	PERCENTAGE LOAD	OFF — HOURS	BALANCE TOTAL	TIME — EFFECT WORK V WEEKS:	
		78.41	5794	4320	138	-1654	-1654	1.3	2
		78.43	2405	4320	55	1915	261	0.9	4
M = WORK IN M/1	4402	78.45	2980	4320	68	1340	1601	0.8	6
		78.47	2536	4320	58	1784	3385	0.8	8
+ = WORK IN PRE—RELEASE	5782	78.49	4836	4320	111	-516	2869	0.8	10
		78.51	5152	4320	119	-832	2037	0.9	12
- = WORK ON SECTION	3763	78.53	3107	4320	71	1213	3250	0.8	14
		79.03	5099	4320	118	-779	2471	0.9	16
* = WORK DUE ON SECTION	3750	79.05	5110	4230	118	-790	1681	0.9	18
		79.07	5620	4320	130	-1300	381	0.9	20
T = WORK PENDING OTB OPS	326	79.09	4739	4320	109	-419	-38	1.0	22
		79.11	4551	4320	105	-231	-269	1.0	24
K = KNOWN FUTURE LOAD	7267	79.13	4784	4320	110	-464	-733	1.0	26
		79.15	4316	4320	99	4	-729	1.0	28
F = FORECAST FUTURE LOAD	81743	79.17	4689	4320	108	-369	-1098	1.0	30
		79.19	5482	4220	126	-1162	-2260	1.1	32
		79.21	4230	4320	97	90	-2170	1.0	34
		79.23	4132	4320	95	188	-1982	1.0	36
		79.25	3722	4320	86	598	-1384	1.0	38
		79.20	4210	4320	97	110	-1274	1.0	40
		79.29	3659	4320	84	661	-613	1.0	42
		79.31	3432	4320	79	888	275	0.9	44
		79.33	2050	4320	47	2270	2545	0.9	46
		79.35	3985	4220	92	335	2880	0.9	48
		79.37	2760	4320	63	1560	4440	0.9	50
		79.39	3473	4320	80	847	5287	0.9	52

Figure 8.3   The forecast loading for the work-centre for the period October 1978 to September 1979. Note that the codes printed on the left refer to the print-out shown in Figure 8.4

S 03 H.MILL SCHEDULED WORK

F SEC W/CENTRE PART NUMBER	SER/ SCHED	S P PROD QNTY	ALLOWD HRS–MN	STORES DATE	WKS O/D	OP NO	LAST F W/C	THIS F W/C	DATE LAST MOVE	COMMENTS
* 018.2 3	S12PAJY	4	1.04	78/50-	1	02	S MH28	S MH28	24/11/78	
018.2 3	S12PAJY	4	2.28	78/50	0	03	S MH28	S MH72		
* 018.3 4	S02PFSE	1	0.43	78/50-	1	01	S MH28	S MH28	24/11/78	
018.3 4	S02PFSE	1	6.50	78/50	0	02	S MH28	S MH72		
0 60.20.1	PAV	1	2.56	78/49-	3	04	S GE12	S MH28		
* 0111.24	PAV	1	0.53	78/49	2	04	S MH28	S MH28	8/12/78	
* 011.25	PAV	1	1.03	78/49-	2	04	S MH28	S MH28	8/12/78	
C/P 13975	HKW	150	10.36	78/49-	5	02	S CPA2	S MH28		& FOR ASSEM
29130AA	BTX	11	1.43	79/05-	3	02	S CB7	S MH28		
353316B	HWW	15	2.20	79/05-	1	02	S CB7COM	S MH28		
* 38703	HWW	5	4.10	79/05-	1	02	S MH28	S MH28	27/11/78	
* 31000-622	HVX	14	5.27	79/05	0	03	S MH28	S MH28	7/11/78	
* 31002-891	HWX	20	32.30	79/05	0	04	S MH28	S MH28	2/11/78	
31086-390	HZX	20	23.40	79/01-	2	02	S CC7	S MH28		
31087-501	HTX	100	12.25	79/01-	1	04	S JBAC	S MH28		
31091-312	RM	25	11.55	79/02	0	02	S CB7COM	S MH28		
31092-080	HTX	25	27.00	79/01	0	02	S CC7	S MH28		
C/P * 31098-246	PBW	1	2.00	79/02-	6	03	S MH28	S MH28	6/11/78	
* 31098-250	HWY	12	4.48	79/05	0	03	S MH28	S MH28	30/10/78	

Figure 8.2   Manufacturing schedule of week 50 of 1978 for the work-centre

```
03 MH28 MILLING-H
* * * * * * * * * * * *
              0%      100%    200%    300%    400%

WK.NO.       + ......  + .......  + .......  + .......  + .......

78.41        - - - - - * * ** * TMMK
78.43        - * * +M
78.45        - * +MK
78.47        -++MKKF
78.49        +++MMKKKFFF
78.51        ++MKKFFFFFF
78.53        KFFFFFF
79.03        +MKFFFFFFFFF
79.05        +MKFFFFFFFFF
79.07        KFFFFFFFFFFF
79.09        MFFFFFFFFFF
79.11        FFFFFFFFFF
79.13        FFFFFFFFFF
79.15        FFFFFFFFF
79.17        FFFFFFFFFF
79.19        FFFFFFFFFFFFFF
79.21        FFFFFFFFFF
79.23        FFFFFFFFF
79.25        KFFFFFFF
79.27        KFFFFFFFFF
79.29        FFFFFFFF
79.31        FFFFFFFF
79.33        FFFFF
79.35        FFFFFFFFF
79.37        FFFFF
79.39        FFFFFFFF
```

Figure 8.4   A print-out showing in chart form the percentage loading of the work-centre over the one-year period covered in Figure 8.3. The percentage loading for weeks 41 and 42 is 138, for weeks 43 and 44 is 55, and so on (see column 4 of Figure 8.3)

The figures given, which are reproduced with permission of the cigarette-making machine manufacturer referred to in previous case studies, show computer print-outs in respect of a work centre engaged in milling (It is identified on the left, third line, of the print-outs.) A brief explanation is appended to each table.

Control

The purpose of control is to ensure that plans are achieved. Table 8.2 shows the various types of control that correspond to the types of planning listed in Table 8.1. They are briefly described in the sections below. (Method maintenance is a part of work study and is dealt with in Chapter 9.)

Management By Objectives (M.B.O.)

The need to spell out precise objectives for each part of the organization has been emphasized earlier in this chapter and in Chapter 2. The strategic plan gives the general objectives to be achieved by the business as a whole over the forthcoming planning period, and these will be broken down to form the more detailed specific objectives for the various departments. These objectives form the basis for the departmental budgets that are drawn up; they are also the basis for the targets that have to be achieved by individual managers and work sections throughout the organization. Such targets will be expressed in terms of **quality** of output, **quantity** of output per unit period, and the **time** within which given objectives are to be achieved, and it is against these three types of target that actual performance is assessed as a basis for control.

Management By Objectives is the name given to a technique which applies this process in a formal way to every member of the organization down to supervisor or foreman level. Its features include:

- regular meetings between superior and subordinate to set detailed objectives and to review achievement

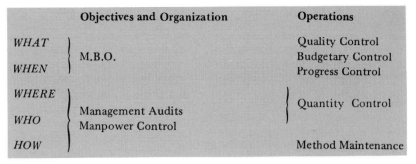

	Objectives and Organization	Operations
WHAT	M.B.O.	Quality Control
WHEN		Budgetary Control
		Progress Control
WHERE	Management Audits	Quantity Control
WHO	Manpower Control	
HOW		Method Maintenance

Table 8.2   The Control Process

- emphasis on ends rather than means – the subordinate is free to decide, within the constraints of company policy, how best to achieve his objectives
- rapid feedback of performance details to assist control
- improved motivation by gearing monetary rewards and promotion prospects to results.

This technique has all the advantages that come from formulating precise objectives at all levels in the company (see page 33), but the rather rigid and formalized procedure can cause staff to apply it in a mechanical manner, and it can result in the achievement of well-defined objectives at the expense of equally necessary but more vague objectives.

Management Audits

These aim to examine and measure the effectiveness of the organization and the overall quality of management. Management auditors visit departments or other units of the organization, examine organization structure and delegation, coordination, lines of communication, quality of decision-making, working methods, and so on, the object being to assess organizational and managerial performance in relation to given standards.

Manpower Control

The object of this is to ensure that reasonable staffing levels are maintained throughout the organization. It involves measuring the number of man-hours of work that each type of task requires, monitoring the number of tasks of each type that are carried out per unit of time in each section of the organization, and adjusting staffing levels accordingly. The application of this technique is described in the case study on page 130.

Budgetary Control

The purpose of budgetary control is to ensure that the input costs for each department are within the budgeted figures. Costs are collected continuously and analysed by the Costing Department, any variance between the actual costs and the standard costs (see page 129) being brought to the departmental manager's attention – it is his responsibility to take whatever corrective measures may be necessary.

Progress Control

The purpose of progress control (also called **progressing**, **progress chasing**, **chasing**, or **follow-up**) is to ensure that tasks are completed on schedule. This is especially important in production, where a delay in one section can have widespread and expensive repercussions in other sections, and a progressing section will normally be set up to deal with this aspect of control.

A typical progressing procedure is as follows. A batch of punched cards will be prepared to accompany each job through the factory, one card per operation that has to be performed on the job (the code number of the operation being recorded on the card by means of a pattern of holes – page 101). As each operation is completed the relevant card is extracted from the batch and sent to the Data Processing Department, where it is fed, with others, into a card reader to update the Work-in-Progress computer file. In this way a check is kept on the progress of the work as it passes from one section to the next, any delays being signalled by the computer. The progress chasers will investigate these delays and decide what action needs to be taken to rectify the situation.

In offices a number of follow-up procedures are used to ensure that jobs are completed on time. For the informal planning and control of personal work, entries in personal diaries are the usual reminder system adopted. For general office work more formal procedures are necessary, three widely-used procedures being:

1 Bring-up procedures (Civil Service). To ensure the progressing of correspondence the relevant file is marked for 'bring up' (BU) on a specified date. The filing clerk notes the file number under that date in his bring-up diary, and if by that date a reply has not been received to the correspondence the file will be retrieved and passed to the appropriate officer for action.

2 Chaser cards (banks, insurance companies, etc.). 'Chaser cards' are made out for files awaiting a reply, and stored in an index under the appropriate chase (bring-up) week number. Within each chase week section of the index, the cards are held in file code number. If a reply is received prior to the chase week, the appropriate card is removed from the index and destroyed. Files for the remaining cards are retrieved for action during the chase week.

3 Diaries (insurance companies, etc.). A diary record sheet is opened for each case, and chase dates are worked out and entered against each of the pre-printed action-events on the sheet. The case code number is entered under the appropriate chase dates in a diary; if relevant correspondence is received or other appropriate action is taken on an entry prior to the chase date, this is indicated on the diary record sheet and the case number is deleted from the appropriate chase date page of the diary. Remaining diary entries are followed up on the chase date.

Quantity Control

The purpose of quantity control is to ensure that each worker or section produces a reasonable volume of output. In factory situations this is often a very precise control tool used to ensure that planned output targets are achieved: targets are carefully calculated using work measurement techniques, the actual daily or weekly output of each worker or section being measured and compared with the targets. Some office tasks are amenable to similar treatment. In a typing pool, for example, the number of lines typed by each operator can be recorded and compared with the target figure. Precise and realistic targets are, in themselves, a strong motivator (this is one of the principles behind Management By Objectives); however, quantity control is normally allied to payment-by-results schemes, under which workers receive monetary rewards for achieving or surpassing the targets.

Quantity control is not often applied in offices, and it is perhaps as a result of this that the output of the typical office worker is as low as it is – studies show that he is actually working for only 50% or 60% of his time. As indicated in Chapter 9, payment-by-results schemes have a number of disadvantages, and in any case they are not applicable in most offices, which can only process the amount of work that is fed into them from other systems. However, quantity control of a more 'relaxed' kind can be exercised by measuring the volume of output on a weekly or monthly basis and comparing this with the allocation of staff to the office. This is the basis of manpower control and is illustrated in the case study on page 130.

Quality Control

Output targets specify not only the *quantity* to be achieved in a given time, but also the *quality* of output. The purpose of quality control is to ensure that the quality of output lies within the specified tolerances. Statistical quality control methods, outlined on page 63, are widely used in production. An account of quality control in the office is given on page 86.

Measuring Input and Output

Effective planning and control are based upon accurate measurements of both output capacity – the amount of work that individuals, sections, or departments can produce – and input – the cost of the resources needed to produce the output. Strategic planning and budgeting rely on both output capacity and input measurements, and organizational planning, scheduling, and loading depend upon output capacity measurements. A brief description of these measurement techniques is given below.

Measuring Input: Costing

This involves the continuous collection of costs for each area of work, or process, or product. Although no department is excluded from the costing process, the main focus of attention is on departments engaged on the production and handling of goods and materials. Companies using job or batch production methods normally adopt a system of costing known as **job** costing: the costs for each job or batch are accumulated as it passes through the various stages of production, the unit cost being determined by dividing the total cost by the job or batch size. Companies using continuous production methods adopt a system known as **process costing**: the costs per unit of time for each part of the process are totalled, the unit cost being determined by dividing the total cost by the number of units produced per time unit.

The elements that make up the overall cost of a product are classified as either **direct** or **indirect**. Direct costs consist of the cost of materials included in the product, as well as the labour and equipment directly expended in its manufacture. Indirect costs are the overheads: administrative costs (administrative salaries, rent, heating, etc.), selling costs (salesmen's salaries and expenses, etc.), distribution costs, factory overheads, and so on. These overheads must be apportioned over the total output of the company, so that each unit of output bears not only its direct costs but also its share of the indirect costs. The apportioning procedure involves the collection of these indirect costs at 'cost centres' (which may be departments, sections, machines, or processes), and sharing the costs of each centre amongst the various processes or products that it supports.

Standard costing is an extension of this technique to the establishment of cost standards (or targets) for each cost centre, process, and product. It involves determining what the direct cost of materials, labour, etc. *ought to be* for the forthcoming period, as well as the indirect costs that have to be apportioned amongst the various processes and products, and it therefore forms the basis of budgeting. It is also the basis of budgetary control: the actual costs incurred over the period are collected and compared with the standard costs.

Measuring Output Capacity: Work Measurement

Work measurement is used to establish the work content of jobs and the capacities of work centres. The main work measurement techniques are as follows.

1 Activity Sampling This is a statistical sampling technique used to determine the proportion of time spent by an office (or other work centre) on general categories of work (filing, telephoning, typing, reception, etc.). At predetermined random times through the day a rapid observation is made of each worker in the office, and the tasks being done are noted in tally form against the list of activities. (The method is described and illustrated on page 62.) The activities will normally be sampled in this way over a period of a few days to ensure that the results reflect accurately the overall work of the office.

The limitations of the technique are that activities are classified into general categories for measurement, so that no figures are produced for the basic job elements, and no allowance is made for the effectiveness with which the activities are performed. However, it is a technique which is well-suited to work measurement in offices, which include many informal and ill-defined activities, and it is very simple to apply. It enables the categories of work which occupy significant amounts of time to be identified, and it indicates the amount of staff savings that can be achieved by reducing, eliminating, or mechanizing these activities.

2 Diaries The use of diaries in work measurement is described in the case study below. They take the form of time sheets, made out in 15-minute blocks, the workers being required to self-record the main activities undertaken in each block (see Figure 8.5). The sheets are normally filled in each day for the course of a month, thus ensuring that the results obtained are representative of the work of the office.

This technique has the same advantages and limitations as activity sampling − it is easy to carry out, but it looks at general categories of work only, it takes no account of effectiveness, and the results obtained are only approximate.

3 Time study This involves the accurate measurement, by stopwatch, of the basic times of each element of the jobs being studied. A job is broken down into small elements, each of which must have a clearly-defined start and end (e.g. 'take hold of pen', and 'release document into out-tray'), and each should last between 5 and 30 seconds. The time study officer records the time taken for each element of the job over a number of job-cycles.

On each occasion he 'rates' the effectiveness (the speed and efficiency) with which the element is performed against a numerical scale (trained time study officers are accurate to within 2% or 3% in this sort of subjective assessment). **Standard rating** is designated 100 on this scale: this is the rate that the operative achieves when he is working at optimum speed and efficiency, such as will make him no more than 'healthily tired' at the end of the day. A rating of 30% less than this is 70, 20% more is 120; few operatives work outside these limits, and it is difficult to assess accurately very slow or very fast rates or work.

Over the course of a job the rate of work of an operative may vary considerably, but over an individual small element it will vary hardly at all. This is one reason why jobs are broken down into elements for time study purposes – by recording both the time and the rating for each element it is possible to calculate the time that would be taken by an operative working at the standard rate of 100. This is called the **basic time**, the formula for it being

$$\text{basic time} = \frac{\text{rating}}{100} \times \text{observed time.}$$

By timing each element on a number of occasions with different operatives, an average, and very accurate, basic time can be determined.

Another reason for breaking down jobs into elements is that many tasks have a large number of elements in common, and by building up a library of elemental times it is possible to determine the basic time for a job without using a stopwatch. In the case study below, *all* the basic times were determined by reference to the manual supplied by the consultants.

Time study is the most difficult and expensive of the work measurement techniques, but it provides accurate and detailed information on the jobs under examination. Precise work targets can be established and staffing levels determined, and, as is shown below, its application can have a marked effect upon productivity in the office.

CASE STUDY: WORK MEASUREMENT AND MANPOWER CONTROL IN THE OFFICE

The company described in this case study is one of the country's leading finance houses, its current monthly turnover exceeding £40 million. It provides facilities for instalment credit and leasing, which enable business customers to finance plant, machinery, commercial vehicles, and computers, and private customers to finance the purchase of cars, other consumer durables, and home improvements.

Since its formation in 1947 with a small head office and four branch offices, the company has experienced very rapid growth, and it has today a large head office with some 500 staff and a further 1000 staff in 96 branch offices. Expansion has not proceeded, however, in a planned and orderly way. Decisions were made to raise staffing levels and increase office accommodation on an intuitive basis rather than as a result of a work measurement programme. (The O & M Unit, set up in the late 1960s, did undertake a certain amount of work measurement and job evaluation, but this was done on a piecemeal basis and studies were not kept up-to-date.)

The success the company has enjoyed in the past stems in part from its policy of recruiting high-calibre personnel to top management posts. Until recently it was not found necessary to extend this policy to lower-level positions, for the routine work of a finance company was fairly straightforward and did not require a great deal of expertise. However, finance work of all types has grown steadily more complex, competition from banks and foreign companies has grown more intense, and to stay ahead it is now necessary to employ high-calibre staff providing the highest standards of service and expertise.

It had become apparent by 1977 that the uncontrolled growth of the past and the filling of low-level posts by staff capable only of routine clerical work and with little management potential could no longer continue. In an effort to alter the course of the company, the post of Director of Management Services was created, his main objective being to ensure that each section of the company was staffed with the right number of the right calibre of personnel at the right grade. Placed under his control were the Personnel Department, the O & M Unit, and the Training Department.

To achieve his objective the Director of Management Services had to institute a programme of work measurement and job evaluation covering every department and unit of the company. Management consultants were called in, and their *Clerical Work Improvement Programme* (CWIP) was installed (see reference on page 143). The main features and steps of this programme were as follows:

1 The success of any reorganization scheme is related to the degree of consultation and participation achieved. The first step in the programme, therefore, was to inform everyone − management, union officials, and staff − of the objectives of the programme and the way in which it was intended to reach those objectives. Throughout the programme, in fact, very full consultations were held with all interested parties, and as a result there was no conflict at any time, and high levels of cooperation were achieved. Both sides adopted reasonable attitudes: management agreed that no redundancies would occur as a result of the programme, any reduction in staffing levels being achieved through natural wastage, and for its part the union agreed that management would be free to move staff within the company in order to even out any workload inequalities that the programme might reveal.

With regard to the job evaluation, staff were assured that in no case would a downward regrading of a post affect the rate of pay of the existing incumbent, but any regrading upwards would result in increased pay. The prospect of increased earnings proved a powerful incentive to everyone to cooperate in the programme.

2 The next step was to recruit, from within the company's own workforce, a team of nine analysts. These were trained by the consultants in the work measurement techniques that were to be used, and two of the team were given additional training in job evaluation.

3 Each unit of the company was then introduced to the analysis team and given a thorough briefing on the programme. Every member of staff was issued with daily diary sheets, to be completed each day for one month (see Figure 8.5).

4 The information recorded on the diary sheets was transferred by the analysis team onto summary sheets, and from these it was possible to identify for in-depth analysis those tasks which occupied significant amounts of time (i.e. in excess of two hours per week).

5 The in-depth analysis involved firstly a critical appraisal of procedures in order to eliminate any obvious inefficiencies, and then a break-down of each task into a sequence of standard elements. These elements were specified in the reference manuals supplied by the consultants, typical elements being 'pick up pencil from desk', 'copy text material − per 5 letter word', 'place paper on desk'. Basic times for all the thousands of possible elements were supplied in the manual, and the task-time was determined by adding up the basic times for the elements that comprised a task. In order to convince staff of the fairness of the results some tasks were

Daily Diary Sheet

SECTION_____POSITION_____DATE_____

Description of job	7 am	8 am	9 am	10 am	11 am	12 noon	1 pm	2 pm	3 pm	4 pm	5 pm	6 pm	TOTAL
	15 30 45	15 30 45	15 30 45	15 30 45	15 30 45	15 30 45	15 30 45	15 30 45	15 30 45	15 30 45	15 30 45	15 30	
Personal													
Telephone calls													
Interruptions													
	STARTING TIME		FINISHING TIME		LUNCH BREAK			TOTAL			TOTAL		

Figure 8.5   Daily Diary sheet

timed by stopwatch. It was found that these were, in general, accomplished some 10% faster than the calculated times, due to allowances built into the basic times. (These allowances are made to allow staff to take short rests as needed and to attend to personal needs, and they account for $16\frac{2}{3}$% (= one sixth of the basic times.)

6 From the records kept by each unit it was known how many tasks of each type were undertaken by each worker on each day, and it was therefore possible to calculate how long each worker should have spent on those tasks. The results of these calculations were compared with the actual times recorded on the daily diary sheets. Usually the calculated times accorded well with the recorded times; where serious discrepancies occurred it was found that the diary sheets had been incorrectly completed, as, for example, where periods of idle time were recorded as dealing with correspondence.

7 For tasks occupying less than two hours a week, detailed work measurement was not undertaken. Instead a time for the job was agreed between the team, the supervisor, and the worker concerned.

8 The total number of man-hours required by each unit to handle its workload was

then calculated, and this was expressed as a percentage of the actual staffing hours available to that section to give a measure of its *effectiveness*:

$$\text{Effectiveness} = \frac{\text{total calculated hours}}{\text{available hours}} \times 100.$$

The target effectiveness is 90%; units that fail to exceed this are considered to have spare capacity, and therefore able to take on additional work.

As a result of the Clerical Work Improvement Programme, areas of overstaffing were pinpointed, and staff reductions were achieved. Within a year Head Office staff was reduced by 14%, and branch staff numbers were increased by only 8% in spite of a 38% increase in the number of transactions processed. It is estimated that the savings achieved in that first year were three times as great as the total cost of the programme — and these savings are continuing.

The programme is now a permanent feature of management control in the company. It is administered by the O&M Unit, under the direction of the Director of Management Services. All procedural changes are monitored and remeasured using the basic times in the consultants' manual. Every month the head of each unit is required to submit a report on the two forms shown in Figures 8.6 and 8.7. The time taken to compile this report is not excessive (about two hours per month), and the information it provides is invaluable for organizational planning and control.

On Form 1 is entered the monthly volume of each type of task (columns 5 to 10), and the standard (i.e. basic) hours for each task (column 4). The total standard hours required for that volume of work is then calculated and entered (columns 11 to 16). From this the total workload in standard hours is calculated for the unit. On Form 2 is entered an analysis of the actual number of man-hours available to the unit, and from this and the total workload calculated on Form 1 the percentage effectiveness is calculated.

At the foot of Form 2 the workload records for previous months are summarized, together with a workload forecast for the next 3 months. This forecast is produced by time series analysis — taking a moving average over the previous 6 months and projecting forward, adjusting the projection in the light of the number of transactions anticipated by the Marketing Department. From this forecast the staffing requirements for each unit can be determined for the next three months, and this is compared with the availability of staff over this period. If temporary under-staffing is forecast (resulting from, for instance, seasonal peaks of work), arrangements will be made to redeploy staff from other units. In the case of anticipated under-staffing of a long-term nature (resulting from increased business), arrangements will be made to recruit and train additional personnel. The forecasts have been found to accurate, overall, to within 2%.

The job evaluation part of the programme has resulted in a revised grading structure which enables management to utilize staff in a much more flexible manner, and which provides staff with an improved career structure. The team evaluated jobs on the basis of a points scheme provided by the consultants. Each post was awarded points under various headings, e.g. knowledge and/or experience required, degree of responsibility, and so on, the total number of points determining the position of the post in the new grading structure. This has transformed what was previously a hotchpotch of grades varying from department to department into a single all-embracing system.

A useful by-product of the programme has been the establishment of an

| Department Monthly Workload Calculation Sheet | | | DEPT. X Y Z | | | | | | | | | | | | |

Ref. No.	Job/Function	Item to Which Standard Time Relates	STD Tim Per Item	VOL 20 A	VOL 20 M	VOL 20 J	VOL 2 J	VOL 22 A	VOL	STD Hrs 20 A	STD Hrs 20 M	STD Hrs 20 J	STD Hrs 21 J	STD Hrs 22 A	STD Hrs
1	Invoices	Payments Received	·076	2298	2142	2165	2033	2564		175	163	165	155	195	
2	Advice Notes	Page of List	·275	1120	1120	1120	1134	856		308	308	308	348	263	
3	Correspondence	Per Item	·084	442	400	575	654	872		37	34	48	55	73	
4	Journals	Per Entry	·09	410	410	395	412	490		37	37	36	37	44	
5	Monthly Duties	Constant	27·50	1	1	1	1	1		28	28	28	28	28	
		Standard Hours Sub-Total							A	585	570	585	623	603	
WORKLOAD		Sub-Total (A) x 10% = Supervision Allowance							B	59	57	58	62	60	
FOR		Sub-Total (A) + 7 x .1666 = Personal Allowance							C	13	14	14	15	14	
MONTH		Unmeasured/Special Jobs Time							D	–	–	4	35	16	
		Sub Total							E	657	641	661	735	693	
		Monthly Factor							F	x 1	x 1	x 1	x ·95	x ·91	x
		Total Workload (E) x Factor (F) to give total on 20 day month							G	657	641	661	698	631	

Factors 18 = 1.11   19 = 1.05   20 = 1.00   21 = .95   22 = .91   23 = .87   24 = .83   25 = .80

Figure 8.6   FORM 1 – Monthly workload calculation sheet

improved regime of training for each new staff member. Training requirements have been determined from the detailed analyses of jobs produced by the analysis team, and in addition comprehensive procedure manuals, based upon the analyses, have been compiled for issuing to all trainees.

EXERCISES

1 Identify the main benefits of this work measurement and job evaluation programme to the company.

2 State the reasons for the success of the programme.

3 What problems would a similar programme conducted in your organization run into? How might these problems be overcome?

FORM 2

Monthly Control Report

DEPARTMENT_____   MONTH_____

Authorized Establishment Including Supervisors Etc. **6**

Staff Included in Control Figure

FULL TIME	8
PART TIME	

Actual Staffing Including Supervisors **8**

Month New Starts Leavers

Analysis of Hours Worked	Calendar Hours	Factor	Factor Hours	Hours
Total Contractual Hours (Always 20 Days)				1120
Less Non-Attendance	301	91	274	
Less Loaned Time	–	–	–	274
Sub Total				846
Add Borrowed Time	–	~	~	
Add Overtime	~	–	–	

Total Workload **631** Hrs

Total Time Attended **846** Hrs

$$= \frac{(Total\ Workload \times 100)}{(Total\ Time\ Attended)} = \boxed{75}$$

Unmeasured Work **16** Hr **2** %

Non-Attendance **274** Hr **24** %

LAST SIX MONTHS WORKLOAD						AVER	Next Three Months Workload			Staffing		
Month	A	M	J	J	A	/	S	O	N	S	O	N
Total Workload	657	641	661	698	631	657	657	660	653	5·3	5·3	5·3
Total Time Attended	1107	1116	1014	1017	846	1020						
Effectiveness	59	57	65	68	75	64						
Work in hand	Volume		Std. Hours						Volume		Std. Hours	

C.W.I.P. 2

Figure 8.7   Form 2 – Monthly control report (Percentage effectiveness and Workload forecast)

ASSIGNMENT GROUP WORK

Assignment 5 Section A (page 192).

Decision-Making Techniques

The remainder of this chapter is devoted to a description of some operational research techniques that are widely used in business decision-making. A knowledge of these techniques is required of students taking BEC Higher National courses and professional courses, but not of BEC National Award students.

As was emphasized in Chapter 2, decision-making must be carried out as an integrated process that takes an overall view of the organization, the aim being to optimize the operations of the system as a whole rather than those of individual subsystems. The mathematical decision-making techniques that have been developed by operational researchers do just this. They adopt the following general approach:

1 *All* the main variables that impinge upon the situation under examination are isolated and analysed

2 A mathematical model of these variables and their interrelationships is constructed, normally using standard computer programs

3 The values of the variables are manipulated in the model and the mathematical outcomes calculated in order to determine the best course of action.

The determination of economic order quantities (a stock control technique) provides a simple example of the approach. The cost of ordering and holding in stores an item of stock is made up of two elements:

(a) The administrative cost (A) incurred by the Purchasing Department in actually placing the order, and (b) The holding cost (H) incurred by Stores in holding a single item for a unit period of time.

The total annual cost varies with the quantity that is ordered each time a purchase is made. The operations of the Purchasing Department would be optimized if just one very large order were placed; the operations of the Stores Department, on the other hand, would be optimized if a large number of small orders were placed, as this would reduce the average quantity held and therefore the stockholding costs. A graph illustrating the effect on overall costs of altering the order quantity is shown in Figure 8.8.

The graph shows the economic order quantity (EOQ) which leads to overall optimization (but to the individual sub-optimization of both the purchasing and stores functions). Using the techniques of a branch of mathematics known as calculus, it is possible to show that this quantity is determined by the formula

$$EOQ = \sqrt{\frac{2AY}{H}}$$

where Y is the rate of usage (i.e. the average number of items consumed by the business per unit period of time).

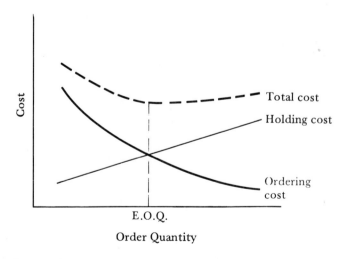

Figure 8.8   Economic order quantity

Deciding Between Alternative Strategies: Decision Theory

Decision Theory embraces a number of techniques. In the method described below, the various strategies facing the decision-maker and the possible outcomes of those strategies are represented as branches of a **decision tree**, and values and probabilities are assigned to these outcomes. The optimum strategy is the one that has the highest **expected value** (E.V.) – the E.V. of an outcome is calculated by multiplying its probability by its value.

The underlying theory is simple. Suppose that, in a dice game, a gambler can choose between (a) receiving £3 if a 6 is thrown, or (b) £1.20 if any other number is thrown. Assuming that the die is fair (unbiased), there is only one chance in six – i.e. a probability of 1/6 – of winning £3, but five chances in six – i.e. a probability of 5/6 – of winning £1.20. It is intuitively obvious that choices of this nature can be compared by calculating the E.V.s:

$$\text{E.V.(a)} = \frac{1}{6} \times £3 = £0.50$$

$$\text{E.V.(b)} = \frac{5}{6} \times £1.20 = £1.00.$$

Over the course of a number of games he can expect to win twice as much by choosing strategy (b) rather than strategy (a).

The value of an outcome is called its **conditional value** (C.V.) – its value 'on condition that' it occurs. Thus the C.V. of strategy (a) is £3, the C.V. of strategy (b) is £1.20. The formula for calculating expected values is therefore

E.V. = probability × C.V.

There are three ways of assessing probabilities of alternative courses of action. In straightforward situations, such as the above, they can often be calculated mathematically. In more complex situations this may not be possible, and past records may then form the basis of the calculations. For example, if the die in the above illustration were biased, then to determine the probability of throwing a 6 it would be necessary to count the number of 6s that had actually occurred over a large number of prior throws. If neither of the above methods are feasible, then the probability will have to be subjectively assessed by those familiar with the situation.

As an example of the application of this decision-making technique, we shall suppose that the Research & Development Department of a British food company has developed a promising new process for manufacturing synthetic meat from vegetable waste. The Board of Directors is not prepared to give the go-ahead for the building of a factory for large-scale manufacture of the product without some form of market test, and the Marketing Department has to decide whether to carry out a market research survey, which it estimates will cost £100,000, or whether to carry out a small-scale test launch of the product, at a cost of £2 million. If the results of either strategy are unfavourable (i.e. if they indicate that the product is unlikely to be successful), then the process will be sold to an American company for £3 million. If, on the other hand, the results are favourable, then the British company will go into large-scale production.

The consensus of opinion of the Sales Committee is that the probabilities of the various outcomes of these strategies are as follows.

Strategy (1) – carry out market research survey:

Probability of a favourable result = 70% = $\dfrac{70}{100}$ = 0.7

Probability of an unfavourable result = 30% = $\dfrac{30}{100}$ = 0.3

If the company goes into large-scale production on the basis of a favourable result, then the possible profits from the project over its anticipated lifetime are
£NIL with a probability of 0.1
£10m with a probability of 0.5
£20m with a probability of 0.4.

Strategy (2) – carry out a small-scale test launch:

Probability of a favourable result = 0.6
Probability of an unfavourable result = 0.4
If the company goes into large-scale production on the basis of a favourable result, then the possible profits over the lifetime of the project are:
£10m with a probability of 0.2
£20m with a probability of 0.5
£30m with a probability of 0.3.

The tree diagram showing the two strategies and their possible outcomes is shown in Figure 8.9. The calculations are shown at the right of the diagram. The C.V.s of each possible outcome are obtained by summing the losses/profits of the successive branches leading to that outcome (losses being indicated by negative amounts, profits by positive amounts); the probabilities are obtained by multiplying the probabilities of the successive branches; the E.V.s are obtained by multiplying each C.V. by the corresponding probability. The expected value of each strategy is calculated by adding the E.V.s of the possible outcomes of that strategy. The test-launch strategy has the highest expected profit (£11.8m), and so this should be the strategy that the company adopts.

Assessing the Value of Additional Information

Any increase in the amount of relevant information at the decision-maker's disposal will tend to improve the quality of the decision made, and this will result in an increased expected value. However, the cost of collecting the additional information has to be offset against the increase in the E.V.

The above example illustrates the effect of increasing the expenditure on information. By choosing the test-launch strategy the company gains better quality information, for which it pays an additional £1.9 million. The effect of that information is to alter the probabilities of the various outcomes, and this affects

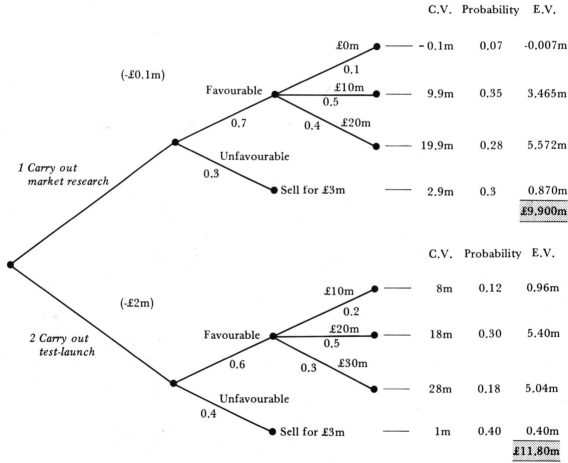

Figure 8.9   Tree diagram for calculating the expected values of alternative strategies

the E.V.s. The mathematical procedure for comparing the cost of additional information with the increase in expected value (in order to determine whether or not the information should be collected) is explained in the writer's text *Quantitative Methods for Business Students*, published by Heinemann.

Deciding Between Alternative Allocations of Resources: Linear Programming

This technique is used to determine how resources of personnel, finance, equipment, transport, etc. should be allocated so that profits are maximized, or costs minimized, or some other optimization criterion achieved. The use of a computer is essential for most linear programming problems; however, if two variables only are involved, then a simple graphical method of solution is possible, and this is illustrated in the example below.

Suppose that a furniture factory makes two products: bookcases and coffee tables. The contribution to profits from each bookcase is £4, and from each coffee table is £6. The factory manager wishes to determine what quantity of each product he should manufacture per unit time in order to maximize profits.

The first step is to determine the limitations, or **constraints**, on the numbers of each product that can be processed per unit of time by the various stages of manufacture. We shall suppose that these constraints are as follows:

1 Woodworking: this section can machine the parts for up to 12 bookcases or 6 coffee tables in an hour, or some intermediate mix (e.g. 10 bookcases and 1 coffee table, or 8 bookcases and 2 coffee tables, etc.)

2 Assembly: this section can assemble 8 bookcases or 10 coffee tables in an hour, or some intermediate mix

3 Finishing: this section can finish up to 9 bookcases or 7 coffee tables in an hour, or some intermediate mix.

The next step is to represent the possible mixes for each section by straight lines on a graph – see Figure 8.10. One axis is used to represent the number of bookcases per hour, the other the number of coffee tables per hour. To represent the possible mixes of output of the woodworking section, a line is drawn joining the

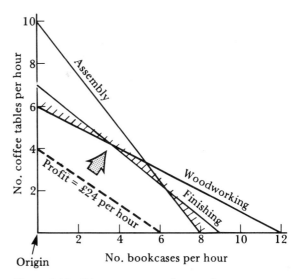

Figure 8.10   Linear programming graph

value 12 on the bookcase axis to 6 on the coffee table axis. All the points lying on this line or below it on the graph represent the various possible mixes of bookcases and coffee tables that can be made by the woodworking section in one hour; however, mixes represented by points *above* this line are not possible – the section cannot, for instance, make 8 bookcases *and* 8 coffee tables in one hour. To show that points above the line are not feasible, that region is hatched on the graph.

The lines representing the possible product-mixes for the assembly and finishing sections are drawn and hatched in the same way.

Next, a line is inserted on the graph to show the possible product-mixes that will result in a specified level of profit. Any profit level can be chosen – say £24 an hour. The factory can achieve this by making 6 bookcases an hour but no coffee tables (each bookcase yields a profit of £4, so the total profit is £24); or by making 4 coffee tables an hour but no bookcases (each coffee table yields a profit of £6, so the total profit is again £24); or by making some intermediate mix such as 3 bookcases and 2 coffee tables. The line joining 6 on the bookcase axis and 4 on the coffee table axis shows all possible product-mixes that will achieve this level of profit.

If another level of profit is chosen, this will generate a line on the graph parallel to the £24 line; if the profit is smaller than £24, the line will lie closer to the origin, and if the profit is higher than £24, the line will lie further from the origin. The line which gives the highest profit within the manufacturing constraints given above will be the one which can be drawn the furthest distance from the origin *which passes through at least one point lying below the hatched region of the graph.*

By taking a ruler and moving it carefully upwards and parallel to the £24 line it can be seen that the maximum profit line passes through the point lying at the intersection of the woodworking and finishing lines. It is this point − 3.6 bookcases and 4.2 coffee tables an hour − which represents the product-mix giving the highest profit to the factory.

Deciding Between Alternative Priorities: Network Analysis

This widely-used technique (also known as **critical path analysis**) was developed in the 1950s to schedule projects in order to minimize their completion time. A complex project involves a large number of activities, many of which take place simultaneously. Slight delays in some activities will not affect the overall project time; some activities, however, will be **critical** − any delay in them *will* increase the project time. Network analysis enables these critical activities to be identified, so that by diverting to them resources of manpower, equipment, or money, or by studying them in detail to find faster ways of completing them, the overall project time is reduced.

To illustrate the technique we shall use the (relatively simple) example of a man purchasing a vacant shop in order to set up a launderette. The steps in constructing and analysing the network for this project are outlined below.

1 List the activities and estimate the time needed for each. We shall suppose that these are as follows:

(a) Draw up contracts for the purchase of the shop, and complete the purchase − 6 weeks
(b) Decide the type and number of washing machines etc. to be installed, and place order − 2 weeks
(c) Await delivery of machines − 6 weeks
(d) Draw up detailed plans showing the location of machines, plumbing, etc. − 3 weeks

(e) Arrange for a plumber to carry out the plumbing work − 1 week
(f) Give the plumber 2 weeks' notice of the work to be done
(g) Obtain all plumbing materials required as specified in the plans in consultation with the plumber − 3 weeks
(h) Carry out plumbing work − 3 weeks
(i) Prepare concrete bases for machines as required and carry out all electrical work − 1 week
(j) When (i) has been completed, install machines − 1 week
(k) When (h) and (j) have been completed, decorate shop and lay flooring − 1 week.

2 Represent the activities by a network of arrows, connected by sequentially numbered nodes (i.e. the circles shown in Figure 8.11).   Each node represents the moment in time when one activity ceases and the next begins. It is conventional to number the starting node (representing the moment in time when the project is begun) by the number 1, and to number sequentially through the network to the finishing node (which represents the moment of completion), making sure that no two nodes have the same number. In the Figure, the arrow joining node 1 to node 5 represents activity (a), the arrow joining node 1 to node 2 represents activity (b), and so on. The duration of each activity is entered below its arrow.

Note that activity (a), activity sequence (b)−(d)−(g), and activity sequence (e)−(f) take place simultaneously, and so are represented on the network by three branches proceeding from node 1. Activity (g) cannot commence until both (d) *and* (e) have been completed: to ensure that this condition is satisfied by the network a *dummy* activity of zero duration is shown joining nodes 3 and 4. Note also that activities (h) and (i) cannot commence until activities (a), (f), and (g) are completed: node 5 represents this moment in time.

3 Calculate for each activity the earliest start time(E). This is done by writing E = O above node 1 and proceeding logically through the network, the earliest start time for each successive node being the sum of the earliest start time of the preceding node and the duration of the activity leading to it. For example, the earliest start time of activity (f) is 0 + 1 = 1, and so E = 1 is written above node 3. When two or

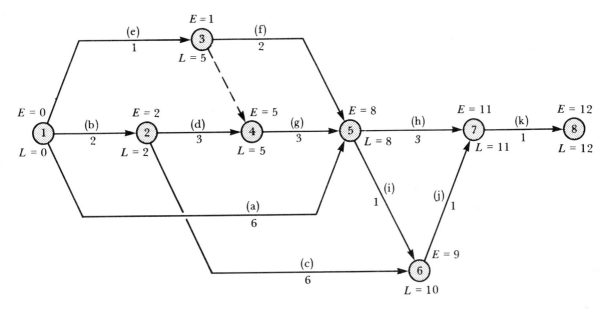

Figure 8.11   Network for setting up laundrette business

more arrows converge on a node (as at node 5), then the highest E-value must be taken for that node. Thus the earliest start of activities (h) and (i) is week 8, since the sequence (b)−(d)−(g) takes 8 weeks to complete.

This calculation is repeated right through the network until the final node 8 is reached, for which, in this example, E = 12. 12 weeks is therefore the overall project time.

4 Calculate for each activity the latest finish time (L). The procedure is to work backwards through the network, commencing at the final node 8. At this node L is set equal to E, so that in this example L = 12. The calculation of successive L-values is similar to that for the E-values, though now the duration of each activity is *subtracted* from the preceding L-value. Thus at node 7, L = 12 − 1 = 11; at node 5, L = 11 − 3 = 8; and so on. Where two or more arrows emerge from a node, as at node 5, the *lowest* L-value must be taken.

5 Calculate the float time for each activity. This is the amount of excess time available for the completion of the activity, and it is determined by subtracting the earliest start for that activity from the latest finish time (to get the available time for that activity), and subtracting from this the activity time. For example, for activity (c) the float is 10 − 2 − 6 = 2 weeks. This means that (c) can be extended by up to 2 weeks without affecting the overall project time.

6 Determine the critical path. This is the sequence of activities with zero float, and is most easily identified in the network by tracing through those nodes for which E = L: 1, 2, 4, 5, 7, and 8. The critical path consists of activities (b), (d), (g), (h), (k): a hold-up in any of these will delay the overall project time. It is these that must be carefully controlled, and it is on these that any efforts to reduce the project time must be concentrated.

9
The
Well-Organized
Job

One quarter of the work of the typical office is unnecessary. Much of the remaining three quarters lacks interest, and is carried out at only 60% effectiveness. If office work were well-organized, so that unnecessary operations were eliminated, necessary operations were put together in ways which provided stimulating jobs, and realistic staffing levels were set, then productivity would double without any change in the technology employed.

In this chapter we examine the organization of work, firstly from the standpoint of the **scientific approach** − this embraces techniques such as work study and O&M, the purpose of which is to analyse work with a view to increasing efficiency and determining realistic staffing levels − and secondly from the standpoint of the **human relations approach** − this embraces techniques such as job enrichment, the purpose of which is to organize work in ways which will provide meaningful jobs and enhanced motivation.

Scientific Management

What is known as 'scientific management' was developed by Frederick Taylor in the 1880s. Originally a shop-floor worker, Taylor had such ability that he rose through the ranks of supervisory and middle management to senior management, and the wide experience of industry that this provided convinced him that enor-

mous savings could be made by applying scientific methods to the working practices of the day. These practices had evolved in a haphazard way, through the transmission of rule-of-thumb working methods from one generation to the next. The typical manager or supervisor had little knowledge of these methods, but relied on the workers under his control to exercise their skills in the most efficient ways, rewarding them for their efforts by financial incentives.

Out of this system had arisen a multitude of methods for doing any one job, none of them particularly efficient, and Taylor resolved that he would make it his life's work to rectify this situation and so eliminate the enormous waste represented by all these inefficiencies. The principles of scientific management that he developed were based upon the premise that managers, not workers, should be responsible for the methods of work, and that the workers' responsibility was limited to carrying out the tasks in strict accordance with the laid-down methods.

Taylor's principles can be summarized as follows:

1 Managers should institute a scientific study of work ('work study'): each job should be broken down into its elemental activities, and each elemental activity should be systematically analysed in order to determine the most efficient way to carry it out.
2 When the new methods have been determined, each revised activity should be carefully timed at a standard rate of work (see page 130) in order to establish the

work-content of each job and thus to fix manning levels and set realistic output targets.

3 Workers should be given financial incentives (bonuses) to achieve the target output, the size of the bonus being directly related to their rate of work. (Under traditional bonus incentive schemes, bonuses begin to be paid when the worker achieves an overall rating in excess of 80% of the standard rate.)

4 Managers should select workers and train them in the laid-down methods.

Taylor's 'work study' principles were quickly adopted and successfully applied in a wide variety of factory situations, and they are now a permanent feature of industrial management.

Scientific Management in the Office

From Taylor's original work study methodology has arisen a number of techniques for use in office situations. The most important of these is Organization & Methods (O & M), which differs from work study in that it addresses itself not only to work methods and targets, but also to organization structure, the provision of management information, and forms design. CWIP (Clerical Work Improvement Programme), described in the case study on page 130, should also be mentioned. Although this includes O&M techniques, it is primarily concerned with work measurement and the establishment of staffing levels, and is available on a consultancy basis only from W.D. Scott & Co. Ltd., management consultants.

The benefits that accrue from eliminating unnecessary paperwork and setting realistic staffing levels in offices can be substantial. The gains that result from the latter are illustrated in the case study on page 130. The gains that result from eliminating unnecessary paperwork are illustrated by the following example, which describes the experience of the Purchasing Department of a shipping company. The processing of each order produced by the department involved no less than 17 documents (requisition forms, quotation requests, etc.), and the cost (including clerical labour) amounted to £10. On average, ten weeks elapsed from the date of initiating the process to its completion, and the amount of paperwork in the office was such that little time was spent on buying decisions (comparing suppliers to select the most suitable, negotiating terms, etc.). As a result of an O & M study the paperwork was

cut by around 70%, orders were processed in a few days, much more time was spent on making buying decisions, and £100,000 per annum was saved.

The Organization of O & M

Work study and O & M is normally carried out by specialists, able to bring to bear on a given situation their experience gained on a number of projects in a variety of departments and organizations. In many organizations the Work Study Section is responsible to the Production Manager, and the O&M Unit to the Accountant or Office Manager; but this can create problems if projects are carried out in departments outside the direct control of these managers. It is generally found more satisfactory to set up a **Management Services Department**, responsible for systems analysis, operational research, O & M, and possibly work study, which exists to provide a service to other departments, and which is controlled by a manager immediately below the Managing Director in organization hierarchy.

The Work Study and O & M Technique

A work study or O & M project may take only a few days to carry out, or it may last for a year or more. For major projects a preliminary survey will normally be carried out with the object of:

1 determining whether the potential benefits are large enough to justify setting up the project;

2 establishing and agreeing with all concerned the terms of reference of the project;

3 drawing up a timetable for the project as a basis for control (even work study officers should have targets to aim for!).

The main stages in a work study or O & M project are as follows:

1 Secure the co-operation of all staff affected by the project. Preliminary meetings should be held with staff in the department in which the project is to be undertaken, and at these the departmental head should take the opportunity to explain the reasons for the project and give an indication of the anticipated benefits, give no-redundancy guarantees, introduce the project team, and invite questions. The success of the project depends, in large measure, upon the degree of co-operation engendered in the staff.

2 *Select the area of work to be studied*. Major areas of work that can be expected to yield worthwhile savings will have been identified and selected in the preliminary survey. As the project proceeds, however, the selection process will be applied in greater depth. The approximate work-content of the various tasks carried out in the areas under review will be determined, either by activity sampling or diaries (page 129), so that those which occupy significant amounts of time and which therefore offer the greatest potential savings can be identified for in-depth investigation.

3 *Record the methods used at present in the selected areas of work*. Recording goes hand-in-hand with selection. First, the broad outline of the job is noted down, usually in the form of a process chart (page 74). At this stage it is often possible to make major improvements by, for example, eliminating entire steps in the job (by altering the sequence of operations, redesigning forms, installing new equipment, combining operations, or eliminating the need for one operation by modifying another). Those parts of the job that cannot be altered in this way are selected for more detailed analysis, and for these more detailed process charts are constructed. Each small activity that is distinguished on these charts will be analysed with a view to reducing its work-content or eliminating it completely. Exceptionally, in the case of highly repetitive tasks, any activities that emerge from this level of analysis are examined in still finer detail.

To illustrate the work study and O & M technique we have chosen as an example the invoice reconciliation procedure described in the case study on page 75. The three levels of recording and analysis described above (broad outline, more detailed analysis, and fine detail) are shown in Figure 9.1.

The techniques used for recording the present method include:

(a) Interviewing and observing the work of the operatives and clerks (which, in the case of very detailed recording, may include filming followed by frame-by-frame analysis)
(b) Following documents through a process and recording the operations that are carried out on them
(c) Recording on a scale plan of the working area all movements of the workers under observation, in order to design a better layout (see page 158).

4 *Examine the present method in order to make improvements*. This stage in the project is carried out concurrently with selection and recording. Major 'chunks' of work are recorded and examined first with a view to making improvements; fine detail is recorded and examined only for those parts of the work that survive this initial broad investigation. The technique is to subject each part of the work (i.e. each step in the process chart) to the questioning process described on page 120. Work study officers and O & M analysts find it helpful to apply the WHAT–WHEN–WHERE–WHO–HOW questions in a formal way by means of a **critical examination chart**, and an example of this is given in Table 9.1.

In the invoice reconciliation example referred to above, one would begin at the first level of analysis shown in Figure 9.1 by examining the overall reconciliation task. The answer to the question 'Why is this done?' (column 2 of Table 9.1) is that it ensures that the company does not pay for goods it has not received and that the invoice total is correct. One obvious alternative course of action would be *not* to carry out invoice reconciliations. To determine whether this alternative is viable one would have to compare the cost of doing it with benefits of avoiding unnecessary payments. At least one company has found that it is more cost-effective not to reconcile invoices but to pay on the basis of a quick scrutiny by the payment clerk to ensure that they are from usual suppliers for the type of goods and materials normally purchased.

If, however, the overall task of invoice reconciliation cannot be eliminated, then it is necessary to drop to the second level of analysis shown in Figure 9.1, and record and examine the procedure in more detail. Again, the WHAT–WHEN–WHERE–WHO–HOW questioning technique must be applied to each step of the (more detailed) process chart. In Table 9.1 the technique is applied to the operation of attaching the sticker to the invoice and copying the invoice details onto it. Both this operation and the work of maintaining the Invoice Register are necessary because the invoices pass from the paying section to other sections and departments (see Figure 5.6); the sticker provides a standard document for use by these sections, and the Invoice Register provides a means of keeping track of the invoices in the event of queries.

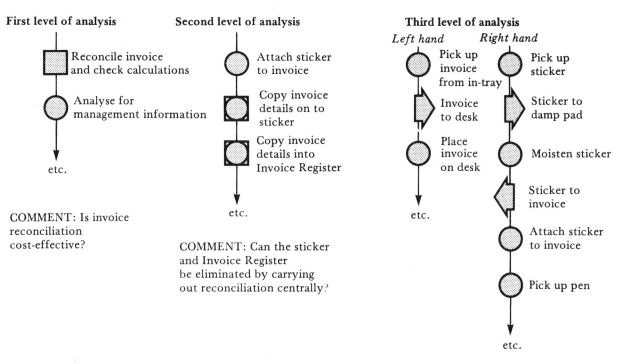

First level of analysis

⬚ Reconcile invoice and check calculations

⬤ Analyse for management information

etc.

COMMENT: Is invoice reconciliation cost-effective?

Second level of analysis

⬤ Attach sticker to invoice

⬤ Copy invoice details on to sticker

⬤ Copy invoice details into Invoice Register

etc.

COMMENT: Can the sticker and Invoice Register be eliminated by carrying out reconciliation centrally?

Third level of analysis

Left hand   *Right hand*

⬤ Pick up invoice from in-tray   ⬤ Pick up sticker

▷ Invoice to desk   ▷ Sticker to damp pad

⬤ Place invoice on desk   ⬤ Moisten sticker

◁ Sticker to invoice

⬤ Attach sticker to invoice

⬤ Pick up pen

etc.

etc.

EXAMPLE OF IMPROVEMENT: Reverse R.H. and L.H., so that 'pick up pen' can take place at the same time as 'attach sticker to invoice'.

Figure 9.1   The three levels of analysis: man-type process charts

The need for these documents would be eliminated if invoice reconciliation were carried out centrally by the paying section. The way in which this could be done is shown in the process chart in Figure 5.7 and the accompanying text.

Since this operation can be eliminated at the WHAT? stage of the questionning process there is no need to proceed through the subsequent WHEN–WHERE–WHO–HOW questions on the critical examination chart.

The process of questioning the various steps shown on a process chart should follow a logical sequence. First, the operations and inspections shown on the chart should be examined. If any of these can be eliminated then any dependent transports, delays, and storages will disappear also. The procedure is to take each operation and inspection in turn, and then any surviving transports, delays, and storages, and subject them to the questioning process by completing a critical examination chart for each one.

Any activities that emerge from this critical examination process can be recorded and analysed in still greater detail in order to find more efficient ways of doing them (this is the third level of analysis shown in Figure 9.1), but this is only worthwhile in the case of highly repetitive tasks.

5 Develop the new method, using the best alternatives arrived at by the above critical examination process. Process charts of the new procedure should be constructed, and forms must be redesigned. Staffing levels must be determined using the results of work measurement (either by determining from an activity sample of the old method how much time the new method will save, or by carrying out time studies of the new method). If a bonus incentive scheme is to be

Question	Information on the present method	Alternatives	Best alternative
WHAT IS BEING DONE?	(WHY is this done?)	(What could be done?)	(What should be done?)
Sticker is attached to invoice, and invoice details are noted on it	To provide a standard form for use by the sections and departments involved in invoice reconciliation	1 Departments could indicate checks on the invoice itself 2 Reconciliation could be handled centrally by paying section, thus eliminating need for entries by other depts	Eliminate need for sticker by handling reconciliation centrally
WHEN IS IT BEING DONE?	(WHY is it done at this point in the sequence of activities?)	(When could it be done?)	(When should it be done?)
WHERE IS IT BEING DONE?	(WHY there?)	(Where could it be done?)	(Where should it be done?)
WHO DOES IT?	(WHY this person?)	(Who could do it?)	(Who should do it?)
HOW IS IT BEING DONE?	(WHY this method?)	(How could it be done?)	(How should it be done?)

Table 9.1   Critical examination chart.

installed, then accurate time studies must be carried out, either by stopwatch or by looking up standard times in a manual.

6 Submit proposals to management. A description of the proposed method, the reasons for it, and the financial savings and other anticipated benefits, should be incorporated in a report. The report should be prefaced by a summary of the main recommendations and the expected benefits: only the departmental managers and supervisors who are to be directly involved in the implementation of the recommendations need read beyond this.

The responsibility for accepting the recommendations and authorizing their implementation rests with management. Provided an appropriate area of study was selected and the project was carried out in an efficient way, then management will normally accept the recommendations as they stand, with perhaps a few minor modifications.

7 Install and maintain the new method. The responsibility for implementing the agreed recom-

mendations rests with the departmental manager(s) concerned, though the O & M officers who undertook the project will generally be called upon to assist.

The installation of the new method should be properly planned and organized, and a time-table should be drawn up. New equipment may have to be purchased, forms printed, structural alterations made, and training in the new procedures given. The physical changeover of equipment and layout may have to be carried out over a weekend, to minimize disruption, and close supervision will have to be exercised during the first few days of operating the new procedures. Some details of the new method may not work out quite as planned, and minor modifications may have to be made.

'Maintaining' the new method involves ensuring that undesirable variations in the proposed procedures are not introduced. There may be a tendency, initially, for workers to revert to old practices, and a periodic review of procedures should be carried out. Any changes which are an improvement upon the recommended method should, of course, be accepted.

CASE STUDY: O & M IN A GENERAL OFFICE

During an O & M survey carried out a number of years ago by the writer for an overseas government, the procedure described below was observed in the General Office of one department. It was carried out by the Clerical Assistant responsible for handling mail.

Incoming letters are opened, rubber-stamped with the department's name, and stamped again with the date. For each letter the following information is entered in the Inwards Mail Register: the date, the code number of the file into which the letter is to be inserted, and a brief synopsis of the contents of the letter. All of these details are copied from the letter apart from the file code number, which is looked up in a card index.

When a batch of letters has been dealt with in this way, the files in which they are to be inserted are removed from the filing cabinets, each letter is inserted in its file, and a slip of paper with 'ACTION REQUIRED' printed on it is pinned to the front of the file jacket.

The files are then placed in the out-tray on the Clerical Assistant's desk. The Clerical Assistant periodically clears this tray and distributes the files to the appropriate officers for action. They draft replies, which are subsequently typed by a typist (an original plus two carbon copies), who also addresses the envelopes. Each reply with its envelope is attached by a paper clip to its file, and every so often a batch is returned to the Clerical Assistant.

For each file in the batch the Clerical Assistant removes the ACTION

REQUIRED slip and copies the following details from the typed reply into the Outwards Mail Register: the date, the file number, the addressee, and the subject heading of the reply. The typed original is then inserted in the envelope, the first carbon copy is inserted in the file (which is replaced in the filing cabinet), and the second carbon copy is placed in a 'Running File' which contains copies of all outgoing correspondence in date order. The envelopes are sealed, stamped with the department's name, stamped again with the date, and placed in the despatch tray.

The examination of this procedure comprised a tiny part only of the overall project, but being straightforward and self-contained it provides a simple illustration of the application of the principles of O & M. Every operation in the procedure has to be subjected to the critical examination technique, the key question always being WHY? (column 2 of Figure 9.2). For example:

- **WHY** the 'action required' slips, when the mere presence of the file in the outtray shows that it has to be passed on for action? Some time previously a file had inadvertently been replaced in the cabinet before action had been taken, and the slips had been introduced to avoid the (remote) possibility of this happening again. Similar reasons had been found for the various rubber-stamping operations.
- **WHY** the 'running file', when a copy of the outgoing correspondence is held on the ordinary departmental files? The head of the department stated that this was 'invaluable' if correspondence went missing or additional copies were required — but another part of the investigation showed that this happened only about five times a year.
- **WHY** the Inwards and Outwards Mail Registers? The laws of the land insisted that these be kept, but they did not specify what details had to be recorded in them — the date and the relevant code numbers of the correspondence would suffice.

As a result of the survey many of the operations were eliminated, and the Clerical Assistant, who previously was overloaded with work, found that he could now cope easily with the existing throughput of letters. Similar savings were achieved in other areas in the department, and the head of the department dropped the request that he had previously made for a staff increase.

EXERCISE

Construct a man-type process chart of the above procedure, suggest ways in which it might be improved, and chart the proposed method.

ASSIGNMENT GROUP WORK
Assignment 5 Section B (page 193).

Disadvantages of the Scientific Approach

The scientific approach described above tends to 'deskill' and 'dehumanise' work – jobs are reduced to a sequence of mindless and repetitive operations, requiring reduced levels of skill and training, and workers are given little or no responsibility for planning, organizing, and controlling their own work. The basic assumption on which the approach rests is that all the worker needs or desires from his work is the pay-packet at the end of the week, and so the method adopted to motivate workers to give of their best is bonus incentive payments.

By the early years of this century it had become apparent that, although Taylor's approach was effective enough in eliminating waste, it did little to increase the motivation of workers. In fact it sometimes had the reverse effect, and in some sections of British industry 'work study' is still anathema. The main drawbacks of Taylor's approach can be summarized as follows:

1 Authoritarian attitudes are fostered in supervisors and initiative is stifled in workers by limiting the responsibility of workers to carrying out the laid-down procedures. Workers are not encouraged to seek ways of raising output or finding solutions to problems.

2 Any sense of achievement is destroyed by breaking down jobs into tiny tasks. The individual worker does not produce an end-product with which he can identify his efforts, and so work loses its meaning.

3 Workers are subjected to considerable pressures, and friction is created with management, by bonus incentive schemes. Such schemes encourage workers to seek only material rewards from their work, and they can destroy the social fabric of life on the shop floor. Many organizations have introduced instead **merit-rating schemes**, which entail the subjective assessment of the employee's effort and ability, usually by his immediate superior. Points are awarded for quality and quantity of output, dependability, co-operativeness, and other factors. The assessment is carried out once a year, and pay is adjusted in accordance with the total number of points earned.

4 Job-interest is reduced and fatigue is induced by the reduction of tasks to small sequences of repetitive steps carried out over and over again. The effect of monotony and fatigue upon output is illustrated in Figure 9.2, which is based upon a study carried out by the writer in the microscopy laboratory attached to the Malaria Eradication Programme in a tropical country. The microscopists had the task of inspecting slides of blood samples for evidence of infection, and the graph shows how the average rate of slide-reading rose to a peak an hour or so after the start of work, and then declined during the remainder of the day.

The solution suggested by the author to this problem was **job rotation**. Employed in the laboratory were some slide cleaners, and it was suggested that these be trained in microscopy work and that slide cleaning be carried out in turn by each of the microscopists during the day in order to introduce variety into the work and reduce fatigue.

Job rotation was the only practical means, in this instance, by which work could be improved. The human relations approach, with which the remainder of this chapter deals, shows that in many cases much more radical and effective solutions can be found to the problem of the dehumanization of work.

The Human Relations Approach

By the beginning of this century the wealth created by the industrial revolution had resulted in considerable improvements in the pay and working conditions of workers in industry. It had been assumed that these material rewards would motivate workers to give of their best, but experience proved otherwise. In 1924 the Western Electric Company of Chicago addressed itself to the problem of finding more successful ways of motivating workers in order to improve performance. It commissioned the services of Elton Mayo, professor of industrial research at the Harvard Graduate School of Business, and for five years he investigated the problem at the company's Hawthorne works.

The results of this research had far-reaching consequences, for it brought home to industry a fundamental truth that had not hitherto been appreciated:

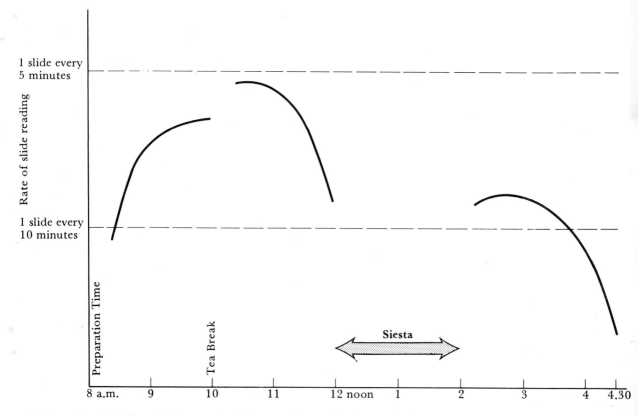

Figure 9.2   The effect of fatigue on performance: microscopists in a tropical country

that people are motivated to perform well at work not only by material factors (pay and working conditions) but by social and psychological factors also. Behavioural scientists in many parts of the world followed Mayo's lead and undertook their own investigations, confirming and extending his conclusions. The findings of a few of the main workers in the field are outlined below.

Maslow's Hierarchy of Needs Theory

One of the principal researchers into motivation at work was Abraham Maslow. His investigations led him to the conclusion that an individual will be motivated to give of his best only if his work leads to the satisfaction of five categories of need. These needs, he found, form a hierarchy: the individual will first seek the fulfilment of his low-level (material) needs; having

done so, he will experience the desire to satisfy high level (social and psychological) needs, and these needs will then motivate (drive) him. He will be fully motivated only if work provides him with the means of satisfying every category of need. The hierarchy of needs proposed by Maslow is as follows.

1 Physiological needs (food and shelter). The individual's first concern is to feed, clothe, and house himself and his family to an acceptable standard. When this basic need has been met through the provision of an adequate wage, the next need in the hierarchy will be aroused, namely:

2 Safety and security. This includes job security, 'social' security, and protection from the arbitrary actions of others (e.g. superiors). The effect of the threat of redundancy on morale (and on workers' willingness to moderate their wage claims!) has been witnessed in many businesses in recent years, and illustrates the power of this need. High morale and co-operative attitudes will be secured only if workers' job security is assured.

3 Social needs (belonging and affection).
The power of these and higher level needs is evidenced by the considerable psychological problems that unemployment brings. Once his low-level needs are met, relationships with others assume great importance for the individual. He desires to be accepted, valued, and supported by his work group, and he will often forego the satisfaction of other needs in order to conform to the values and standards of the group and thus secure its approval.

4 Ego needs (esteem and self-respect).
When the above needs are satisfied the need to perform work that earns the esteem of others and gives the individual a sense of status and personal worth makes itself felt. Arising from this need will be the desire for an income which is high enough to allow him to reinforce his sense of status through the purchase of luxury goods and services. Many higher managers have attained their positions through the driving force of this need, and for such people expensively-appointed offices, personal secretaries, and other status symbols are of great importance.

5 Self-actualization needs (self-fulfilment and release of potential).
When all the above are satisfied, the need to realise one's full potential will demand fulfilment. Work will become truly satisfying only if it enables the individual to become in actuality what he is potentially.

Superimposed upon this hierarchy will be the idiosyncrasies of the individual. The life of one individual, for example, may be dominated by the need for safety and security, and that of another by an overwhelming need for belonging and affection. Differences of this sort will affect the individual's choice of job, but they do not invalidate the general principles proposed by Maslow.

Herzberg's Motivation/Hygiene Theory

Maslow's theory does not provide a complete answer to the problem of motivation at work. It postulates a 'satisfaction threshold' which, when reached, marks a falling off of the desire for the need which is now satisfied, and the arousal of the desire to satisfy the next need of the hierarchy. In fact, needs − in particular material needs − are rarely satisfied to the extent that no more is desired. People have ever-increasing levels of material aspiration, and no sooner is a need met than more is desired.

Herzberg's great contribution to motivation theory was to show that to cater for these increased aspirations does not motivate people to give of their best and does not lead to job satisfaction, but that failure to cater for them creates dissatisfaction. His studies (carried out in the late 1950s and since confirmed by other investigators) led him to conclude that satisfaction and dissatisfaction at work are not opposites, but arise from two different sets of factors in the work situation.

What he called **hygiene factors** are those whose presence avoids dissatisfaction: these are external to the job itself and include good pay and working conditions, satisfactory company policy and administration, and good supervision and interpersonal relations. (These correspond to Maslow's physiological, safety, and social needs, and are discussed in Chapters 10 and 11.)

Herzberg drew an analogy between these factors and medical hygiene factors. The absence of the latter causes disease, but their presence will not cure the disease. So, Herzberg said, something more than just the presence of the above hygiene factors is needed to create satisfaction at work, and this 'something more' he referred to as **motivation factors**. His researches showed that these factors are intrinsic to the job and include the nature of the work, the sense of achievement and recognition resulting from the work, and the responsibility entailed in the work. (These correspond to Maslow's ego and self-actualization needs, and are discussed in the section 'Job Design' below.)

Herzberg's theory indicates that the motivation factors only take effect when the hygiene factors are present. The workforce will not be motivated to give of its best by removing the causes of dissatisfaction; however, these causes have to be removed before the factors that *do* motivate can take effect.

Herzberg's theory, like Maslow's, cannot be applied in every case. Some people are 'maintenance seekers', that is they are mainly influenced by hygiene factors (pay, working conditions, quality of supervision, etc.), while others are 'motivation seekers', being mainly influenced by motivation factors. Again, differences of this sort will affect the individual's choice of job, but they do not invalidate the general applicability of the theory.

McGregor's Theory X and Theory Y

The extent to which Herzberg's hygiene and motivation factors are present in a work situation is governed by the attitudes of the management towards the workforce. Manager X, who believes that workers are naturally indolent, shun responsibility, and desire nothing from the work other than the weekly pay-packet, will control his subordinates quite differently from manager Y, who believes that workers do desire satisfying work, do find fulfilment in a job well done, and can be relied upon to exercise responsibility and self-control. If workers are performing poorly, then manager X will ask himself, 'What disciplinary measures should I take to improve performance?' Manager Y, on the other hand, will ask, 'What should I do to improve the work and the conditions of work so that motivation and performance are improved?'

Douglas McGregor, in his book *The Human Side of Enterprise* (published 1960), called the first set of managerial assumptions *Theory X*, and the second set *Theory Y*. Drawing on the considerable body of research evidence that had been built up by that time, he observed that most manager's assumptions tend towards Theory X, whereas most workers, under the right conditions, behave in a way which supports Theory Y.

McGregor listed the main features of the two sets of assumptions as shown in the table.

McGregor pointed out that managers and supervisors who lean towards Theory X (the majority) adopt patterns of behaviour that tend to alienate workers, thus causing them to dislike work, perform poorly, and so on. In this way Theory X becomes a self-fulfilling prophecy. What the research evidence in fact shows, McGregor suggested, is that man is inclined by nature towards Theory Y, and that if workers lack motivation, then this is due to management's inability to provide the right conditions for the manifestation of their true nature.

THEORY X	THEORY Y
Most people dislike work.	Under the right conditions, work is as natural and enjoyable as play.
Most people must be strictly controlled and if necessary threatened with punishment to ensure that they put adequate effort into the job. Motivation occurs at the physiological and security levels only.	If people are committed to their work then external force is not necessary. They will exercise self-direction and self-control. (This commitment is achieved if Herzberg's motivation factors are present.)
Most people are not ambitious, avoid responsibility, and wish to be directed by others. Their overwhelming desire is for security.	Under the right conditions most people will exercise imagination and creativity in the solution of organizational problems, and will accept (and indeed seek) responsibility. Most people are rarely given the chance to achieve their creative and intellectual potentials.

Theory X and Theory Y are, of course, the two extreme ends of the spectrum of possible managerial assumptions. As McGregor indicated, the type of supervisory behaviour that is based upon Theory X assumptions – authoritarian attitudes, threats, and failure to allow subordinates a measure of self-control – is not normally appropriate. However, the Theory Y extreme of the spectrum is not normally entirely appropriate either. Most people want freedom to exercise self-direction and self-control only within certain limits, and a measure of external control seems to be a psychological necessity. A well-defined authority structure engenders a sense of security in the individual, whereas lack of authority and unfettered liberty result in insecurity and, in some cases, psychological disorders. Again, for most people a measure of responsibility does provide for the possibility of ego-satisfaction and achievement of potential, but too much responsibility can result in the inability to cope, which can be psychologically destructive.

It should also be pointed out that in many jobs,

particularly production-line jobs, it is not possible to provide for the satisfaction of higher level needs, and in these situations a supervisory approach approximating to that implied by Theory X gives the best results. However, with the increasing automation of routine work in the factory and office, such jobs will largely disappear over the next decade or so.

Job Design

The human relations approach has demonstrated quite clearly that good pay and working conditions do not motivate people to give of their best at work. Nor, indeed, does a good 'atmosphere' (social relationships). These factors are necessary, but only because their absence causes dissatisfaction which hinders the operation of those factors that *do* motivate.

The genuine motivators are to be found in the work itself: the job must impart a sense of achievement and give the individual self-respect; it must present him with a (surmountable) challenge and provide him with a means of satisfying his creative and problem-solving skills; and it must enable him to exercise some responsibility and a measure of control over his own work.

Jobs which contain these motivators in full measure are rare; Maslow estimated that only one person in a hundred is 'self-actualizing', i.e. achieves his full potential through his work. In order to rectify this situation Herzberg developed the technique of *job enrichment*, the purpose of which is to enable managers to design jobs which provide for workers' needs and which truly motivate. The technique specifies three design steps:

1 Enlarge jobs horizontally so that each individual is given a 'whole' task. There are many workshop and office situations in which this can be done. For example, in a sales office organized on traditional 'division of labour' principles one individual or section might deal with enquiries and issue quotations, another might handle credit control, another might prepare the invoice and despatch documentation, and so on. In a sales office which is organized on job enlargement principles each individual or section will deal with a certain sales area or group of customers, carrying out all tasks generated by those customers from the initial quotation or order through to the despatch documentation. The theory is that each individual or group will

become familiar with the particular sales area or group of customers dealt with, and because he is able to identify his efforts with the 'end-product' of the task (expediting the orders of these customers) he will be motivated to progress the work. Morale and motivation in the office will thus be enhanced, and customer service will be improved. The drawback of this approach is, of course, the loss of the advantages that result from high degrees of specialization: reduced training, the development of high levels of expertise, and no loss of time switching from one type of task to another.

It should be noted that job enlargement does not contradict the general principles of division of labour or the scientific approach to work, but it does counter the tendency to take these principles to extremes.

2 Enlarge jobs vertically so that some of the control functions previously carried out by the supervisor are incorporated into them. Short-term objectives that the individual should aim for should be defined by consultation between superior and subordinate (or groups of subordinates), the subordinate then being free, within the limits of company policy, to plan and control the way in which he achieves these objectives. The increased responsibility will often involve the subordinate in liaison with other sections, thus providing for increased satisfaction of his social needs.

3 Provide feedback information on achievement, so that the individual knows how well he is doing. This is necessary if he is to control his own work effectively, and it also enables his superior to monitor his progress and thus to give appropriate recognition for work well-done, through merit-rating schemes, for example.

Limitations of the Human Relations Approach

The above account touches on only one aspect of the human relations approach. In the face of the almost infinite complexity and diversity of humanity, no one theory of human behaviour can be expected to give all the answers or to work all of the time. The principles outlined above have been applied in a large number of work situations, and the results have been generally favourable and sometimes remarkable. They cannot, however, be regarded as a panacea for all our industrial ills. Many jobs are not amenable to the sort of approach proposed by Herzberg, and it would be true to say that the impact that this approach has had upon working methods and productivity has, so far, been small compared to that of the scientific approach described earlier in this chapter.

The Micro-Electronics Revolution and Job Design

Although the micro-electronics revolution will reduce the amount of work available for people, it will do so in a way which tends to improve the quality of working life. Repetitive and mindless work will be automated, and each individual will have a wider area of responsibility (and therefore an enlarged job). Feedback information on achievement can be provided automatically and speedily. The increased flow of relevant information through the organization will increase both the individual's knowledge of the organization's activities and his sense of involvement.

In America, where wealth has risen in line with the increased productivity of the workforce, the revolution has not measurably reduced the total number of jobs. Instead, the drop in the number of boring and demeaning jobs seems to be matched by an increase in jobs at higher levels in organizational hierarchies. Whether this pattern is repeated in Britain depends upon whether we, as a society, are prepared to exploit the opportunities offered by the new technology in ways that countries such as America, West Germany, and France are doing.

Quality Circles

Japanese companies have been much more successful than their Western counterparts in motivating their workforce. One of the reasons for this success has been the practice of grouping workers into what are known as **quality circles**. About ten million Japanese workers – a significant proportion of the total workforce – belong to such circles.

Spurred on by the Japanese experience, a number of Western companies (including Ford, Marks & Spencer, and ITT) have installed quality circles in their establishments. Each circle consists of about ten workers drawn from the same work area who meet together on a regular basis (usually once a week) to discuss and find solutions to any technical or organizational problems that affect their work area. The objective is to improve quality, efficiency, and productivity, and to promote motivation and involvement in decision-making on the shop-floor or in the office. No financial rewards are offered to circle members for productivity or quality improvements; instead, the whole approach is based upon McGregor's Theory Y (that under the right conditions people will exercise imagination and creativity in the solution of organizational problems, etc.).

The main features of quality circles are as follows:

1 Membership is voluntary; however, a supervisor or foreman of the work area concerned is expected to belong to the circle and to act as its leader.
2 Each member of the circle is given training in problem-solving techniques.
3 The circle meets for about one hour a week to discuss and seek solutions to problems affecting the organization, efficiency, quality, safety, and other aspects of the work area's activities. If necessary management specialists can be called in by the circle to advise.
4 If possible the circle implements the solutions itself, and in the case of solutions which impinge upon other areas it tries to persuade management to implement its suggestions.

ASSIGNMENT GROUP WORK

Discuss and prepare notes for Assignment 7 Section A (page 193).

10
The
Well-Planned
Office

In the last chapter we saw how scientific management and human relations principles can be applied to the design of jobs. In this chapter and the next we see how these principles can be applied to the design of the work situation surrounding the job (Herzberg's hygiene factors). These include company policy and the quality of supervision (discussed in the next chapter), and the working environment (discussed below). It is with the planning and design of the *office* working environment that we are concerned in this text, although the principles outlined here apply to all work situations.

The Main Considerations

A badly-planned office will adversely affect performance because

- efficiency will be impaired through poor workflow and communications
- dissatisfaction will be generated and motivation hindered through poor working conditions.

In planning the office account must therefore be taken of:

1 Efficiency considerations – office furniture and equipment should be physically laid out in the way which best facilitates the flow of work and of information between individuals and between sections.

2 Ergonomic considerations – the results of ergonomic research (the study of the effect on workers of the various environmental factors, such as lighting, heating, decorations, chair design) must be taken into account in choosing heating, lighting, furniture, and other office environmental systems.

A third set of considerations must also be taken into account:

3 Legal considerations – the provisions of the various Acts of Parliament that impinge upon the office must be complied with; these include, in particular, the Health and Safety at Work Act 1974 (referred to in this chapter as HASAWA), and the Offices, Shops and Railway Premises Act 1963 (referred to here as the Offices Act).

The Planning Steps

The broad approach to office planning outlined below is not dissimilar to that advocated for organizational planning in Chapter 3. First, the primary workgroups are built up by grouping the basic operations in ways which promote efficient working methods and a good workflow, and then the workgroups are positioned about the office in such a way that the flow of information is facilitated. We can summarize the planning steps as follows:

1 A preliminary method study of the activities to be carried out in the office should be undertaken in order to eliminate unnecessary operations and to determine how the operations that *are* necessary should be carried out and how they should be grouped. This should be coupled with work measurement to determine the number and type of posts required for each work group.

2 The area required for each post and its associated furniture and equipment should be calculated, and the results summed to give the totals for each workgroup.

3 The flow of information between workgroups should be analysed and the layout which best assists this flow determined.

4 Furniture, lighting and heating arrangements, colour schemes, wall and floor coverings, and other environmental factors must be planned.

5 A check should be made that health, safety, and other legal requirements have been complied with.

Step 1 has already been dealt with (part of Chapter 8 and Chapter 9); the other planning steps are dealt with in turn below.

Step 2: Space

Having established what staff and equipment are necessary, the next essential is to determine the amount of space needed for each post and item of equipment. Too little space will lead to inefficiencies arising from inadequate working and storage areas, and also to dissatisfaction and reduced motivation; too much space represents wasted resources, and it can reduce efficiency through unnecessary movement.

The Offices Act specifies that there should be at least 40 sq. ft. per person. This is minimal, and the amount of working space provided should, ideally, vary from about 60 sq. ft. for clerks and typists, through 100 sq. ft. for supervisors, up to around 200 sq. ft. for senior managers (this greater space being mainly needed for visitors and to satisfy their ego needs). Up to 15% should be added to the calculated working space to allow for access to and circulation among the various working areas, and, if the accommodation is to consist of a number of small 'closed' offices (rather than a single large 'open' office), a further allowance of 15% should be added for corridor space.

A single open (or 'general') office will utilize the available space in the most efficient way. It has the fol-

lowing advantages over 'closed' offices:

(a) Up to 30% of the space requirements of closed offices is for corridors and for doorway access; open offices therefore offer substantial space savings

(b) Space can be used in a very flexible way, and layouts can be easily rearranged

(c) Fewer partitions, radiators, and other fittings are required

(d) Workflow and communications between sections is facilitated

(e) Supervision is more easily exercised

(f) Common services and equipment can be more readily provided.

However, open offices have a number of potential disadvantages, and, unless such offices are planned with great care, these can outweigh the advantages. Distracting noises and movements can seriously impair mental effort and reduce output; any activities which offend in this respect should therefore be excluded from an open office. Also, open offices are not suitable for dealing with confidential matters. Most open offices have desks arranged in regimented rows parallel to the office walls, as this gives the most efficient use of space; most people, however, prefer a more informal layout which provides them with a clearly-defined territory and affords some privacy. And some people, especially in higher management, have strong ego needs and resent the lack of a private office.

Large open offices, accommodating upwards of fifty people, can be **landscaped**. This is a technique which aims to make the office as aesthetically pleasing as possible. Landscaped offices combine the advantages of the open office with the lack of regimentation, the privacy, and the status provided by small closed offices; and they can successfully house the entire administration, from typists to top management. Workgroups are arranged in a carefully-planned but deliberately informal way, the air of informality being enhanced by the ample provision of indoor plants and foliage. An adequate degree of privacy is secured by partially enclosing workgroups with shoulder-height screens and filing cabinets. Distracting noises are largely eliminated by high standards of soundproofing. A further feature of such offices is the detailed attention given to ergonomic aspects – lighting, ventilation, furniture, decorations, carpeting, etc. (See Figure 10.1.)

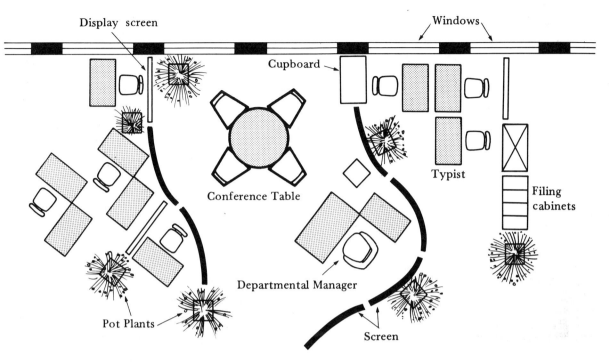

Figure 10.1   Part of a landscaped office

In general, offices have to be planned to fit within the confines of an existing structure, the dimensions of which may be far from ideal for the purpose at hand. In these circumstances it is often possible to convert a number of unpromising and perhaps dingy small offices into a spacious open office in which the various activities and workgroups can be laid out in a way which promotes efficient working, and which, when suitably decorated and furnished, forms a pleasing working environment.

Step 3: Layout

The layout should be planned so that workgroups that communicate frequently are located near each other. The extent to which individuals and workgroups communicate with one another can be measured by means of a **relationship chart**. A relationship chart showing the frequency of communication in a production control office is shown in Figure 10.2. If an office includes copiers, central storage areas, or other common services, these should be included in the chart.

It is not difficult to construct such a chart − all that is necessary is to ask each member of staff in turn to estimate the frequency of contact that he or she has with other individuals in the office. From it a **balloon diagram** can be drawn to show the relative importance of the various information flows in the office. The balloon diagram that derives from Figure 10.2 is shown in Figure 10.3. From this the general layout of the office can be determined − those workgroups that intercommunicate most frequently should be located near one another, whereas those with infrequent communications can be relatively remote. Thus, in the example given in the Figures, the Stock Planning, Stock Records, and Data Control sections should be located close to one another, and Typing should be close to both Stock Planning and Contracts Issue. (For an exercise based on this example see page 200.)

The detailed layout of the office is best decided by making scaled-down cardboard templates of the desks, chairs, filing cabinets, etc., and juggling these around

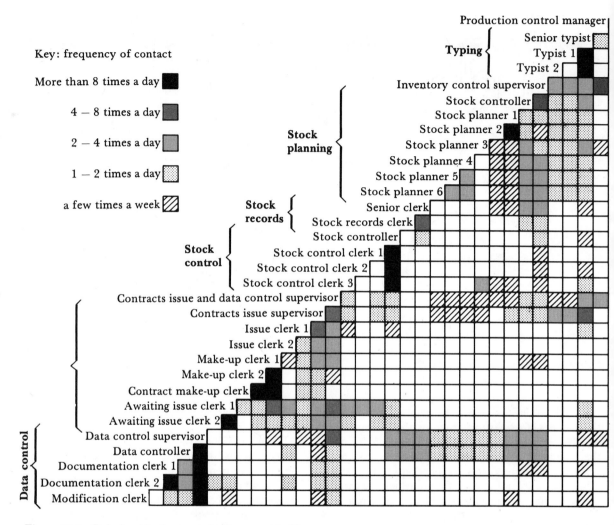

Figure 10.2   Relationship chart: production control office

on a scale plan of the office. Once the office is set up and working, the layout can be 'fine-tuned', if this is considered desirable, by constructing a **string diagram**. This consists of a scale-plan of the office lay-out attached to softwood, with pins inserted at the workstations, filing cabinets, and other items of office equipment. The journeys made by the office workers between the various fixtures are reproduced on the plan by means of cotton wound from one pin to another. If a particular route (e.g. from workstation to filing cabinet) is traversed by a clerk 10 times during the observation period, the length of cotton will be

wound from one pin to the other and back again 10 times. This enables the amount of movement between the various items of furniture and equipment to be determined, and from this a detailed layout that mini-mizes total movement can be designed.

Step 4: Furniture, Heating, Lighting, and other Ergonomic Considerations

There is wide range of **office furniture** available, and choice should be governed primarily by efficiency

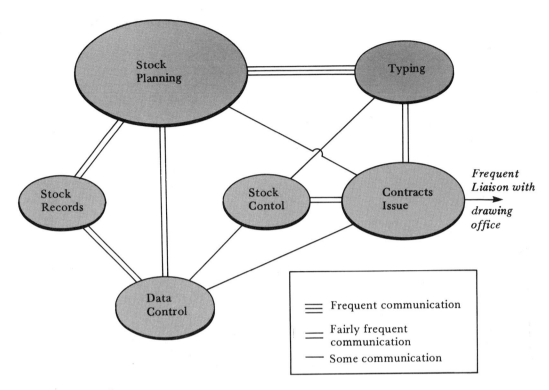

Figure 10.3 Balloon diagram

and ergonomic considerations. The more expensive high quality furniture is generally the most economical in the long run: its ergonomic superiority over cheaper furniture makes for reduced fatigue and therefore higher productivity, and its superior design makes for more effective use of (expensive) office space, with perhaps telephones and other items of equipment incorporated into the design.

A number of manufacturers produce office furniture designed on a 'modular' basis, so that the desks, chairs, storage units, shelving, screens, etc. link together to form an integrated furniture system. Such a system can offer distinct efficiency and aesthetic advantages over an arrangement of unrelated pieces of office furniture.

The possible health hazards of cathode ray tubes and other equipment in the office fade into insignificance compared to the greatest health hazard of them all: the fact that office workers spend most of their time seated at desks. This is a major cause of back complaints, which account for more lost working days than strikes! Besides being a health hazard, unsuitable desks and

chairs cause fatigue and therefore reduced productivity. In order to alleviate these problems a great deal of ergonomic research activity has been devoted to determining the optimal design of desks, chairs, and desk-top equipment. Figure 10.4 gives the key dimensions indicated by this research for electronic workstations.

Heating, lighting, and **ventilation** are the most frequent causes of environmental dissatisfaction in the office. The planning of these is complicated by the fact that lights generate a significant amount of heat, which has to be taken account of, and the positioning of screens and partitions can create marked variations, particularly in temperature, in different parts of the office. If screens exceed shoulder-height, then the heating, lighting, and ventilation arrangements will be very seriously disturbed.

Ergonomic studies indicate that the optimum temperature for office work is 19 – 20°C (67 – 70°F); that lighting intensity should be 500 lux (750 lux for typing pools and drawing offices); and that

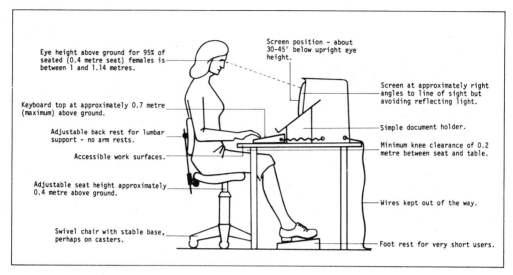

Figure 10.4   Good workstation principles (Reproduced from Word Processing Now *by kind permission of Tom Stewart)*

fresh air (without draughts) is essential if fatigue is to be avoided.

A number of office heating systems are available: radiators, storage heaters, convectors, and ducted air. Ducted air systems have a number of points in their favour:

(a) They heat all parts of the office evenly (other systems give rise to substantial heat variations, caused by the masking effects of filing cabinets and other furniture)
(b) They ensure a continuous supply of fresh air
(c) They can incorporate humidifiers (most heating systems reduce the relative humidity of the air, and this can result in an unpleasant dryness in the nose and throat, and lowered resistance to infection).

With regard to lighting, desks should be arranged to take full advantage of the natural light available. Fluorescent tubes or bulbs are the most satisfactory form of artificial lighting: although more costly than conventional incandescent bulbs to install, they are cheaper to run, they provide a more even illumination, and the light they emit is similar in character to natural light.

Naked tubes and bulbs are not desirable as they cause glare and also harsh contrasts of light and shade, and shades or grids should be fitted to diffuse the light.

However, some variation in the light intensity, if carefully planned, can add to the visual interest of the office environment.

Some of the best modern office blocks are constructed on a modular basis. The ceiling of each level consists of an array of ceiling modules, each of dimensions 5 ft by 7 ft (approximately) and comprising the following elements:

(a) A fluorescent tube located centrally along the length, with a grid fixed below to eliminate glare
(b) Air ducts on each side of the tube for heating/ventilation
(c) A metal surround (about 1 inch wide) into which modular partitioning can be fitted.

This system, besides providing a satisfying working environment, enables offices to be expanded or contracted at will simply by relocating partitioning (although the dimensions of each office must be a multiple of the module size).

Considerable attention should be given to **acoustics**, particularly in open offices. Distracting noises − loud noises, intermittent noises, speech, etc. − hinders mental processes and leads to fatigue. The most effective cure is to treat such noises at source by providing remedies such as sound absorbing screens. Although word processors are quiet in operation, conventional typewriters are not, and the distraction that these cause can be cut down by the use of desk screens (which sit at the rear of the typewriter and partially enclose it). Thick carpeting and sound-absorbent wall and ceiling coverings also help to reduce noise.

A complete absence of sound, however, is not desirable. The best office acoustic environment seems to be a low level of background noise − this has the effect of masking sounds which might otherwise be distracting.

Colour schemes and **decorations**, if well-planned, can have a positive effect on morale. Soft, warm colours seem to be most satisfactory for working areas; excessively bright or contrasting colours, if used, should be restricted to corridors and other non-working areas.

Apart from cost, the main factors governing the choice of floor, wall, and ceiling coverings are attractiveness, ease of cleaning, and wear-resistance. Carpet tiles are a very popular form of floor covering, for they can be moved around to even out wear, and they can also be moved easily if partitioning is relocated.

For walls, vinyl papers are hard-wearing and are easily cleaned, and they can be obtained with foam-backing if increased insulation is required. At the more expensive end of the wall covering range are timber slats and veneers. These are very long-lasting and can be very attractive.

ASSIGNMENT GROUP WORK

Assignment 6 (page 190).

Step 5: Legal Requirements

One in every two workers can expect to suffer, over the course of his working life, a serious industrial accident or disease. Each year more than 1,400 workers in this country die from these causes. In order to provide minimum health and safety standards for the various groups of workers a large body of government legislation has been built up over the past 100 years. Two examples of this legislation are the Factories Act 1961 (covering factory workers) and the Offices, Shops and Railway Premises Act 1963.

These Acts deal with health and safety at work in a rather fragmented way, and prior to 1974 more than five million workers were not covered by any legislation whatsoever. In order to rectify this situation the government passed the Health and Safety at Work Act 1974, which provides an integrated approach to the health and safety of *all* people at work.

In planning and maintaining the workplace the provisions of these various Acts must be complied with − and so far as the office is concerned this means primarily the provisions of the last two Acts referred to above, namely the Offices Act and HASAWA.

The Health and Safety at Work Act (HASAWA) is an *enabling* act. It does not replace any existing legislation, but it provides a co-ordinating framework for this legislation, it gives powers to the authorities to make additional regulations in the future, and it lays down the principles that should underlie such regulations.

In brief, these principles are that everyone − employers and employees − have a duty to play an active role in maintaining health and safety at work. So far as the employer is concerned, the Act states that he should ensure, so far as is reasonably practicable, the health, safety, and welfare at work of all of his employees. ('Reasonably practicable' means that the employer may take cost considerations into account in framing any health and safety measures to be adopted.) So far as the employee is concerned, HASAWA states that he has a general duty to take reasonable care for the health and safety of himself and of others who may be affected by his acts or omissions at work, and that he should co-operate with his employer and with others so that they can discharge their health and safety duties.

The main weight of the Act falls upon the employer, and in the event of a legal dispute the onus is upon him to prove that it was not reasonably practicable to do more than was actually done. The employer's duties can be summarized as follows:

1 To maintain a safe and healthy working environment − it must be kept clean, lighting must be adequate, temperature must be kept above 16°C, there must be adequate ventilation, dust must be controlled, and toilet facilities must be available for male and female staff with hot and cold water, soap, and clean towels.

2 To maintain corridors, gangways, entrances, and exits in a safe condition

3 To provide and maintain plant and systems of work that are safe and not detrimental to health

4 To provide first aid boxes and personnel trained in first aid

5 To control noise and air pollution, to provide for the safe storage and use of dangerous substances, and to provide protective clothing as necessary
6 To provide such information, training, and supervision as is necessary to ensure the health, safety, and welfare of employees
7 To provide employees with a written statement of the employer's policy on health and safety.

Under the Act, **safety representatives** must be appointed from among the employees, either by the employer, or by the local authority or a recognized trade union. Such representatives must be granted time off work with pay in order to perform their functions, which are:

1 To make representations to the employer on matters relating to health and safety in the workplace
2 To formally inspect the workplace at intervals of three months or less, after giving reasonable written notice to the employer
3 To inspect at any time the scene of an accident.

The Offices Act (1963) covers office and shop staff only (about 8 million workers) and for these it lays down precise standards of cleanliness, space, temperature, etc. Many of its regulations overlap the (more general) provisions of HASAWA. The main regulations are:

1 Floors, stairs, and other areas used by employees must be cleaned at least once a week
2 In working areas the lighting must be adequate for safety and to avoid strain
3 The temperature must reach 16°C within one hour of starting work, and ventilation must be adequate for health
4 The space provided per person must be at least 40 sq. ft. (or 400 cubic feet if the ceiling is under 10 feet high)
5 A specified number of toilet facilities must be available, with hot water and towels, according to the number of workers on the premises
6 Fresh drinking water must be available for all employees
7 Cloakroom facilities must be provided for overcoats and other clothing not worn during working hours
8 A suitable room must be provided if food is eaten on the premises
9 Suitably designed chairs must be provided for workers who sit while working, incorporating foot rests if their feet are off the ground. If workers normally stand, at least one chair must be provided for every three employees, and whenever possible the workers should be allowed to sit down
10 Stairs must have an outside railing, and must not be slippery
11 All dangerous parts of machinery must be securely fenced, and no employee is to be allowed to work such machinery unless he has been properly instructed and trained, or is adequately supervised
12 All premises where more than 150 people are employed must have a properly trained first aid person on hand, and first aid boxes must be provided
13 Premises must have an effective fire alarm system which is tested or examined once every three months. Escape routes must be kept free from obstructions, and fire fighting equipment must be readily accessible. If more than 20 people are employed (or more than 10 people on other than the ground floor) a fire certificate must be obtained and displayed on the premises.

The Fire Precautions Act (1971) extends the provisions of (13) above. It demands that there are adequate means of escape and that these are kept free from obstructions; that all doors out of the building can be opened from the inside (push-bars are reckoned to be the best type of opening mechanism for doors which are normally locked); that all employees are familiar with the means of escape and the routines to be followed in the case of fire; that there is an effective fire alarm system; and that fire extinguishers and other fire-fighting equipment is kept in readily accessible locations.

The Health and Safety Executive, local authority inspectors, and the Factory Inspectorate are responsible for enforcing these Acts. An Inspector is empowered to enter at any time premises to which the Acts apply in order to carry out whatever examinations are necessary, to require any person to answer questions, and to issue Improvement Notices requiring infringements of the regulations to be put right within a given time. If necessary he may issue a Prohibition Order ordering the activity to cease until remedial action has been taken.

If an accident occurs that causes the death of an employee or disables him from doing his usual work for more than three days, then, under the Offices Act, this must be reported to the appropriate authority. *All* accidents, however minor, should be recorded in an accident record book. (Failure to do so will hinder any claim for compensation that may subsequently be made by an employee.)

Causes of Accidents

Common causes of accidents are incorrect use of equipment, poorly maintained equipment or electrical points, sharp corners on desks and equipment, slippery floors, and trailing electrical leads. All these are obvious defects and most are easily remedied: furniture should have rounded edges, the legs of desks can carry electrical leads, non-slip floor coverings should be used, etc.

Many individuals, workgroups, and sometimes entire offices are, however, indifferent to safety. They refuse to take the most elementary precautions, and they become 'accident-prone'. Research has shown that this is caused by low morale and fatigue, and that a company with a bad accident record is not cured overnight merely by enforcing the provisions of the above Acts. It is necessary to raise morale and to reduce fatigue by ensuring that Herzberg's hygiene factors are present in the work situation – by providing a good working environment (as explained in this chapter), and by providing good pay, good working relationships, good supervision, and other factors (see next chapter).

11
The
Well-Managed
Worker

The control of the most important business resource of all, human labour, is the subject of this chapter. To many, the use of the word *control* in connection with human beings will seem unfortunate. The theory of control – systems theory – was originally applied to engineering systems, and its terminology is such that, when applied to human systems, it appears to dehumanize the individual. The worker is a business 'input', to be 'controlled' in such a way that he achieves his 'target output'. This language smacks of the attitudes of a century ago, which have since been vigorously countered by the proponents of the human relations approach.

In fact systems theory, far from denying the validity of the human relations approach, provides it with a valuable theoretical framework:

1 It emphasizes the need to give people responsibility for the way in which they achieve objectives (targets). It therefore stresses self-control as against external control, and the need to organize work so that people produce identifiable end-products and are provided with feedback on their performance – Herzberg's motivation factors.

2 It emphasizes the need for managers and supervisors to investigate the causes of under-achievement and to make rational input adjustments. To the manager who adopts Theory X attitudes a major cause of under-achievement will appear to be the natural laziness of workers; however, the human relations approach indi-

cates that it is far more likely to be the failure of management to provide the right conditions – Herzberg's hygiene factors – for the objectives to be achieved. Given this finding, the systems approach emphasizes that the conditions should be adjusted in such a way that the objectives will be achieved.

Herzberg's motivation factors – (1) above – have been dealt with in Chapter 9. In this chapter we examine the hygiene factors: that is, those factors which must be present in the work situation to avoid dissatisfaction (and the consequent inhibition of the operation of the motivation factors). These hygiene factors are:

- Good pay
- Good working conditions
- Good company policy
- Good administration
- Good supervision
- Good interpersonal relations.

Good Pay

Dissatisfaction over pay arises when people perceive themselves as unfairly treated in comparison to others. These comparisons are made when similar work is being done for different rates of pay, that is, when the duties and skills of one job overlap those of another (differently paid) job. Inter-job comparisons are most

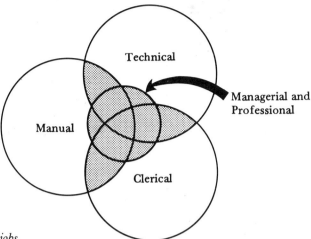

Figure 11.1   Overlapping jobs

commonly made in the areas of overlap between manual, clerical, technical, and managerial and professional jobs (the grey areas shown in Figure 11.1).

To give an example: in a manufacturing company, components may be assembled by manual workers and tested by technical workers. The technicians feel that they must have rigid lines of demarcation between themselves and the manual workers to protect their jobs and their salaries, but the manual workers see these lines as artificial, perceiving their work as being similar in nature to that done by the technicians, and making the inevitable comparison between their rates of pay (and status) and those of the technicians.

These demarcation problems are resolved by an equitable grading structure (to minimize pay differentials where overlaps occur) combined with a fairly-administered promotion policy which provides a means for every employee to progress up through the grades (for details *see* page 21).

Good Working Conditions

The provision of good working conditions (i.e. a good office or workshop environment) has been dealt with in detail in Chapter 10.

Good Company Policy

To avoid dissatisfaction company policy should include the following:

1 Job security. The ultimate penalty of dismissal should only be applied in the case of grave misdeeds (e.g. defrauding the company, or continual insubordination), and redundancies should be made only if absolutely essential. Staff reductions should normally be achieved by natural wastage. Dismissal for trivial offences and over-hasty staff cutbacks are frequent causes of industrial disputes.

2 Consultation in all matters affecting the workforce. In some companies worker representatives are appointed to the Board of Directors, the philosophy being that the general objectives and policies pursued by the company are of great concern to the workforce, which should therefore have some say in decision-making at the highest level. However, the idea has not really caught on, either with management or with workers. The general view is that it is the responsibility of management alone to take these high-level decisions, and that worker participation in management should be encouraged only at lower decision-making levels in the company.

Greatest success in worker participation is achieved by companies that operate joint consultation schemes. Committees made up of representatives of workers and management are set up at the various company sites to discuss all matters affecting the workforce: rates of pay, working conditions, productivity agreements, changes in organization and working practices, and welfare. The joint consultative system offers the following benefits:

A PAY DISPUTE IN ANCIENT TIMES

A landowner went out early in the morning to hire men to work in his vineyard. He agreed to pay them a denarius for the day and sent them into his vineyard.

About the third hour he went out and saw others standing in the market place doing nothing. He told them, 'You also go and work in my vineyard, and I will pay you whatever is right'. So they went.

He went out again in the sixth hour and the ninth hour and did the same thing. About the eleventh hour he went out and found still others standing around. He said to them, 'You also go and work in my vineyard'.

When evening came, the owner of the vineyard said to his foreman, 'Call the workers and pay them their wages, beginning with the last ones hired and going on to the first'.

The workers who were hired about the eleventh hour came and each received a denarius. So when those came who were hired first, they expected to receive more. But each one of them also received a denarius. When they received it, they began to grumble against the landowner.

But he answered one of them, 'Friend, I am not being unfair to you. Didn't you agree to work for a denarius?'

(Extract from Matthew's Gospel, Ch. 20, *New International Version*)

(a) Every employee of the company has access to a representative on his site

(b) Workers are involved in the decision-making process, which leads to enhanced motivation and improved decision-making

(c) The attitude of managers to the decision-making process is changed: consulting with staff *before* decisions are taken becomes a natural part of the process, and this minimizes the possibility of conflict.

Further details on the workings of the joint consultative system are given in the case study below.

3 An equitable promotion policy. The importance of this cannot be overstressed, for promotion is the means by which an employee gains recognition and esteem for his work. Promotion should be primarily on the basis of merit, and all employees should have the opportunity to reach the highest grades.

4 Good training arrangements. It is a natural human desire to do jobs well, and training improves morale and motivation because it enables this need to be satisfied. It also makes the employee feel that he is valued by the company, and it increases his sense of commitment to it. Notes on training are given on page 21.

5 Good social and welfare amenities. These are a further important hygiene factor. They engender in the employee a feeling that he is valued by the company, and they promote good personal relationships and informal communication between staff at all levels in the organization.

CASE STUDY: JOINT CONSULTATION AND STAFF BRIEFING IN AN INSURANCE COMPANY

The joint consultative system described in this case study was introduced by an insurance company in 1974 to provide a means of communication and consultation between staff and management on all matters of mutual interest. The briefing system which is also described here extends over all levels of staff and is designed basically for the downward transmission of management decisions and information to staff.

The joint consultative system operates on a two-tier structure whereby groups of head office departments or local branches are represented on eight committees, organized on a geographical basis, which in turn elect representatives to the Joint Consultative Council. There are four committees for head office staff and four committees for branch staff. Each committee consists of a chairman, a secretary, and one or two management representatives, all appointed by the company, and a number of elected staff representatives. The Council consists of a chairman, a secretary, and up to four management representatives, all appointed by the company, and eleven representatives elected by the committees.

The committees and the Council each meet at least three times a year. The committees and the Council have no negotiating rights or decision-making functions, other than deciding whether or not to refer any matters discussed by the committees to the Council (or, if appropriate, to local management) or any matters discussed by the Council to general management. However, the consultative system provides an important forum for discussion and for making known staff views prior to decisions being made by management.

All matters of mutual interest to staff and management can be discussed at the consultative meetings, including:

1 Salaries and terms of service generally, except matters affecting particular individuals
2 Productivity and efficiency
3 Physical conditions of work, welfare, and social amenities
4 Changes to the constitution and rules of the consultative system and consideration of other forms of staff representation.

Specific issues discussed have included remuneration settlements, the staff pension scheme, the staff development programme and the staff house purchase loan scheme.

The briefing system extends over all levels of staff. The information communicated to staff consists mainly of matters raised at the management level briefing groups which may include matters discussed at Board level. Other items of information briefed include clarification of information generated by circulars and matters of particular and general importance within a department or branch.

EXERCISE

Compare the objectives and powers of the consultative committees described above with those of the staff/management Review Committee described in the British Airways case study on page 43.

What are the advantages and disadvantages of these two approaches to consultation?

Good Administration

This is a further important hygiene factor. The most obvious symptoms of poor administration are:

1 Excessive bureaucracy and paperwork, which occupy staff on mundane and trivial matters, clog the communication channels, and hinder decision-making on important issues. The result is that initiative is stifled and morale is depressed. One solution is to call in the services of O & M analysts to review organization and procedures.

2 Disharmony between the various parts of the organization, caused by unco-ordinated or unrealistic objectives. The departmental manager and the supervisor are at the centre of this type of conflict (see Figure 11.2). There will be antagonism between himself and colleagues in other departments or sections if what he is trying to achieve is at variance with their objectives, he will be under pressure from his superior to achieve his objectives, and he will be faced with resentment from his staff as a result of the pressure that he in turn has to exert on them. The solution to this problem is properly co-ordinated objectives, and realistic output targets based upon work measurement.

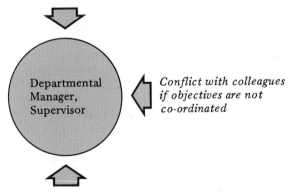

Pressure from superiors to achieve objectives

Departmental Manager, Supervisor

Conflict with colleagues if objectives are not co-ordinated

Friction with subordinates if objectives are too diificult to achieve

Figure 11.2   Conflict between different levels and departments in an organization

3 Conflict over changes in organization and working methods, e.g. changes in structure, working methods, equipment, and staffing levels. Change represents a threat to the individual's security, and to avoid conflict in this area it is necessary to provide for this security by giving job guarantees and to involve the individual in planning the change through joint consultation (see page 43).

In administering change the following steps can be taken:

(a) Staff reactions to possible changes can be tested out in joint consultative committee discussions, or by releasing information on an unofficial basis to the 'grapevine' (the informal communications network). If reactions are unfavourable, the ideas can be modified or shelved without loss of face to management.
(b) If reactions are favourable, meetings should be held with all affected staff to explain management's intentions and the reasons for the change, to give no-redundancy guarantees, and to set up consultative procedures.
(c) When the proposals have been fully discussed, modified as necessary, and a reasonable measure of agreement reached, implement the change (if necessary for a trial period of 3 to 6 months − even the most change-resistant individual cannot reasonably object to a trial, and by the end of the trial period the resistance to change will operate in the reverse direction, i.e. against reverting to the old practices).

Good Supervision

Individuals tend to adopt unconsciously the attitudes of the group to which they belong, which will be based largely upon the attitudes of those who play a leadership role in the group. If the supervisor or manager has the leadership qualities desired by the group and is fully accepted as the leader, then the attitudes and objectives of the group will gradually conform to his attitudes and objectives. He can motivate it to seek actively the solution to problems, and to achieve a high output. A poor supervisor or manager, who lacks these leadership qualities, will cause low morale, low productivity, and conflict.

The requirements of a good supervisor or manager are:

1 an appropriate leadership style

2 appropriate personal qualities
3 the ability to take appropriate disciplinary action.

1 Leadership style. The three main leadership styles are authoritarian, democratic, and *laissez-faire*.

The *authoritarian* leader is one who makes decisions and sets objectives without consulting subordinates. He will tend to hold 'Theory X' assumptions about his subordinates, and he will tend to exercise control by constantly monitoring the way in which they work. This type of leadership style is most appropriate in situations like production-lines in factories, where the work is not satisfying and the only real incentive to the worker is the pay-packet at the end of the week.

Supervisors or managers who adopt this style must have strong, domineering personalities. Some supervisors tend to be extremely authoritarian and dictatorial, and ensure compliance with their wishes by humiliating or dismissing subordinates who do not toe the line; this extreme style causes antagonism and tends to be unsuccessful in the long-term.

The *democratic* leader is one who delegates as much authority as possible to subordinates, and involves them in decision-making and in setting objectives. He makes 'Theory Y' assumptions about his subordinates, and exercises control by monitoring results − subordinates are free, within limits, to determine the way in which they will achieve their objectives. This type of leadership style is reckoned to be the most successful, and is generally applied above the foreman level and in many office situations.

The *laissez-faire* leader is one who lets his subordinates determine their own objectives and control their own work, intervening only when asked for advice. He tends to avoid any planning or control responsibilities, and so the activities of the members of the group are uncoordinated (since each sets his objectives independently of the others). In general, this is the least successful leadership style, and it will only work if the individuals in the group are highly motivated.

2 Personal qualities. A number of studies have been carried out on the qualities required of a successful leader, and these indicate that the following are essential:

(a) **Intelligence** − too high a level of intelligence can create a barrier between a leader and his subordinates, and can bring about his rejection by the group, but a sufficient level of intelligence to make sound decisions and to command the respect of subordinates is essential.

(b) **Confidence** − a successful leader must have sufficient confidence to make firm decisions − if necessary on the basis of inadequate information − and to instill in his subordinates a belief in the rightness of those decisions.

(c) **Motivation** − successful leaders are highly motivated towards the achievement of the objectives of the group, and will pursue them, if necessary, at the expense of personal popularity. This strong inner drive will tend to infect the group with the same enthusiasm, causing it to be highly achieving.

(d) **Technical ability** − the natural leader in any situation is the individual who can best enable the group to achieve its objectives. Thus in times of industrial unrest it may be the hot-headed militant who emerges as the group leader. Generally speaking, a successful leader must have a high level of expertise in the area of work in which the group is engaged. In some organizations leadership rotation is encouraged − the group leader at any given time is the individual who is best able to guide the group in the project on which it is currently engaged.

3 Disciplinary action. The third main requirement of a good supervisor or manager is the ability to take appropriate disciplinary action. Individuals and work groups vary greatly in the way in which they react to a given situation, and in some cases these reactions amount to insubordination or neglect of duties. It then becomes necessary for their superior to take disciplinary action. (He may choose to avoid the problem by turning a blind eye, but this will generally lead to greater insubordination and neglect of duties later on and more acute authority clashes).

The most appropriate course of disciplinary action can only be determined by a thorough examination of the facts of the case, and by taking full account of the effects of that action both on the individual(s) concerned and on others in the work group. It involves the following steps:

(a) **Establish the facts** − the facts about the individual and his misdemeanour must be established by talking not only to him but to his colleagues. Any gaps or contradictions in the story should be isolated and further facts obtained.

(b) **Determine the objective of the disciplinary**

action – the desired effect of the action on the individual, his colleagues, and the work of the section should be defined.

(c) **Decide on the action to be taken** – the various alternatives should be formulated, and the one chosen which best conforms to the policies of the organization and which will best achieve (b) above.

(d) **Take action** – the most appropriate person to take the disciplinary action should be determined, senior managers and Personnel should be notified if necessary, and the timing of the action determined.

(e) **Follow up the action** – the subsequent attitude and work of the disciplined individual should be monitored to determine the effectiveness of the action.

CASE STUDY: DISCIPLINE

Derek is a middle manager employed by a company making rubber products. He is in charge of four departments, one of which – the Sterilizing Unit – was placed under his control only a few weeks prior to the date of this case study (March 1980). The manager previously responsible for the Unit had only been with the company for seven months, was absent for most of this time owing to personal problems, and resigned in February 1980.

The Unit had therefore been without an effective manager for about eight months, and the supervisor in charge, Jane, had taken advantage of this situation by spending most of her time in the canteen, where she did her paperwork while being fed cups of tea by the canteen supervisor, and, according to rumour, by hitting the bottle on the premises. (Smoking and drinking alcohol are both strictly forbidden in the Sterilizing Unit, the penalty for infringement of this rule being instant dismissal). The effect of this on the morale of the Unit was considerable – it was at an all-time low, and the output was only 65% of the target.

Derek visited the Unit every day during his first week in charge, and on no occasion was Jane in evidence supervising the work. Nor was she in her office adjoining the Unit; instead she was in the canteen, surrounded by her paperwork. It quickly became clear to Derek that none of the workers in the Unit had any respect for Jane, and the low morale was evident and was reflected in the general attitude to work.

Towards the end of the first week Derek told Jane that she had to do her paperwork in her office, and that she had to spend more time in the Unit so that the work could be properly supervised and the output increased to somewhere near the target output. He did not mention the drinking matter, because he had no evidence other than rumour. Jane did not respond in any way to these instructions, and she did not alter her behaviour.

In the early afternoon of the Friday of his second week in charge, Derek interviewed a worker who had just handed in her notice. He asked her why she wanted to leave, and although she gave no direct answer, she did indicate that she was dissatisfied with Jane's attitude. Immediately after this interview Derek spoke to Jane – he found her in the canteen – and asked her for her opinion of the worker, and whether she thought a higher wage should be offered to induce her to stay. Jane's only comment was: 'Good job she is leaving – maybe the atmosphere in the department will get better.'

As she said these words, Derek suddenly realised that her breath smelt strongly of alcohol. He knew that she had not been off the premises all day, and he accused her of drinking on the job. Jane hotly denied this, and in a fit of anger rose from her chair to leave.

EXERCISE

What should Derek do next?

(Historical note: The action that Derek actually took resulted in Jane completely altering her attitudes and behaviour. Within a month, her relationships with the workers under her were much improved, she was exercising effective control over them and doing her paperwork in her office, and the Unit's output had reached 92% of target. She had also sought help with her drink problem.)

Good Interpersonal Relations

Good personal relationships between members of a workgroup are a further important hygiene factor. Disagreements of a minor nature will always occur in any group of people; most amount to no more than differences of opinion over trivial matters, and are usually resolved quite amicably. Some, however, blow up into major rows, and these can have a disastrous effect on morale.

If conflict does occur, then those involved should take stock of the situation and ask themselves the following questions:

1 Is the issue really worth fighting over? (It is a sign of strength of character if you are willing to give way over inessentials − this removes a cause of the conflict, and damps down the aggression of the other party.)

2 Why am I standing up for my point of view? Is it really important that the other party accepts my position? (It is a sign of weakness if you feel that you have to stand up for yourself because you cannot afford to lose face.)

3 Is my point of view really the right one? (It is a sign of strength if you are prepared to admit that you are wrong.)

Individuals with overbearing personalities can be a problem in a workgroup, especially when two such people work closely together. A conflict between them can result in a violent personality clash, which can permanently sour their relationship and mar the atmosphere of the office. The only solution in such a case may be to move one of the individuals to another department.

CASE STUDY: A PERSONALITY CLASH IN A BANK AND ITS EFFECT ON PRODUCTIVITY

This case study describes how a personality clash led to a prolonged conflict and prevented method improvements in the sub-branch of a bank. The organization chart of the sub-branch is shown in Figure 11.3. The two sections referred to in the study are the *cashiers*, who undertake the branch's counter work, and the *machine operators*, who work in the machine room − they man the computer terminal (which is linked to the bank's regional computer) and deal with the receipt and despatch of mail.

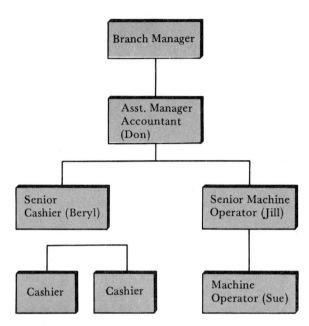

Figure 11.3   Branch organization chart

The manager of the branch has a 'laissez-faire' leadership style. He makes no attempt to train the staff or to improve the efficiency of the branch, and does not intervene in any way in the day-to-day running of the sections, in spite of a long-standing feud that exists between them. This has led to an almost complete breakdown of co-operation between the two sections; for example, if one section is overloaded with work, the other will make no attempt to help out.

The feud developed when Jill (the Senior Machine Operator) started work in the branch about four years ago. Both she and Beryl (the Senior Cashier) have strong personalities, and a conflict flared up when Jill took over Beryl's job while Beryl was away for a week. Beryl is the oldest member of staff — she is coming up to retirement — and many of her working methods are out-of-date, although she is a conscientious worker. Upon her return Jill told her that the methods she had used for the past 25 years were inefficient, and that she should go about her work in a different way. Not unnaturally, Beryl resented this, and the resulting row between the two has never been patched up.

About three months prior to the date of this case study the Assistant Manager was promoted to the position of Manager at another branch, and the present Assistant Manager (Don) took his place. Don is an accountant in his early thirties. During his first few weeks at the branch Don examined all the working methods and devised a number of improvements. He discussed these with the Manager, and requested permission to put them into effect. The Manager readily agreed — he was only too pleased that Don wanted to take on this responsibility. It did not occur to the Manager to mention the rivalry that existed between the two sections (he did not consider it to be of great importance), and Don had failed to observe, in the short time that he had been in the branch, that such rivalry existed. Unfortunately, however, most of the proposals depended, for their success, upon co-operation between the two sections.

A few days later Don called a staff meeting at which he put forward his proposals. The reception they received was mixed, for Beryl and Jill used them as a vehicle to express their mutual hostility by adopting opposing positions on each. A few of the proposals that were discussed, and the reactions to them, were as follows:

1 *Statements*. It is the bank's policy to issue statements every month. In order to save on postage, Don proposed that statements for regular customers (i.e. people — mainly in business — who come in every week) should be held by the cashiers and handed to the customers when they called at the bank. About a third of all statements would be handled in this way (the remaining two-thirds being posted as at present), and substantial savings would be achieved. The proposal involved about ten minutes a day extra work in the machine room, and some additional work for the cashiers.

Beryl was against this proposal, Jill was in favour.

2 *Standing Orders*. There was an imbalance of work between the cashiers and the machine room. The cashiers had built up a considerable backlog of work, while the machine operators normally finished their work with time to spare. In order to eliminate this imbalance, Don proposed that the work of dealing with standing orders be transferred from the cashiers to the Senior Machine Operator. (The work involves checking customers' standing order requests against any existing standing orders held in their folders, amending the latter as necessary, and completing computer amendment slips.)

Beryl was in favour of this proposal, Jill was opposed. However, Jill grudgingly agreed to do the work until the backlog was cleared, when it should be returned to the cashiers.

3 *Outgoing Mail*. There are eight mailbags held in the machine room for the various categories of mail: first class, second class, overseas, head office, regional centre, registered post, recorded deliveries, and internal. Staff bring mail into the machine room and deposit it in the appropriate bags. It is the job of the Machine Operator (Sue) to frank the mail and enter details in the Outgoing Mail Register. Don proposed that a pigeon-hole system be installed outside the machine room, one pigeon-hole for each category of mail, and that towards the end of the day Sue should clear these, frank the mail, and place it in the appropriate bags.

Jill was in favour of this proposal (because the traffic through the machine room would be reduced), but Beryl expressed doubts about it.

In spite of the mixed reactions, Don decided to implement the proposals. The results have been disastrous:

1 *Statements*. The cashiers failed to hand out the statements to the regular customers, and after several weeks they were all passed back to the machine room for posting.

2 *Standing Orders*. Jill processed these, as agreed, but when the backlog was

cleared Beryl refused to take the work back into her section. The outcome has been increased animosity between the two sections.

3 *Outgoing Mail*. Under the old system, mail was never placed in the wrong bag. Immediately the pigeon-holes were installed many envelopes were deposited in the wrong hole and so were incorrectly franked and bagged. Sue, who had the job of franking and bagging the mail, had taken up employment with the bank only a few months previously, and she had insufficient experience to detect that mail was incorrectly sorted. Some of the mail, in fact, was knowingly placed in the wrong pigeon-hole — on one occasion a cashier made no attempt to sort a bundle of mail into the correct holes but placed it all in one. The result was that complaints about mis-routed mail started to flow into the branch at the rate of about ten a day, and the pigeon-hole system has finally had to be abandoned.

The other changes instituted by Don have suffered similar fates, and the old ways of working have had to be restored.

The final outcome of this difficult situation is that Don has moved to a post at another branch, where he has successfully installed similar changes. Jill has also moved to another branch and Sue has been moved up to fill her post. There was never any real antipathy between Beryl and Sue, and the relationship between the two sections is now quite amicable.

EXERCISES

1 To what extent would the conflict described in this case have been ameliorated if the branch manager had adopted an authoritarian or democratic leadership style?

2 How should Don have proceeded in order to get his proposals accepted, installed, and working?

ASSIGNMENT GROUP WORK

Assignment 7 (page 193). For Section A, use the notes you have prepared for the exercise on page 154.

Industrial Relations

Although management has a social responsibility towards the workforce to ensure that the hygiene factors discussed above are present in the work situation, its primary responsibility is economic: the production of goods and services at a profit. Whether the enterprise is publicly or privately owned, there will inevitably be some conflict between these social and economic responsibilities, and when this occurs management will tend to sacrifice the interests of the workforce in favour of its main economic objectives.

Some mechanism is therefore needed to ensure that the collective interests of employees are safeguarded. In non-unionized establishments elected representatives of the workforce might discuss pay, conditions, and other hygiene factors on joint consultative committees (see page 165); in unionized establishments elected employee representatives known as **shop stewards** will negotiate with management to ensure that these factors are provided.

The formal relations that exist between employers and the body of employees are known as **industrial relations**, the main force on the industrial relations front being, of course, the trade unions. The remainder of this chapter is devoted to a discussion of the role played by the unions in industrial relations and in ensuring the provision of the hygiene factors − in particular good pay, physical conditions, and employment policy.

The History of the Trade Union Movement

The trade unions grew out of the terrible social conditions that marked the early years of the industrial revolution. The political doctrine of the time was 'laissez-faire' − the non-intervention of government in economic and social matters − and this led to great wealth being amassed by entrepreneurs and enormous business growth on the one hand, but the exploitation of workers on the other. 'Combinations' of workers were illegal, and so the workforce was powerless to take collective action to improve its lot. However, new political ideas were stirring at this time − in France they had led to the Revolution − and these, together with the prevailing social climate, brought about the emergence of trade unionism.

The first trade unions were formed in 1824, immediately after the repeal of the Combination Acts, and they quickly made their presence felt by striking for improved pay and conditions. In an attempt to curb these activities the government passed a further Act in 1825, but the force of popular pressure caused it, in subsequent years, to revise the law in favour of the unions.

The original unions were small local craft unions, formed to protect the interests of workers in a particular trade. A number of these still exist today − one example is the United Patternmakers' Association − but they represent a tiny proportion of the total unionized workforce. Over the years many have amalgamated to form large multi-craft unions, typical of which is the Amalgamated Engineering Union.

A further development has been the formation of a few very large general unions representing a wide range of workers over a variety of trades and industries. The two main general unions today are the Transport and General Workers Union and the General and Municipal Workers Union, which together represent about a fifth of all unionised workers.

During the first quarter of this century many unionists felt that the union movement should be restructured on an industrial basis, so that for each industry there would be one union representing all workers, and in 1924 the Trades Union Congress passed a resolution encouraging such a move. This type of union structure has obvious advantages, for it avoids negotiations involving several unions and it eliminates inter-union disputes. However, the T.U.C. had great difficulty in implementing this proposal, caused partly by the conservatism of many unionists and partly by the difficulties involved in defining the various industries. Only a few industrial unions have in fact been formed − two are the National Union of Mineworkers and the Union of Post Office Workers.

The latest stage in the steady expansion of union influence on the industrial relations front has been the unionization of clerical and administrative staff, the most important white collar unions being the National and Local Government Officers Association in the public sector and the Association of Scientific, Technical and Managerial Staffs in the private sector. But in spite of this steady growth, only about half of all workers in this country belong to unions.

Trade Union Organization

Internal organization varies greatly from union to union, but for many the chart shown in Figure 11.4 is fairly typical. The majority of union officials are part-time and unpaid (though their employers normally compensate them for time spent away from work on union business).

At the bottom of the organization are the shop stewards, elected by a show of hands at the workplace. These deal with shop-floor problems and they conduct local negotiations over pay and conditions. Most negotiations used to be carried out further up the union hierarchy at the district level, but during the last 30 years there has been a shift away from this in both directions − to national pay bargaining on the one hand by the union executive, and to workplace bargaining by local representatives on the other.

90% of unionists belong to trade unions which are affiliated to the Trades Union Congress. Delegates from all affiliated unions attend the T.U.C. annual conference, which elects the General Council. This Council represents all organized labour in the country, and it enters into discussions on its behalf with the government and with the equivalent employers' association, the C.B.I. It is also responsible for deter-

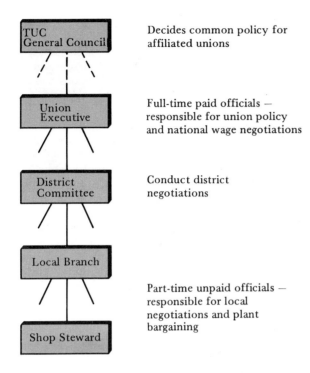

TUC General Council — Decides common policy for affiliated unions

Union Executive — Full-time paid officials — responsible for union policy and national wage negotiations

District Committee — Conduct district negotiations

Local Branch

Shop Steward — Part-time unpaid officials — responsible for local negotiations and plant bargaining

Figure 11.4   Union organization

mining the overall policy of the trade union movement.

Collective Bargaining

Collective bargaining is the process of negotiating agreements on pay and conditions between employers and the workforce, and it is conducted by representatives of the employers and representatives of the workers. It is a process which, in the last analysis, is based upon the ability of the union to withdraw labour, on the one hand, and on the other, upon whether the employer is able to pay the wage desired by the union negotiators while maintaining an adequate level of profitability.

In spite of the ultimate strike weapon which is available to the union side, the majority of disputes are resolved reasonably amicably through the agreed negotiating procedures that exist in every industry. Strikes or other forms of industrial conflict impair the employer's ability to pay high wages, and responsible

union negotiators always try to avoid recourse to them.

The main collective agreements are those that are negotiated at the national level between employers' representatives and full-time union officials. These agreements set the national wage levels for particular industries and groups of workers. However, there is an increasing tendency for these national agreements to be modified at local level by workplace bargaining between the local management and shop stewards. This has had the effect of introducing wide variations in the wages paid at different establishments and of downgrading the importance of nationally negotiated agreements.

As mentioned above, most disputes between unions and management are settled without the union having to resort to strike action; Britain's record compares favourably with that of other countries in this respect. It is an accepted part of the official bargaining procedure that unions will only resort to strike action when the agreed negotiating process has been exhausted. The majority of stoppages suffered by British industry are *unofficial*, and this country has more than its fair share of these. They are caused when local negotiators (shop stewards) resort to strike action *before* the agreed negotiating process is exhausted, and they are called in the face of official union opposition.

This type of stoppage tends to be concentrated in those industries and establishments where inadequate provision is made for Herzberg's hygiene factors: where company administration and employment policy are poor, working conditions are inadequate, and so on. They are also more likely to occur if the negotiating procedure is rather bureaucratic and slow, or if the union appears to be following government or T.U.C. policy rather than seeking to promote members' interests.

Unions and the Micro-Electronics Revolution

Prior to the introduction of new technology into the workplace, management may have to enter into **productivity agreements** with the unions involved. The essence of these agreements is that management offers the workforce improvements in wages and conditions, in return for which it secures cooperation in the introduction of the new equipment, the revision of working practices, and the reduction of manning levels.

The widespread introduction of microprocessor-based machines will dramatically increase the productivity of workers, especially office workers, and this will have serious repercussions on their long-term employment prospects. The material benefits offered by the new technology are enormous, but so is the social threat it poses.

In introducing microprocessor-based equipment, industry is starting down a road leading towards a substantial proportion of the working population being unemployed, with all the attendant problems that this brings, while those who have jobs are very well paid and able to enjoy to the full the fruits of the new technology. The unions, however, want an equitable distribution of the benefits on offer, and are calling for full discussions with employers' representatives. They are unlikely to stand idly by if industry travels too far down this road. The type of productivity agreement that they are likely to press for will lead industry down a different road towards a 'work-sharing' situation in which the majority of the workforce retain their employment but with a much shorter working week.

The problem that this poses for industry is basically organizational. Employees may work alternate weeks, or $2\frac{1}{2}$ days in 5, or some other work-sharing pattern, and this will cause tremendous problems of co-ordination. Nevertheless, management will have to talk to unions, and this sort of problem will have to be faced and resolved, if business is to enter the new computer age.

Appendix I:
A Small Business Computer System

INPUT:	DISK STORAGE RETAINING:	OUTPUT:
Customer orders Good returned Cash received Goods inward	**Sales ledger records:** Customers' names and addresses Delivery details Terms Credit details Account balances. **Stock ledger:** Product reference and description VAT code Discount details Price details Stock levels **Representatives file:** Sales value at cost prices Sales value at selling prices **Sales transaction file**: Individual transaction details for period	Invoices/credit notes Journal listing Aged debtors listing Statements Transaction summary Customer activity and turnover reports Representatives' sales report Stock summary and analysis reports

Figure A.I.1   A small business computer system

Small business computer systems cost under £10,000 (including software) and will carry out all the usual data processing functions. The figure shows the application of such a system to the invoicing/sales ledger/stock control and the purchase ledger/nominal ledger/cash control sides of a business. (By courtesy of *Adler Business Systems Ltd.*)

SAMPLES OF PRINT-OUT INFORMATION

Transaction listing

```
DPN60                          S U P P L I E R S   T R A N S A C T I O N S                    PAGE 0001
DATE 01.12.77  RUN NO 0001

SUPPLIER NO      NAME                   PMT   DATE     TYPE   PGM     REFERENCES    GDS/CSH · VAT/DISC   TAKE DISC

   100   GENERAL ELECTRIC LTD.,          0  20.07.77   CHQ  21-0001       0          265.00   10.00DR
                                            20.07.77   INV  30-0001   123 345        100.00    8.00       0.00
                                            20.07.77   CHQ  21-0001       0          100.00    8.00DR
                                            20.07.77   CHQ  30-0001     1 DFGH        18.00    2.00DR
                                            18.11.77   INV  30-0002   5369 PHONE     100.00    8.00       0.00
                 106.50-   CURRENT          18.11.77   CSH  30-0002   5369 PHONE     200.00   14.50DR
                   0.00    MONTH 1
                   0.00    MONTH 2
                  58.00    MONTH 3
                 --------
                  48.50-   BALANCE


   101   THE GAS BOARD                   0   1.06.77   CHQ  21-0001       0           54.00    0.00DR
                                            20.07.77   INV  30-0001   2587 P0987     100.00    8.00       0.00
                                            20.07.77   INV  30-0001   1254 3456       50.00    4.00       0.00
                                            20.07.77   CHQ  21-0001       0          100.00    8.00DR
                   0.00    CURRENT          20.07.77   CHQ  30-0001   10001           54.00    0.00DR
                   0.00    MONTH 1
                  54.00-   MONTH 2
                  54.00    MONTH 3
                 --------
                   0.00-   BALANCE


   103   LONDIS PAPER MILLS              0  20.07.77   INV  30-0001   1254 DFGHJ       25.00    2.00       0.00
                                            20.07.77   CHQ  21-0001       0           27.00    0.00DR
                  12.56-   CURRENT          18.11.77   CRN  30-0002   5369 257        12.00    0.56DR
                   0.00    MONTH 1          24.11.77   CHQ  21-0001       0           50.00    0.00DR
                 112.00    MONTH 2
                  50.00-   MONTH 3
                 --------
                  49.44    BALANCE
```

Turnover report

```
DPN60                   S U P P L I E R S   B A L A N C E S   ( A F T E R   A G E I N G )          PAGE 0001
DATE 01.12.77  RUN NO 0001

SUPPLIER NO      NAME                   CURRENT   MONTH 1   MONTH 2   MONTH 3   BALANCE  (PER) T'OVER (YTD)

   100   GENERAL ELECTRIC LTD.,           0.00    106.50-     0.00     58.00     48.50-    1025     1025
   101   THE GAS BOARD                    0.00      0.00      0.00      0.00      0.00-     200      200
   103   LONDIS PAPER MILLS               0.00     12.56-     0.00     62.00     49.44     163      163
   104   ADLER BUSINESS SYSTEMS           0.00      0.00     48.50      0.00     48.50    1634     1634
   105   RYMAN CONTRACTS LTD.,            0.00      1.40      0.00     -0.00      1.40      301      301
   106   LONDON BOROUGH OF EALING,        0.00    149.17      0.00      0.00    149.17     650      650
   107   JONES BROS BUILDERS MERCHANTS,   0.00   3000.25-     0.00    109.50   2890.75-    125      125
   108   HARRY LAWRENCE LTD.,             0.00      0.00      0.00    108.00    108.00     620      620
   109   L:ONDON BOROUGH TAX OFFICE,      0.00      0.00    100.00-   108.00      8.00     300      300
   110   JOHN SMITH & CO. LTD.,           0.00      0.00      0.00      0.00      0.00   369901   369901
```

```
DPN60                          S U P P L I E R S   B A L A N C E S                              PAGE 0001
DATE 01.12.77  RUN NO 0001

SUPPLIER NO      NAME                   BALANCE  (PER) T'OVER (YTD)

   100   GENERAL ELECTRIC LTD.,          48.50-    1025     1025
   101   THE GAS BOARD                    0.00-     200      200
   103   LONDIS PAPER MILLS              49.44      163      163
   104   ADLER BUSINESS SYSTEMS          48.50     1634     1634
   105   RYMAN CONTRACTS LTD.,            1.40      301      301
   106   LONDON BOROUGH OF EALING,      149.17      650      650
   107   JONES BROS BUILDERS MERCHANTS, 2890.75-    125      125
   108   HARRY LAWRENCE LTD.,           108.00      620      620
   109   L:ONDON BOROUGH TAX OFFICE,      8.00      300      300
   110   JOHN SMITH & CO. LTD.,           0.00   369901   369901
```

Aged creditor listing

Appendix II
Pinecrafts: A Case Study and Assignment Programme based upon the Proposed Expansion of a Small Business Making Pinewood Kitchen Furniture

The Programme

This one-year assignment programme consists of seven business administration assignments and two cross-modular assignments. Students should work in groups of 3 or 4, and although limited interchange between groups is possible after the programme has

started, it is intended that as far as possible students remain in the same groups throughout the programme.

The programmes for both 3- and 4-student groups are shown in the charts below. For each group the names of its members are entered at the top of the chart; the assignment parts that each member is to write up during the programme are indicated by the

ASSIGNMENT PROGRAMME CHART
3-Student Groups

WEEK WHEN DUE	Student's Name: ASSIGNMENT No.	1 Part	Objective	Grade	2 Part	Objective	Grade	3 Part	Objective	Grade
4	C.M.A.	(c)*			(a)			(b)		
6	1	(b)	A4		(c)*	A5		(a)	A1,2	
10	2	(a)	B1		(b)	B1		(c)*	B1	
14	3	(a)*	B2,3,4,5		(b)	B2,3,4,5		(c)	B2,3,4,5	
17	C.M.A.	(b)			(c)*			(a)		
18	4	(a)	C2		(b)	C3		(c)*	C2	
21	5	(c)*	D3,E2,F2		(a)	D3,E2,F2		(b)	D3,E2,F2	
24	6	(b)	G1		(c)*	G1,3		(a)	G1	
27	7	(a)	H1,3,J1		(b)	H1,3,J1		(c)*	H1,3,J1	

letters in the column below his name. By following this each student will cover every general objective of the BEC National Award module *Administration in Business*, although variations will occur in the coverage of individual learning objectives.

The overall solution to each assignment should be arrived at by group discussion and research, and class time will be set aside for this activity. One aim of the programme is to develop in students the ability to think creatively in groups. Another aim is to develop leadership skills: leadership of the groups will rotate, the leaders for each assignment being indicated by the asterisks in the programme charts.

The group leader will lead and coordinate the group's activities, and it is his responsibility to control the general quality of the assignment submission, and to ensure that it is handed in on time. The grade that he is awarded will be related to the overall quality of the ideas developed by the group and exhibited in the assignment submission, as well as to the quality of his part of the submission. Also, his grade will be adversely affected if the assignment is handed in late. The grades awarded to the other group members will be related solely to the quality of their individual submissions, not to the assignment as a whole.

Each assignment should take the form of a report to the management of Pinecrafts, with a contents page at the front giving the titles of each part, the contributors, and a suitable space for grades and comments by the lecturer. In the case of 4-student groups the first part of the report should be a summary (of a few hundred words) outlining the main conclusions of the group and bringing together the main threads of the argument underlying the assignment solution. The summary (indicated by 'S' on the programme chart) will be produced by the group leader − it will be his only written contribution to the assignment submission. In the case of 3-student groups a summary will not be required.

ASSIGNMENT PROGRAMME CHART
4-Student Groups

WEEK WHEN DUE	Name: ASS. No.	1 Part	Objective	Gr.	2 Part	Objective	Gr.	3 Part	Objective	Gr.	4 Part	Objective	Gr.
4	C.M.A.	S*			(b)			(c)			(a)		
6	1	(c)	A5		S*	A		(b)	A4		(a)	A1,2	
10	2	(a)	B1		(b)	B1		S*	B1		(c)	B1	
14	3	(a)	B2,3,4,5		(b)	B2,3,4,5		(c)	B2,3,4,5		S*	B2,3,4,5	
17	C.M.A.	S*			(c)			(a)			(b)		
18	4	(a)	C2		S*	C2,3		(b)	C3		(c)	C2	
21	5	(b)	D3,E2,F2		(a)	D3,E2,F2		S*	D3,E2,F2		(c)	D3,E2,F2	
24	6	(c)	G1,3		(a)	G1		(b)	G1		(d)	G2	
27	7	(a)	H1,3,J1		(b)	H1,3,J1		(c)	H1,3,J1		S*	H1,3,J1	

CASE STUDY: PINECRAFTS

INTRODUCTION

The idea of forming a partnership to make pinewood furniture was first discussed by Mick, Paul, and John in January 1979. Mick was a skilled woodworker employed by a large furniture company making prototypes from original designs; Paul was a technical sales rep. for a machinery manufacturer, able to bring into the partnership his technical knowledge; and John was an accountant with both administrative experience and a flair for carpentry.

The three men gave up their jobs in the summer of 1979 and set up business in a small workshop in Great Missenden in Buckinghamshire, trading under the name 'Pinecrafts'. They were able to acquire all the equipment they needed secondhand for a little over £2,000 (the new price would have been many times that figure). It comprised:

1 Dominion Universal Machine (for planing, thicknessing, through-sawing, and morticing) for £540;
1 Bandsaw (for sawing) for £400;
1 Spindle Moulder & Tenoner (for rebating, moulding, and tenonning) for £400;
1 Double-Drawn Sander (for sanding large surfaces) for £420;
1 Lathe (for turning and drilling) for £350;
1 Bobbin-Sander (for shaping work) for £10;
and Mick already owned his own handtools (new value £1,000).

The business was an immediate success. The three partners started by making small articles such as wall-racks and small wall-cupboards, which they displayed at local craft shows. Here they got orders for larger cupboards, wooden fireplaces, and a complete fitted kitchen (i.e. sink unit, cupboards, working surfaces, etc.), and from these beginnings their business has steadily grown. Although their market is limited to the South Bucks area, they have found that there is a big demand for fitted pinewood kitchens, which they currently produce at the rate of about 15 per year. Kitchens comprise about 70% of their business, the remaining 30% being smaller items.

The work is divided among the three men in the following way:

1 Mick machines parts (panels, legs, etc.) and assembles the parts into units of furniture. He also visits potential customers to discuss their requirements and works out quotations.
2 Paul also machines and assembles, and in addition he maintains the machinery.
3 John spends about half his time on finishing the assembled product (polyurethaning, polishing, etc.) and preparing it for despatch, and the rest on general administrative duties, including buying raw materials (mainly wood) and parts (such as screws).

There are a number of other jobs that are shared out on an informal basis among the partners. The complete list of tasks, and the percentage of time spent on each, are as follows:

Machining	28%
Assembling	28%
Finishing	10%
Inspection and Despatch	2%
Maintenance	1%
Delivery to customers	3%
Installing	10%
Marketing, Design, Quotations and Liaison with customers	6%
Purchasing	2%
Accounts, Invoicing, and Credit Control	4%
Miscellaneous (costing and other management information, telephone, writing letters, etc.)	6%

They design the fitted kitchens themselves, in consultation with their customers. At the time of writing the price charged for a typical kitchen is £1,400. They reckon they could charge about £400 more, but they are keeping their prices low to establish a reputation and to build up business as a basis for future expansion.

The materials for a kitchen cost about £600, leaving £800 gross profit. From this they pay their overheads of £120 per month (£100 for rent and rates, £20 for electricity and sundries), their transport costs of £30 per month (they hire a van for one day a fortnight for deliveries), and their wages, and also put money aside for future growth.

EXPANSION

The great success of the firm and the large market for pinewood kitchens have prompted the three partners to think seriously about embarking upon a substantial expansion of the business in the near future. John has recently inherited £50,000 which he will put into the business. The plan is to make only kitchens, producing them at the rate of one per working day. They intend to charge £1,800 for the typical kitchen, and they estimate that the material costs will decrease to £450 (because it will be possible to bulk-buy timber in large uncut sections). 80% of the material costs will be wood, the remainder will be screws, glue, polyurethane, laminate, etc.

To produce kitchens at this rate they estimate that they will need to employ the following staff:

3 foremen, earning £150 per week each
22 woodworkers, earning £120 per week
4 driver/installers, earning £120 per week
4 (experienced) office staff, earning £120 per week.

The woodworkers will supply their own handtools, but a substantial investment will have to be made in woodworking machines. The existing machines will be inadequate for the greatly increased volume of work and will be sold (Paul reckons for about 20% less than the price they paid). The following machines will have to be purchased, probably new:

1 Tenoner	£5,000	1 Dimension Saw	£1,500
1 Morticer	£5,000	1 Borer	£1,000
1 Thicknesser	£3,000	1 Dovetailer	£2,000

1 Overhead Planer	£2,000	1 Straightline Edger	£5,000
1 Router	£4,000	1 Dust-Extraction Unit	£2,500
1 Bandsaw	£3,000	Spray Guns and Booth	£2,000

The partners estimate that it will cost £1,500 to install the machines. Additionally, they estimate that £10,000 will be required to equip and furnish the office area. A large van will be required by the installers to deliver the completed kitchens, and this will cost £7,000, its running costs amounting to £2,600 per annum. Premises of about 8000 sq. ft. will be needed to house the business, the expected rental being £4 per sq. ft. per annum. Electricity and other overheads are expected to amount to £2,600 per annum.

ORGANIZATION

It is planned to split the enlarged business into three departments: Sales, Production, and the General Office (including Purchasing). Paul will be the Sales Manager, Mick the Production Manager, and John will be the General Manager, having overall control of the business as well as looking after the General Office. The Sales Department will incorporate a small showroom.

Production will be split into three sections, each under a foreman: machining, assembly, and finishing (including inspection and despatch). The machines listed above will be used by the machining section, with the exception of the spray guns and booth, which will be used by the finishing section. Timber will be held in the raw materials store, which will be attached to the machine shop and under the control of the machine shop foreman. The parts produced by the machining section and the bought-in parts (screws, hinges, etc.) will be held in the parts store, which will be under the control of the assembly foreman. Finished kitchen units will be stored under the control of the foreman of the finishing section.

PRODUCTION AND STORAGE

The main steps in the production of a fitted kitchen are:

1 Designing the kitchen in consultation with the customer and calculating the price. Once the enlarged business is set up it is anticipated that most customers will purchase standard units, as displayed in the showroom or advertised in a catalogue.
2 Purchasing and storing the raw materials and the bought-in parts.
3 Machining and storing the made-in parts (door panels, shelves, legs, etc.).
4 Assembling the parts to make the kitchen units.
5 Finishing the kitchen units (polyurethaning, polishing, etc.) and despatching (packing).
6 Delivering and installing the finished kitchen.

Raw materials and bought-in parts (2 above) are bought on a bulk basis. Once the enlarged business is set up it is reckoned that the amount purchased of each item (the reorder quantity) will be equivalent to eight weeks' usage of that item, and that an item will be reordered when the amount in stock falls to the equivalent of six weeks' usage (the reorder level). This will give adequate leeway for delivery delays (the average time between placing an order and receiving delivery being three weeks).

Made-in parts (3 above) are produced in bulk, so that long production runs and therefore greater output is achieved. It is intended that the reorder level in this case will be two weeks' usage, and that the reorder quantity will be six weeks' usage.

It is estimated that the raw materials store will contain some 40 different sizes of timber; and that there will be 300 different types of bought-in parts and 1,000 different types of made-in parts in the finished parts store. There will be about 10 orders per day placed for raw materials and bought-in parts.

ADMINISTRATIVE PROCEDURES

At the moment very little paperwork is required to plan the work, coordinate activities, and progress customers' orders. Once the enlarged business is set up, however, formal administrative procedures will have to be installed. It is anticipated that, in outline, these will be as follows:

1 Some fitted kitchens will be produced on a made-to-measure basis, and in response to an enquiry for one of these the Sales Manager will visit the house to discuss the design and take measurements. Back at the office he will draw up a *quotation* for the kitchen (if necessary in consultation with the Production Manager), and send it to the enquirer. Many kitchens, however, will consist of standard units, selected by customers in the showroom or by post from the catalogue, and only if special parts are required will a quotation be necessary.

2 Following the acceptance of a quotation by the customer, or the placement of an order for standard units from the showroom or catalogue, the Sales Department will produce a *sales order*, listing the standard parts required plus a description of any special parts that need to be made.

3 Since kitchens will be installed at the rate of one per working day, the delivery and installation date of a kitchen can be booked by the Sales Department by means of a simple *diary system* and confirmed with the customer at the time the order is placed. The booked date will be noted on the sales order, one copy of which will be handed or sent to the customer, another copy being passed to the Production Department. (This copy will form the *works order* and subsequently the *receipt note*.)

4 *Stock records* must be kept for the raw materials store to record materials received from suppliers, materials issued to the machining section, and the balance left in the store. Similar records will be kept for the parts store, to show receipts from suppliers and from the machining section, issues to the assembly section, and the balance.

5 The foremen in charge of the stores will be responsible for maintaining the stock records and for noting any items which fall to the reorder level, together with the standard reorder quantities, on a *reorder suggestions list*. These lists will be sent to the Production Manager every week, and as a general rule he will authorize the ordering of the standard reorder quantities from outside suppliers or from the machining section, as appropriate. Sometimes, however, he may decide not to order the standard quantities — if, for example, a part is to be phased out, or stock levels are to be reduced to ease a cash flow problem.

6 The Production Manager will notify the purchasing clerk of orders to be placed. This clerk will decide which supplier to use, referring to records of previous purchases kept on *purchase record cards*, and will make out a *purchase order*.

7 On the basis of the works orders received from the Sales Department and the reorder suggestions lists received from the parts store, the Production Manager will plan the work of his department.

(a) It is the job of the machining section to produce the made-in parts required by the parts store, as indicated on the reorder suggestions lists. The Production Manager must ensure that each machine is correctly *loaded*, so that the work is fairly distributed, or balanced, between the machines (to avoid bottlenecks caused by a build-up of jobs each requiring the same machine); and he must ensure that the work is properly *scheduled*, i.e. the various jobs must be programmed through the machine shop so that the required parts are produced prior to the assembly date. The workers must be given *job cards* for each part to be made, specifying the operations that have to be carried out.

(b) It is the job of the assembly and finishing shops to assemble the required kitchen units from the parts stored in the parts store, and to polyurethane, polish, or otherwise finish the units in accordance with customers' requirements. The work of these shops will be programmed in fortnightly batches: a fitted kitchen involves one full day's work in each shop, and so ten kitchens can be assembled and finished in a fortnight. Prior to the assembly fortnight the Production Manager will send the works order for the ten kitchens to be built in that fortnight (and which are therefore due for delivery and installation in the following fortnight) to the assembly foreman, who will informally schedule the work through his section in batches, e.g. ten sink units, followed by ten cupboards, and so on. The foreman of the finishing shop will do no scheduling — he will deal with the work in the order in which it leaves the assembly shop.

8 The foremen in each shop will be responsible for the detailed allocation of jobs to the workers. For each worker he will make out a *time sheet*, on which he will enter the jobs to be done and the standard times of the jobs. This sheet, besides providing the worker with a list of jobs and items, will form the basis of the wages calculation.

9 The installers' programme of work will be shown in the diary system kept in the Sales Department. They will collect the appropriate kitchen units from the store adjoining the finishing shop, together with the works order/receipt note, load them onto the van, deliver to the customer's house, and install. The customer will sign the works order/receipt note to confirm receipt and installation.

10 The final step is to send an *invoice* to the customer requesting payment.

The Assignments

Cross-Modular Assignment: Setting up the Business

(a) The three partners are considering setting up the enlarged business as a limited company, to be called Pinecrafts Ltd. Advise them of the advantages and disadvantages of this course of action.

(b) The main stages in setting up the enlarged business and getting it going are:

(i) Forming the company
(ii) Calculating and raising the finance required.
(iii) Acquiring premises and equipment
(iv) Obtaining planning permission
(v) Installing the fixtures and equipment
(vi) Obtaining staff
(vii) Obtaining raw materials and bought-in parts to commence operations
(viii) Designing and printing the company stationery.

Find out and list the tasks involved in each of these stages, and estimate the duration of each (in weeks). For example, under 'obtaining staff' the tasks might be:

Advertise vacancies in the local press (1 week)
Await replies (1 week)
Call suitable applicants for interview (1 week)
Interview applicants and select (1 week)
Await expiry of notice that selected applicants must give employers (4 weeks).

(c) Using the list drawn up in (b) construct a plan, covering an appropriate number of weeks, for setting up the enlarged business. Show against each week of the plan the tasks that must be done in that week.

Business Administration Assignment 1: Organization and Coordination

(a) The case study gives the departments into which the enlarged company is to be divided, the number of posts, and the proportions of time currently spent on the various tasks. Using this information, construct an organization chart (assume that the proportions hold for the enlarged business).

(b) Produce job descriptions for the General Manager, the Sales Manager, and the Production Manager, and write down the main tasks that each of the four office workers will undertake.

(c) The orders received by the Sales Department will determine the jobs to be done by the Production Department, which in turn will determine the raw materials and bought-in parts to be bought by the purchasing function in the General Office. In other ways too the work of the three departments must be closely coordinated. Using the lists of responsibilities and tasks drawn up in your answer to (b) above you are required to carry out the following exercise:

For each department write down five tasks for

which co-ordination is required with either or both of the other departments, and state the results of non-co-ordination. In each case suggest how co-ordination might be achieved (e.g. by a documentation system, or by a meeting, or by a verbal message or memo, etc).

Assignment 2: Management Information

Six important decisions that have to be made in a business of this type are:

(a) For Sales: pricing, advertising policy
(b) For Production: work schedules, equipment replacement policy
(c) For Purchasing: reorder quantities, sources of supply.

For each of the above functions carry out the following exercises:

(i) Write down another important decision that has to be made.
(ii) List the information needed to make each of the three decisions. For example, in order to determine the most suitable supplier for a certain item comparative information is needed on prices, credit offered, delivery times, reliability of supply, and so on.
(iii) Indicate against each category of information whether it can be obtained from the firm's internal records, or whether it must be obtained from external sources. In each case state briefly the procedure to be used in obtaining the information (for the purpose of this exercise assume the firm will not be using a computer system). For example, in order to determine the reliability of various suppliers, the firm's internal records can be used: purchase record cards can be held for each item, with details of previous transactions noted on them.

Assignment 3: Documentation Procedures

Refer to the 'Administrative Procedures' section of the case study, and consider the following sequences of steps:

(a) 1, 2, 3, 9, and 10
(b) 4, 5, 6
(c) 7, 8.

For each of these sequences you are required to:

(i) Develop the procedure in detail and design the forms and other documents required
(ii) State the purpose of each item of data to be entered on each form
(iii) State the methods by which any copies are to be produced
(iv) State the filing method and classification system to be used for each form, or whether it should be destroyed after use: for example, the stock record cards might be held in a visible card index in part number order.

Cross-Modular Assignment: Financial Planning

Before setting up the enlarged business it is necessary to draw up its long-term plans and objectives. These will determine, for example, the choice of premises and equipment, the price/quality bracket of the product, and the amount of finance needed. Such plans must be based upon market research and upon sales forecasts, and they are made operational by being translated into short-term budgets.

(a) Find out and write down how the potential market for the firm's products might be researched and on what basis sales forecasts might be made.

(b) Assuming that market research indicates that the enlarged business will sell every fitted kitchen that it can make during its first year of operation, draw up a cash budget covering this first year (using the data given in the case study). For simplicity divide the year into 13 four-week months, and assume that the only breaks are the summer holidays, when the business closes down for one complete month, and Christmas, when it closes for one week. Assume also that capital equipment is paid for during the first month of operation, that raw materials and bought-in parts are paid for one month after delivery, that customers pay in the month following installation, and that the three managers draw from the business a salary of £7,800 each. Exclude VAT and other governmental contributions from the calculations.

Comment on the final situation.

(c) Draw up a forecast manufacturing trading and profit-and-loss account for the first year of operation, and a forecast balance sheet.

Assignment 4: Data Processing

The price of small business computer systems is falling dramatically, and such a system is, today, a viable proposition for a firm such as Pinecrafts. If installed, a small business computer will automate many office tasks, it will increase the speed and accuracy of data processing, and it will improve the quality of information available to management. For example, customer orders and payments received by Pinecrafts can be keyed into the computer, and on the basis of these it will maintain the delivery diary, work out the production programme, print the invoices, maintain the sales ledger, produce aged debtors lists for credit control purposes, produce sales analyses, and so on.

(a) Estimate the volume of paperwork of various types that the General Office will have to handle (e.g. numbers of invoices, purchase orders, letters, ledger entries, etc.). On the basis of this estimate and your answer to Assignment 3, decide what items of office furniture and equipment should be installed (i) if the firm decides not to computerize any procedures, (ii) if the firm decides to install a small business computer system.

(b) Advise management on how a small business computer system would modify the procedures and documentation you have described in Assignment 3 (parts (a), (b), and (c)), and how it would modify the firm's accounting procedures.

(c) State in what ways a computer system would improve the quality of each category of information you have listed in your answer to Assignment 2(c).

The summary of the report should include a brief discussion of the advantages and disadvantages to Pinecrafts of installing such a system (4-student groups only).

Assignment 5: Control, Work Measurement, and O & M

Section A

For the firm to operate efficiently all aspects of its work must be properly planned and controlled, and this involves setting realistic standards of *quantity*, *quality*, and *time* for the activities of all departments. One example activity is credit control: the targets include (i) the total amount of money owed to the firm should not exceed a specified sum, (ii) the number of bad debts

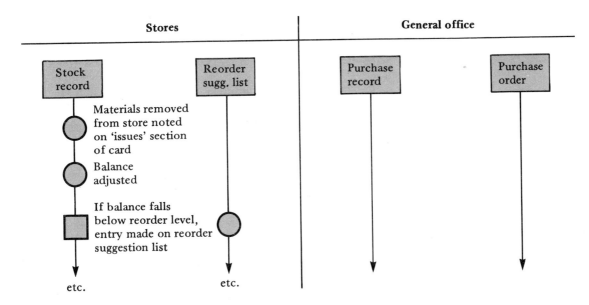

Figure A.II.1   Suggested design for the process chart (material-type)

should be as few as possible, (iii) letters requesting settlement of accounts should be sent out within a specified time after the payment-due date.

Choose two major activities in

(a) The Sales Department
(b) The Production Department
(c) The General Office

and advise how, in each case, targets might be established, and how performance might be monitored and controlled.

Section B
To be efficient the firm should also seek ways of improving its methods of work.

Examine the solutions to Assignment 3(b) produced by the class, and then carry out the following exercises:

(a) Construct a process chart to describe the procedures you have devised in your solution to Assignment 3(b). A suggested design for this process chart is given in Figure II/1.

(b) Construct an X-chart to show the duplication of data in the documents you have designed in Assignment 3(b). Draw up and fill in a critical examination chart for the process chart operation 'entry made on reorder suggestions list' and use the charts to determine how this part of the procedure might be improved (e.g. by eliminating the reorder suggestions list). Can other parts of the procedure be improved? (Assume that the firm will not be computerizing this procedure.)

(c) Construct a process chart of your revised procedure, and redesign forms as necessary.

Assignment 6: Office Planning

In order to promote the coordination of activities in the enlarged business it has been decided that all the managers and office staff will be housed in one office, with screening or partitioning as necessary. Adjoining this office on three sides will be the stores, the workshops, and the showroom.

Using your findings in Assignment 1 and Assignment 4 Part (a) you are required to:

(a) (i) Determine the area required for the office.
   (ii) Obtain a catalogue of office furniture and list

the items that you recommend should be purchased for the office, and the dimensions of each item.

(b) (i) Construct a relationship chart showing your estimated frequencies of communication between each post and every other post in the office. Give brief reasons for your estimates.
(ii) Draw a balloon chart linking the posts by communication lines, the thicknesses of these lines representing the estimated frequencies of communication.

Include the computer in your relationship chart and in your balloon chart.

(c) Draw a scale plan of the office, showing your suggested locations for the posts, and including the partitions, screens, furniture, and equipment (including the computer). Mark on this plan your suggested locations for the adjoining stores, workshops, and showroom.

(d) (To be done by 4-student groups only.) Advise on the effect of relevant legislation – such as the Offices, Shops and Railway Premises Act – on the design and planning of the business premises.

Assignment 7: Motivation and Conflict

Section A
Motivation studies have emphasized the need to give people 'whole' tasks leading to identifiable end-results, a sense of fulfilment and pride in their work, and a measure of responsibility and self-control. Advise management on how the work of

(a) the machining and assembly shops
(b) the finishing shops and the driver/installers
(c) the office staff

should be organized to ensure that staff are well-motivated.

Your recommendations will probably result in a modified organization chart. If so, this should be shown in the summary to the report (4-student groups only).

Section B
Enlarging the business introduces many areas of potential conflict. (For example, conflict may arise between Sales and Production if the latter is unable

to meet delivery deadlines or the product specification.)
List for:

(a) the Production Department
(b) the General Office
(c) the Sales Department

the ways in which conflict might arise, both within the department and between it and the other departments. In each case advise management of the steps that might be taken to minimize the possibility of such conflicts.

Appendix III:
Additional Assignments and Revision Questions

1 An activity sample carried out in an accounts office revealed that the percentage of time spent on the various activities was as follows:

Payments and purchases ledger	24%
Invoicing	9%
Receipts and sales ledger	17%
Credit control	9%
Wages	23%
General ledger accounts	6%
Internal audit	5%
Statistics	3%
Idle	4%

It is estimated that twenty staff, including supervisors, are needed to man the office. In addition there is an accountant in charge (whose work is excluded from the activity sample.)

(a) Design an organization chart for the office, giving reasons for your design
(b) Give a job description for any one of the supervisors shown on your chart
(c) State the section(s) and department(s) with which credit control will need to liaise (coordinate), and indicate the results of failure to coordinate.

2 The club you belong to has decided to raise money by holding a grand fête and jumble sale. You have been put in charge of organizing and running this event, and thirty members of the club have volunteered to help.

(a) State what forecasts you might attempt to make prior to planning the event (numbers likely to attend, etc.). How might you arrive at realistic forecasts?
(b) State what is involved in planning the event. List the tasks that must precede the event (e.g. collecting jumble), and list the stalls and activities that you think might be run.
(c) State what is involved in organizing the event, and in controlling the work of the volunteers.
(d) On the basis of the lists you have produced in (b), analyse the jumble sale system: write down the main subsystems (advertising for jumble, collecting jumble, etc.), together with the inputs and outputs of each and the decisions that have to be made in respect of each. Draw a diagram showing these subsystems connected by a network of inputs and outputs.
(e) Using the analysis carried out in (d) suggest a suitable division of duties and structure of authority.

3 You are the Senior Machine Operator in charge of the computer operations section of a bank branch. The branch organization chart is shown in Figure A.III.1 − you have five computer terminal operators under you, their job being to enter all transactions (such as cash drawn, cheques paid in) on the branch's computer terminals. Some transactions are incorrectly entered, sometimes through keying-in errors, sometimes because the operators have not been informed of the change in status of an account (e.g. closed, transferred). The computer is programmed to pick up these errors. Some errors are detected immediately, and the operator informed; other errors, however, cannot be

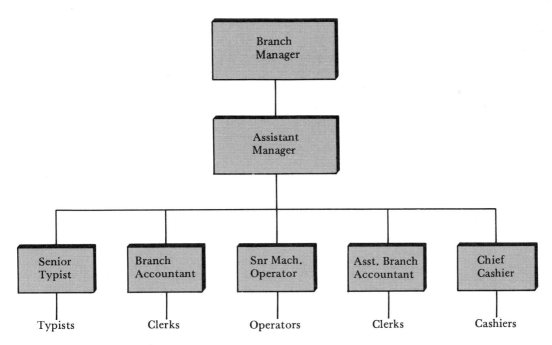

Figure A.III.1   Branch organization chart (Posts shown here on the same level are not necessarily of the same grade. The Senior Machine Operator, for example, is below the Branch Accountant.)

picked up until the computer's files are updated at the close of each day's trading, and these will be indicated on the computer print-out of the day's transactions.

Your first task each morning is to balance the previous day's work. This involves inspecting the computer print-out and making out correcting vouchers for all erroneous entries. There are, on average, twenty such entries per day, and this task is normally completed by 10.30 a.m. The vouchers, together with the print-out, are then passed to the Assistant Manager for checking and authorization.

The purpose of these checks by the Assistant Manager is to ensure that the vouchers are error-free so that the processing of the previous day's work by the computer is not further delayed. Time is of the essence at this point as the work-peak for the computer operations section is in the afternoons, and it is desirable therefore that the correcting entries be keyed in in the mornings. The necessary checks can be completed in about half-an-hour – indeed, when the Assistant Manager is away and the Branch Accountant looks after his work, the vouchers are normally returned to you by 11.30 a.m. The Assistant Manager, however,

rarely manages to get the vouchers back to you before 3 p.m.

Part of the reason for the delay is that the Assistant Manager is dealing with other matters; the main reason, however, is that he wishes to investigate the cause of each erroneous entry and will, on occasion, reprimand the machine operator responsible. This investigation, and the daily problems caused by the late return of the vouchers, has led to a great deal of dissatisfaction in your section. In addition, problems have been caused in other sections of the branch, for the time spent by the Assistant Manager on your work has led to a substantial backlog of other work building up.

Today, however, tempers are badly frayed, and at 3.30, when the Assistant Manager finally returns the vouchers (having previously reprimanded two of the operators), you can no longer control your anger and have a major row with him. The Branch Manager intervenes and calls both of you into his office. The Assistant Manager explains that he is merely carrying out his proper duties by checking the vouchers and investigating the causes of the errors to try to prevent their re-occurrence, and he implies that he does not think that you are capable of properly supervising the work of your section.

The Manager thanks him for his explanation and asks him to leave the room. He then turns to you and asks you to account for your behaviour.

(a) Write the reply you would give, including a reasoned explanation as to why, in your opinion, the Assistant Manager is not carrying out his duties correctly.
(b) The Assistant Manager is only a few years off retirement, and is unlikely to change his attitudes. What change in the organization might be made to solve the problem described above? (Refer to the chart.)

4 During your final term at college you apply for a junior management post in a company. You are short-listed, and at your interview you are asked what you learned at college that you think might be relevant for this post. The chairman of the interviewing panel is a senior manager, and he pricks up his ears when you mention computing and management information systems. 'Maybe you can help us,' he says, and he goes on to explain that he knows very little about the subject, but feels that his company needs to improve on its ability to get the right information to the right people.

It transpires that morale in geographically-remote units of the company is low and efficiency is impaired because of poor communication of information about company activities from headquarters. The senior manager also explains that, although he personally gets regular reports on the units under his control, most of the information they contain is of little value to him: a sizeable proportion of the reports tell him what he already knows – and in skimming through this material he finds that he sometimes misses important items; and many items of information reach him too late to be of much value to him.

He feels that a radical solution is required, and asks you to explain to him how a management information system should operate and what it could achieve, and whether the use of a computer would solve the problems being encountered. 'If you can give us some good advice', he declares, 'the job's yours. We'll adjourn for half-an-hour for you to marshall your thoughts and prepare some notes for what you have to say.'

Write notes for your talk.

5 By referring either to Pinecrafts Ltd (Appendix II) or the company you work for, carry out the following exercises:

(a) Construct a flowchart showing the main operations from the receipt of an order from a customer to the collection of payment from a customer
(b) State the main decisions that have to be made in respect of each operation
(c) State the information needed for the decision 'Choose suitable supplier' and the decision 'Pay supplier'.

6 You have recently left college and joined the staff of a mechanical engineering company. It has rather old-fashioned ideas on the way a company should be run, particularly on the office side. You work in the General Administration and Accounts Department, which deals with the accounts, invoicing and credit control, purchasing, mail-handling, filing, customer complaints, the telephone switchboard, messenger services, reception, and the typing pool. The most advanced piece of equipment in the department is an electric typewriter. You have already caused a few ruffled feathers by pointing out various inefficiencies and by suggesting to the Accountant that all his neatly written-up ledgers should be replaced by magnetic discs and that the bookkeeping procedures should be computerized.

One day the Managing Director calls you into his office and admits to having some sympathy with your ideas, although he is displeased with the way in which you have voiced them to other members of staff. It transpires that he is becoming increasingly dissatisfied with the standard of service that the office is providing: telephone messages are often not passed on, late deliveries of materials and parts that have been ordered are not being properly chased, management information is being produced too late to be of much use, and paper-work is frequently being mislaid.

As he sees it the problem is caused partly by the fact that the department is housed in a number of smallish rooms, and there is a great deal of to-ing and fro-ing of people and paper, and partly by the fact that business has steadily increased over a number of years, without any commensurate increase in the size of the department (there simply isn't any more space available). The result is that the department is now in an almost permanent state of crisis – urgent problems only are being dealt with, non-urgent matters are being left.

He has called you in because he has just read an article describing the impact that the micro-electronics revolution is likely to have on businesses. It refers in particular to the impact of 'communicating word processors' and other microprocessor-based office machines. He feels that the time has come to revolutionize the General Administration and Accounts Department. However, he knows very little about the new developments, and he wants you to prepare a report advising him and the Board of Directors of what changes should be made and what equipment should be installed. He wants the following included in the report:

(a) The pros and cons of converting the floor on which the department is housed to an open-plan office
(b) An explanation of 'communicating word processors' and an account of the impact that they could have on the business

(c) A list of the equipment that could be considered for each section of the department, with reasons for your choice
(d) A statement of what the problems of changeover might be, and how these might be minimized
(e) In view of the fact that you have caused some antagonism in the past by your suggestions that the existing methods be scrapped, he wants included in the report an indication of the way in which the proposals could be sold to the staff and conflict avoided.

You are required to write the report.

7 The BEC assignment system requires that the programme of assignments covers every general objective of each module studied by the student. In the *Administration in Business* module, for example, there are nine general objectives, A to J, and you must achieve every general objective over the course of your assignment

BEC_____ AWARDS   MODULE_____

ASSIGNMENT PROGRAMME   *Student's Name:*

ASSIGNMENT NO.	1	2	3	4	5	6	7	8	9	10	
Learning Objectives											NOTES
GRADING											Overall Grading ___

Figure A.III.2   Form 1

programme in order to pass. If you fail to achieve an objective in one assignment then you must be given the opportunity to achieve it in another assignment.

This particular exercise will enable you to achieve General Objective F: 'Appreciate the need for constant review and possible changes in procedures.'

Each general objective is broken down into a number of specific learning objectives. For this general objective there are just two, F1 and F2:

F1: describe the role of Organization and Methods;
F2: given a description of a work situation or an organizational task, together with the administrative systems and procedures employed, identify possible shortcomings in these and suggest improvements.

The student does not have to achieve every learning objective, and so the assignment programme can cover a representative selection only of such objectives. This exercise covers F2 only. When the lecturer marks your assignments, he has to:

(a) assess whether or not you have achieved the objectives covered (an assessment of *general* objective achievement only is sufficient), and
(b) grade your work.

The procedure for recording and processing the lecturers' assessments of students' work that has been devised by one college is as follows. The heart of the procedure is Form 1 (see Figure A.III.2); each lecturer completes one of these for each student on his course, and keeps them in alphabetical sequence within classes in his student records file. He lists the specific learning objectives of the module that he teaches down the side of each form.

When he marks a student's assignment, he locates the student's form in his file, and ticks, under the appropriate assignment number (1, or 2, etc.), the objectives that the student achieves. If the student fails to achieve an assignment objective, this is indicated by a cross. Many assignments cover perhaps half-a-dozen learning objectives, in which case half-a-dozen ticks/crosses are entered. The grade that the lecturer awards the assignment is entered at the foot of the column.

Once or twice a term the course coordinator passes Form 2 to the lecturer (see Figure A.III.3), one form for each class that the lecturer teaches. The students' names are listed down the side, and the lecturer updates the form by copying from Form 1 the grades achieved by each student since the previous update. He then returns Form 2 to the course coordinator.

The course coordinator maintains one Form 3 (see Figure A.III.4) for each student, held in alphabetical sequence within classes in his student record file. He

BUCKINGHAMSHIRE COLLEGE OF HIGHER EDUCATION
School of Business Studies

COURSE:_____   YEAR:_____

LECTURER:_____   MODULE:_____

STUDENTS' NAMES	ASSIGNMENT GRADES															FINAL GRADE
	1	2	3	4	5	6	7	8	9	10	11	12	13	14	15	

Figure A.III.3   Form 2

BUCKINGHAMSHIRE COLLEGE OF HIGHER EDUCATION
School of Business Studies

COURSE:_____   YEAR:_____

STUDENT'S NAME: _____   BEC NUMBER:_____

MODULE	ASSIGNMENT GRADES													EXAM GRADE
	1	2	3	4	5	6	7	8	9	10	11	12	OVERALL	

RECOMMENDATION:_____

COURSE CO-ORDINATOR:_____   MODERATOR:_____

Figure A.III.4   Form 3

updates these forms from the Form 2s received from the lecturers − he copies all grades achieved by students since the previous update on to the form. Form 2 is then filed until the time of the next update, when it is passed again to the lecturer. It is these Form 3s that the course coordinator and the BEC moderator use to assess student progress.

At the end of the academic year the overall grade that each student has achieved in each module is determined, and this is entered in the column at the right of Form 3. The exam grade is also entered, and when these have been agreed with the moderator they are copied on to the BEC computer input form and despatched to BEC.

You are required to EITHER:

(a) Construct a material-type process chart of this procedure
(b) Critically examine the process chart steps to determine what improvements can be made

(c) Construct a material-type process chart of your proposed procedure

OR:

(a) Construct a flowchart of this procedure
(b) Suggest how a microcomputer might be used to replace the three forms (include in your account an indication of the computer files that would be necessary).

8 Design an open plan layout for a production control office using the information given in Figures 10.2 and 10.3 (pages 158 and 159) and the space guidelines given on page 156. Assume that much of the work is carried out at computer terminals located on the desks.

9 (a) The older Mr Marx of Marx Bros., clothing manufacturers, is very cost-conscious. He has always insisted that tight control be exercised over purchasing, and that all the buying for the business be carried out by the Purchasing Department. This

policy worked well enough in earlier years, but now that the business has grown so large the purchasing system has become quite unwieldy. Departmental managers are complaining that delays are occurring and that they are constantly completing requisition forms for low-value items which, they feel, they should be allowed to buy for themselves.

'But,' Mr Marx counters, 'most of our expenditure is on high-value items. If responsibility for purchasing these is delegated to departments, unnecessary expenditure is bound to occur − it always does. And if we allow departments to do their own purchasing, all sorts of different forms and procedures will be introduced − every department will do its own thing. Things are much simpler left as they are. And,' he concludes triumphantly, 'what will happen when the person responsible for purchasing in a department is sick or on leave? Who will look after that department's purchasing then, eh? The delays will be far worse than they are now!'

How can purchasing be organized to meet both the requirements of the departmental managers *and* the objections of old Mr Marx?

(b) Your friend Henry is in charge of Marx Bros.' sales office. An important part of the work of this office is the processing of customer orders, and he is having a lot of trouble with the three clerks who comprise the order-processing section. Although rates of pay are reasonable, the productivity of the section is terribly low. A large backlog of work is building up and many mistakes are being made.

He explains that the section handles the work for all three sales areas of the company, and that in organizing the work he has put into practice all the accepted principles of specialization of labour:

- one clerk carries out all the credit control work;
- one clerk maintains the stock records (she updates the records, makes sure that there are sufficient stocks in hand to meet the order, and liaises with production to replenish stocks if necessary);
- one clerk prepares the invoice and despatch documentation.

In an effort to boost productivity, Henry has given each clerk a separate office, with their names on the doors, new office furniture, etc., but this seems merely to have made matters worse. Productivity and morale are at an all-time low.

Write a memo to Henry suggesting how he should reorganize the work of the section.

10 Many business studies students are poorly motivated at college. Using the findings of research workers in the human relations field, analyse the causes of this, and suggest ways in which motivation might be improved.

Index

199